THE STORY OF MUSIC

*Big Bangs: The Story of Five Discoveries
that Changed Musical History*

The Story of Music

HOWARD GOODALL

Chatto & Windus
LONDON

Published by Chatto & Windus 2013

2 4 6 8 10 9 7 5 3 1

First published in Great Britain in 2013 by
Chatto & Windus
Random House, 20 Vauxhall Bridge Road,
London SW1V 2SA
www.rbooks.co.uk

Addresses for companies within The Random House Group Limited can be found at:
www.randomhouse.co.uk/offices.htm

The Random House Group Limited Reg. No. 954009

A CIP catalogue record for this book
is available from the British Library

ISBN 9780701187521

The Random House Group Limited supports The Forest Stewardship Council (FSC®),
the leading international forest certification organisation. Our books carrying the FSC label
are printed on FSC® certified paper. FSC is the only forest certification scheme endorsed by
the leading environmental organisations, including Greenpeace. Our paper procurement
policy can be found at www.randomhouse.co.uk/environment

Illustrations by Roger Walker

Typeset in Dante MT Std by
Palimpsest Book Production Limited, Falkirk, Stirlingshire

Printed and bound in Great Britain by
Clays Ltd, St Ives plc

To Val, Daisy and Millie, with love

Contents

Introduction

Perhaps your favourite music was written by Monteverdi in 1600, Bach in 1700, Beethoven in 1800, Elgar in 1900, or Coldplay in 2000. Whichever it is, it is a sobering fact that everything that had to be discovered to produce that music – its chords, melodies and rhythms – had already been discovered by around 1450.

Of course I don't necessarily mean the instruments people used, or the countless quirky creative decisions that make each song, concerto or opera sound distinct and characterful, but rather the raw material: the building blocks of music. In order for Mozart to thrill audiences with just three dramatic chords at the start of his opera *Don Giovanni*, someone had to come up with the idea of playing more than one note at a time. In order for Gershwin to give his song 'Summertime' its enchanting see-saw accompaniment, with the high solo voice gliding in way above it, someone had to work out the alchemy of harmony and the seductive lilt of rhythm. And in order for me to sit at a piano and play those two masterworks in the comfort of my own home – instantly and just as the composer intended – someone had to work out a way of writing the notes down, alongside performance instructions.

Indeed, it is easy to overlook how utterly spoiled for musical choice we are in the twenty-first century. We can listen to almost anything we want at the press of a button. But as recently as the late nineteenth century, even the most devoted music lover might hear his or her favourite piece just three or four times in his or her whole life. Unless you happened to be a virtuoso musician with access to both sheet music and instruments, it was almost impossible to bring large-scale forms of music into your own home. Not until the dawn of recording and radio technology did our ancestors have any great choice as to what they listened to and when. If you like, it is only since recorded music has been available to buy that music has become democratic, something that everyone can influence and participate in by showing their preference for one song, or one style of music, over another.

Inevitably, though, this democratisation brought along with it its own new problems. Once, musical fashion and taste were dictated by a few wealthy patrons and institutions who might, in prosperous times, allow composers some degree of freedom to experiment without fear of starvation. But what became known as the 'popular' age unexpectedly threw up a division between modernist music in the classical tradition and contemporary music of a more accessible kind. Even within the classical tradition the weight of the past bore down heavily on living composers, as the vast repository of 'old' music was recorded and rediscovered. Classical music might well have died out entirely had composers not turned their resentment into resourcefulness and reconnected with audiences by cross-pollenating with other genres; modern film music is just one example of classically inspired sounds being aligned with popular art forms of the present day. This instinct to adapt and move with the flow has been particularly vehement – and particularly necessary – in the past hundred years or so, but it has always been a fact of musical life. If composers of all eras had been unwilling to learn, invent, borrow and even steal, we might still be listening to plainchant. Collectively, they made the mainstream sounds of contemporary Western music possible.

What we call 'Western' music – the medium in which nearly all music on earth is now conceived, recorded and performed, and which has in the past hundred years or so absorbed into its fold most of the 'other' music cultures of the world – started out as merely one localised branch of a global musical map. European-Mediterranean tribes had their particular brand of music much as African, Asian, American and Antipodean tribes did (and still do). What became the generic category 'Western music' was an amalgam of, among others, Egyptian, Persian, Greek, Celtic, Norse and Roman strands of music. It started, though, just like all the world's traditional music cultures: improvised, shared, spontaneous and transient.

The other great musical cultures of the world, because they continued to be improvised, aural traditions handed down from parent to child, have carried on to the present day much as they had for millennia. Indonesian and Balinese music, for instance, can still be heard in forms that have remained unashamedly unchanged for centuries. The branch of music that thrived from Iceland to the Caspian Sea, though, did not stand still. A series of revolutions took place that gave it remarkable new capabilities. This is not to say that Western music, as we have inherited it, is *better* than, say, Indonesian music. Rather, it is an unavoidable historical truth that the Western branch of musical activity developed in ways that were not paralleled in other musical cultures. Gradually, but with a great spirit of determination and invention, the language and method of Western music became universal standards that could be adapted to accommodate, so it now seems, every musical idea on earth.

And yet the telling of music's extraordinary unfolding story is – for anyone, more or less, who hasn't taken a degree in it – a mystery. Worse, it seems to be a *deliberate* mystery, shrouded in arcane jargon and bewildering categorisation, the shrine and preserve of a club of privileged insiders.

We have inherited a series of inaccurate and confusing historic labels by which classical music is catalogued, almost none of which describes what was actually happening in music at the time. Take the Renaissance – 'rebirth' – a period between about 1450 and 1600 in which art, architecture, philosophy and social attitudes made enormous leaps forward. While it is true that music underwent its own transformation in this period, its greatest revolutions – the invention of notation, of metrical organisation, of harmony and of instrument construction – had already taken place during what was, in many other aspects of life, the long, dark, ignorant night of the Middle Ages. The chief movers and shakers of the Renaissance (none of whom, by the way, was a musician) were inspired by the example of Ancient Roman and Greek – 'Classical' – civilisation, although it is not until the later eighteenth century that we come to the Classical era in music, which has inconveniently lent its name to the entire branch of Western music that isn't 'popular'. Between the two we have the Baroque era, characterised by gaudy excess and decorative indulgence in art but by purity and economy in music.

Then there is the chaotic mislabelling of the notes themselves. Music's longest-duration note, for instance, is called a *breve*, meaning 'short'. A *breve* can be subdivided into 4 *minims*, meaning 'shortest of all' – even though it can be further broken down into up to eight subdivisions. The note known as a *quaver* in English is in French called a *croche*, the Anglicisation of which, *crotchet*, has come to mean a note of double the value of a *croche*. The Germans and Americans call two crotchets a *half-note*, while the French call half a *croche* a *double-croche*, a crotchet a *noire* (black) and a minim a *blanche* (white) – even though they are not the same as the black and white notes on a keyboard. The list goes on.

Anachronisms and blind alleys blight all the road signs classical music has given itself. I will tackle them one by one as we progress and attempt to unpick the tangled knot of confusion that they have left in their wake.

More than anything, though, my story of music focuses on the changing sounds and innovations of the music itself – as it has occurred, chronologically – rather than on musicians who had a high profile simply because they had a high profile. Of course it was often the big-name composers who brought about musical revolutions, but sometimes the agents of change were obscure men and women whose names are not carved in the decorative panels of the world's concert halls. They will all be represented as part of the vast jigsaw of Western music. There are already plenty of books out there that can tell you what Beethoven had hidden under his piano or what killed Elvis. I am only interested in either of them if they brought about musical change. (You will see in due course whether either or both of them qualify.)

While the primary focus of this book is the uniquely rapid progress of Western music, it will necessarily and freely dip into the concepts and techniques of other musical cultures, and unashamedly oscillate between 'popular', 'folk' and 'art' music styles. At its heart lies a mission to retell the history of music in such a way that normal music lovers can relate to it. My resolve to do so is fortified by the belief that music, when all is said and done, is a unity and that the divisions we place between periods and categories are often artificial. Musicians who play a variety of styles every day of their lives, transferring their skills across genres as a matter of course, take this as a given. It is high time this truth was shared with everyone else.

The story of music – successive waves of discoveries, break-throughs and inventions – is an ongoing process. The next great leap forward may take place in a backstreet of Beijing or in a basement rehearsal space in Gateshead. Whatever music you adore – Monteverdi or Mantovani, Mozart or Motown, Machaut or Mash-up – the techniques it relies on did not happen by accident. Someone, somewhere, thought of them first. To tell this story we need to clear our minds of the complicated cacophony that makes up our daily soundtrack and try to imagine how revolutionary, how exhilarating, and, yes, even how utterly bewildering so many of the innovations we take for granted today were to the people who witnessed their birth.

Not that long ago, music was a rare and feeble whisper in a wilderness of silence. Now it is as ubiquitous as the air we breathe. How on earth did that miracle happen?

I

The Age of Discovery
40,000 BC–AD 1450

You may think that music is a luxury, a plug-in to make human life more enjoyable. That would be a fair supposition in the twenty-first century, but our hunter-gatherer ancestors wouldn't have agreed. To them, music was much more than mere entertainment.

The famous rock paintings in Chauvet, France, made by cave-dwelling people of the Upper Palaeolithic period, or European Ice Age, are 32,000 years old. They are among the oldest surviving examples of human art ever found anywhere in the world, although, like other cave paintings, they mostly depict animals and the odd symbolically fertile female figures; these were, after all, people who daily diced with extinction. It is thought that the paintings were created and venerated as part of a ritual, and we now know that music of some kind played an important part in these rituals, since whistles and flutes made from bone have been found in many Palaeolithic caves.

A particularly ancient find was a flute made of bear bone, discovered in a Slovenian cave in 1995, which was dated at roughly 41,000 BC. More impressive still, in May 2012 a joint team from Oxford and Tübingen Universities unearthed flutes made from mammoth ivory and bird bones at Geißenklöterle Cave in the Swabian Jura region of southern Germany, carbon dated at between 43,000 and 42,000 BC, making them the oldest musical instruments ever discovered. They may be simple in sound and limited in range, like tiny penny whistles, but it is nevertheless from dusty artefacts such as these that Duke Ellington's horn section and the massed woodwind of the Berlin Philharmonic would one day grow.

Although these deceptively simple ancient flutes are almost all that survives of Palaeolithic music, acoustic scientists have recently made an extraordinary discovery about the lifesaving importance of music to cave-dwellers of this period. In 2008, researchers from the University of Paris ascertained that the Chauvet paintings – which lie within huge, inaccessible, pitch-black networks of tunnels – are located at the points of greatest resonance in the cave network. From these special points, then, human voices would carry, echoing and ricocheting, throughout the whole subterranean system. It has been suggested that people would sing not just as an adjunct to communal ritual, but more crucially as a bat-like form of sonar to provide location bearings in the vast labyrinth of the cave – rather like a musical SatNav.

Our own day-to-day survival may no longer depend on our ability to sing, but our ancient ancestors were on to something that applies to modern lives, too. Study after study around the world has shown that singing enables infants to train their brains and memories, to recognise pitch differentiation as a preparation for the full development of spatial awareness. In the Palaeolithic Age this was an absolutely crucial skill, if survival depended on knowing from which direction a wild animal's cry was coming, what size it was and what mood it might be in, but even now, singing and the mastery of pitch play a large part in a child's development of language. For an infant in China, for example, pitch recognition is an essential building block of language – but in all languages it is certain that sound modulations enable us to enhance the sophistication, tone and meaning of our words.

Even though we now know that early music played an important part in ritual, communication and language development, piecing together a coherent picture of our early musical past is a notoriously difficult task because musical notation was not a

common practice until much later. Fortunately, we do have
evidence of music's perennial importance to public and private
life. The considerable body of art left to posterity by the Ancient
Egyptians, for instance, shows us that by their time (3100–670 BC),
the playing of music was closely associated with the exercise of
power and homage, with religious and secular rituals, and with
state ceremony, dancing, love and death. These pieces of art depict
a variety of instruments, from the simple *sistrum* or *sekhem* – a
hand-held, U-shaped shaken percussion instrument – to harps,
ceremonial horns, flutes and wind instruments whose sound is
made by blowing across strips of reed, the same technique that
produces the sound of the modern oboe, bassoon and clarinet
families. They also depict expert performers of high status,
including members of royal dynasties and deities. The prevalence
of music in Ancient Egyptian life is demonstrated by the fact that
over a quarter of all the tombs at the necropolis found at the site
of the city of Thebes are decorated with iconography of music-
making of one sort or another.

The Egyptians were not alone in their reverence for the power
of music. Psalms sung by the priests of King David, who united
the kingdoms of Israel and Judaea in 1003 BC, are riven through
with references to instruments and to singing. (The Greek word
'psalm' itself, strictly speaking, refers to a religious song with
accompaniment by plucked stringed instrument.) In one psalm
alone, number 150, *tof* (timbrel or tambourine), *ḥaṣoṣerah* (trumpet),
shofar (horn), *kinnor* (triangular-frame harp or lyre), *nebel* (psaltery),
ʿuḡav (possibly a type of organ or alternatively a flute), *meṣiltayim*
(cymbals) and *minnim* (an unspecified group of stringed instruments) are invoked in praise of God.

The Psalms of David, *Sefer tehillim* (book of praises) in Hebrew,
are still sung today, to more recent melodies; as such they can
claim to be the oldest continually performed tradition of religious
singing in human history. David's successor, Solomon, set up a
music school attached to the temple at Jerusalem for the training
of musicians.

And yet we have absolutely no idea what this music sounded like. Nor do we know what the music of the earlier Sumerian civilisation sounded like (c. 4500–1940 BC), nor that of the Egyptians, nor – save for a few tiny fragments of tunes – that of the (more recent) Ancient Greeks (c. 800–146 BC). The informative paintings and impressive pyramids of the Ancient Egyptians have survived remarkably well, but their music has disappeared completely. They simply had no way of writing it down for us.

The Ancient Greeks, to be fair to them, did at least leave a few tantalisingly scattered remains of a form of musical notation, the most complete example being some lines engraved on a first-century burial tomb. This 'Epitaph of Seikilos' has an accompanying decipherable tune that lasts about ten seconds in all. But in general, it just would not have occurred to them that having musical notation mattered. This is because the Greek musical tradition, like all the musical traditions of the Ancient World, was one of improvisation. Setting music in stone, as it were, so that it stayed the same for each performance, year in and year out, would have struck them as a contradiction of music's function and enjoyment. They did not *need* a musical notation. All of which is particularly frustrating for us, since we have so much evidence of the wonderful-looking instruments of the Ancient World, but no way of bringing them to life.

The oldest list of musical instruments ever discovered, including a few instructions on how to play them, was found on a clay tablet in Mesopotamia (modern Iraq), and dated to 2600 BC. The columns on the tablet are made up of cuneiform script detailing various instruments, including the *kinnor*, the hand-held harp-like instrument that is alternatively known as a lyre. A slightly younger Old Babylonian clay tablet, dating from 2000–1700 BC, gives basic details on how to learn and tune a four-stringed fretted lute, including instructions for the notes to play. As such it is the oldest form of decipherable notation – albeit very simple notation – in existence. Sadly none of these lutes survives.

But archaeologists have had moderate success in unearthing

other ancient instruments in all corners of the globe. Several lyres and two harps dating from the same period as the Mesopotamian clay tablet were found at the large excavated royal burial site at the old city of Ur (known today as Tell el-Muqayyar). One of the lyres is decorated with a golden bull's head, complete with large horns, and it was buried alongside the sacrificial body of its (female) player. In Egypt, equally impressive examples of the kind of instruments featured in ancient art have also been unearthed, notably a semicircular five-stringed harp found in the burial tomb of King Amenhotpe's priest Thauenany, who was laid to rest in around 1350 BC.

Around the same time in Sweden – in approximately 1000 BC – it would seem that people were playing brass instruments. Cave paintings from the King's Grave at Kivik show a number of people playing – together – what look like curved horns. Horns of a similar shape, and of roughly the same period, survive to this day in the form of the Brudevaelte Lurs, a set of six Bronze Age *lurs* – curved brass horns – that were found in a field in Zealand, Denmark, in 1797. They were perfectly preserved and are still playable today. We even know how to play them, because their mouthpieces correspond almost exactly with those of later horns, and while we once again have no way of knowing what sort of music was played on them, we know that their sound is loud and penetrating. (In an unusual tribute to this intrinsically Danish instrument, one of the nation's most famous exports was named after it. Packets of Lurpak butter still feature a pair of lurs in their design.)

What the Brudevaelte Lurs tell us is that it is a grave error to describe the musical activity of 800 BC as 'primitive', since these elaborate brass instruments could only have been the handiwork of culturally sophisticated people, warlike though they may also have been. It is important to bear in mind that these artefacts were made and played five hundred years *before* the Romans conquered Europe. All across the continent – and beyond it – people were constantly thinking up new and ingenious ways of making music.

But of all the culturally sophisticated ancient civilisations that were playing and enjoying music in this period, there is one group that emerges head and shoulders above the rest.

No civilisation, except perhaps for our own, has valued, venerated and taken pleasure in music more than the Ancient Greeks, whose culture dominated south-eastern Europe and the Near East for nearly seven hundred years in the first millennium BC, before it was absorbed into the Roman Empire. Even the word 'music' comes from the Greek μουσιή – *mousike*, referring to the fruits of the nine muses in literature, science and the arts.

There are three major things you need to know about the Ancient Greeks and music, and this is before we take into account that they invented one of the most influential instruments of subsequent millennia: the organ. A physicist-engineer named Ktesibios, who lived in Alexandra in the third century BC, described and possibly even invented what was known as a hydraulis organ, which used a tank of water to pressurise the air for the pipes.

The first major thing you need to know is that the Greeks believed music to be both a science and an art, and that they developed theories and systems for music accordingly. Pythagoras was but one of a host of philosopher-scientists who tried to figure out what music was and how it might relate to the laws of the natural world, especially its relationship to the heavenly bodies of the planets and stars. Greek theorists called the orbiting motions they observed in the night sky 'the music of the spheres'. And this curiosity about music is something the Classical-era Greeks wanted to instil in younger generations. When they more or less gave birth to the systematic education of young people, it is worth noting that their first compulsory seven subjects were grammar, rhetoric, logic, maths, geometry, astronomy and music. Much later, but nonetheless inspired by the Greeks, the world's first universities – Al-Karaouine in Fès, Morocco (AD 859), Bologna (1088) and Oxford (c. 1096) – included music in the basic diet of subjects they taught.

The Greeks believed that studying music would produce better, more tolerant and nobler human beings. Plato declared in *The Republic* that 'musical training is a more potent instrument than any other, because rhythm and harmony find their way into the inward places of the soul, on which they mightily fasten, imparting grace, and making the soul of him who is rightly educated graceful'. Young students were accordingly expected to learn an instrument and perform music daily, alongside gymnastics.

Greek philosophies on the beneficial behavioural qualities of music find striking parallels with Confucius-influenced writings of the second and third centuries BC in China. Chinese belief in the potential of music (*yue*) to improve and refine the human condition was so pronounced that in the Zhou and early Han dynasties the control of musical activity was enshrined in a specific government department. Like their contemporaries in Greece, the Han Chinese saw virtue in the relationship between musical pitch in music – the relative distance between notes – and the arrangement of the stars and planets they observed above them. Thousands of pages of theory and instruction survive, detailing how it might be possible through careful calculation, through manipulation of the calendar, through codifying the elements of music and through study of the cosmos, to formulate good governance, based on the correct alignment of these associated forces.

The second major thing about the Greeks and music is that they treated it as an essential part of all their significant rituals. Aristides Quintilianus, who lived some time between the first and third centuries AD, reported of Greek life that, 'To be sure, there is no action among men that is carried out without music. Sacred hymns and offerings are adorned with music, specific feasts and the festive assemblies of cities exult in it, wars and marches are both aroused and composed through music. It makes sailing and rowing and the most difficult of the handicrafts not burdensome by providing an encouragement for the work.' The Ancient Greeks reserved their greatest excitement in relation to music, though, for competitions, of which they had a large number.

Everyone knows that the Ancient Greeks invented the Olympic Games; for the Greeks, though, it wasn't just running, nude wrestling and hurling the javelin that were important. The earliest Olympic Games were religious, as well as athletic, festivals, and as such would have included some music-making. But a distinct tradition of singing competitions grew up separately, and attracted participants from all over the Greek-dominated eastern Mediterranean. Singer-songwriters would gather for festivals and sing their homespun songs for the benefit of a panel of judges and a live audience. (Yes, even *The X-Factor* is a three-thousand-year-old format.) The earliest recorded contest took place at Chalcis in around 700 BC, the poet Hesiod proudly penning a few lines in celebration of his winning a solo singing class there. The Spartan city of Carneia hosted a long series of knock-out talent shows for singers accompanying themselves on the kithara, a form of lyre. (In 670 BC one such competition was won by Terpander, a bardic musician and kithara expert who is said to have died from choking on a fig thrown by an admirer at a concert.) There were also choral competitions, with a festival atmosphere and plenty of group choreography – ancient versions, if you like, of the present-day carnivals in Rio de Janeiro, Trinidad and Notting Hill.

The significance of these competitions is that they prompted the emergence of a new class of elite musicians – individuals and groups striving for musical excellence who could earn money and prizes for their endeavours. Freakishly talented children were paraded at these events, much as they have been ever since. Hitherto, music had been something anyone and everyone might participate in, a communal activity, like the singing of a tribe in the bush. The Greeks began a process that became unusually pronounced in Western music: emphasis on a VIP class of performers whose brilliance was intended to strike awe and enchantment into the hearts of the ordinary listener.

The third thing you need to know about the Greeks and music is that, by inventing European drama, they in effect invented the musical, since their dramas were all accompanied by music and choral singing, declaiming (close to the modern notion of rapping) or chanting. Their surviving amphitheatres, dotted around the eastern Mediterranean, are among the most vivid reminders to us of the artistic sophistication of their civilisation. Whereas we consider the roles of writer, poet, director, actor, dancer, singer and composer to be distinct professions, the lines were rather more blurred in Ancient Greece, with many leading dramatists fulfilling many or all of these functions. The extent to which drama and music were deemed inseparable by the Greeks, an ideal sought time and again in later centuries by opera composers, is suggested by the fact that the word 'orchestra' is the Greek term for the performing area in their theatrical amphitheatres.

A number of noteworthy Greek dramas are even *about* music. The plot of Aristophanes' satirical play *The Frogs* of 405 BC, for instance, like the story of *Orpheus and Euridice*, concerns a life-or-death poetry and singing competition in the Underworld. And it was Greek comedies such as this one (as well as Greek tragedies) that inspired the dreaming up in Italy, in around 1600, of the concept of a sung form of theatre: opera. It is fitting that the first great opera, composed by Monteverdi in 1607, features a hero faced with a life-or-death singing challenge in the Underworld, *Orfeo*. That said, I suspect that the scale and popularity of these amphitheatre dramas among ordinary folk in Ancient Greece and Sparta, and their origin in choral and religious festivals, puts them closer as an experience to Handel's theatre-filling eighteenth-century oratorios, such as his *Messiah*, or even the twentieth-century musical, a form that more often than not created a story out of songs, in contrast to opera, which tended to create songs from a story. But in the absence of surviving notation of the music performed with the plays of Aristophanes and others, we must once again resign ourselves to frustration and speculation.

Hellenistic culture was in due course absorbed into that of the Roman Empire, and though we can see from paintings, friezes and pottery that the Romans were surrounded by music and its trappings, they too had no compulsion to write it down.

The one great thing we do know about the Romans and music is that they had a particular penchant for the organ, which featured as musical accompaniment for gladiatorial contests and other large-scale public entertainments. They had of course inherited the technology from Ktesibios's hydraulis organ – and the name *organum* likewise comes from the Greek *organon*, meaning instrument or tool. The oldest surviving example of the hydraulis organ was discovered in 1931 in the Roman city of Aquincum (modern Budapest) and dates from AD 228, but it was during this same century – the third century AD – that the Greco-Roman method of using water to compress the air was replaced by a system of leather bellows, the prototypes of all subsequent bellows-fed organs.

What the Romans played on their organs is of course a matter of conjecture. The vast body of written material left to us from the Roman era suggests to us that, if they *had* developed some form of notation, some fragment or mention of it would surely have survived, but it has not. Consequently their music is as deathly silent as the empty rooms of Pompeii.

Almost. One fragile musical thread *did* survive the collapse of Greco-Roman civilisation, given impetus by what seemed at first to be insignificant events in a troublesome frontier territory. This was the unstable puppet kingdom of Judaea, or what we now call Palestine and Israel. In the embers of the last days of the Roman Empire we are able, out of centuries of silence, to hear the only living musical bequest of the Ancient World.

In the year AD 70 the Roman Army, exasperated by years of rebellion in Judaea, sacked the city of Jerusalem and destroyed the Israelites' Temple there. This succeeded in silencing a tradition that had been maintained for perhaps as long as a thousand years – that of chanting Hebrew psalms in the Temple – but the interruption was only temporary; for one thing the tradition of chanting, if not the Hebrew chants themselves, was in due course taken on by the splinter sect of Christianity. It was originally supposed that the earliest Christian gatherings must have been heavily influenced by the synagogue services they replaced, but recent scholarship has shown that Christian chant developed from hymn singing rather than from psalms, and that it was different in character – probably intentionally – from its Jewish predecessor. Caution has to be applied to these conclusions in the absence of any surviving Jewish psalmody from before the destruction of the Temple, but what is clear is that, in the seven-hundred-year period during which Jewish chant fell into neglect, Christian chant spread vigorously. It was substantially reinforced when the religion became legal and was openly practised following the Edict of Milan in AD 313.

The gradual retreat of Roman military and administrative authority across western Europe between 300 and 400 AD left behind a chaotic, fragmented picture, but it's an exaggeration to conclude that all culture disappeared with the Romans and that Europeans were left rummaging around in a sea of ignorance and brutality, with a few isolated monastic settlements holding civilisation together. For a start, it very much depends on which Europeans you are talking about.

The Kingdom of Armenia, for example, established Christianity as its official religion in 301, and Armenians held on to their religious independence even when they were subsumed into the later Persian and Arabic Empires. Etchmiadzin Cathedral was completed in 303 under the supervision of Saint Gregory the Illuminator, and can claim to be the oldest purpose-built state church on earth, all earlier places of worship having been adapted from existing religious buildings, including Roman and Jewish temples. Etchmiadzin Cathedral still stands today, an impressive rebuttal to the notion that the period following the fall of Rome meant the temporary end of civilisation. An even more spectacular architectural contradiction of the phrase 'Dark Ages' is the Hagia Sophia basilica in modern Istanbul, then Constantinople, the construction of which began in 537 and whose breathtaking dome – mostly redesigned and shored up in the 560s – was unsurpassed in its grandeur and ingenuity for nearly a thousand years.

Indeed, all that happened as Roman power retreated from western and northern Europe was that its civilisation relocated to Constantinople, which continued to be a place of cultural magnificence for hundreds of years. The singing of psalms and hymns, and the training up of singers to do so, may have been low down on the list of priorities in the anarchic wasteland of France or England immediately after the withdrawal of Roman Imperial administration, but the church in Rome itself set up its School of Singing (*Schola Cantorum*) in 350 and there was plenty of musical activity going on in the Eastern, Byzantine Empire too. Subsequent hostilities between Eastern and Western powers have blinded us to the fact that the 'European' civilisation we have gratefully inherited was nurtured, enriched and developed in places that now are associated with the Arabic, Islamic and Eastern Orthodox world.

We know chanting, or religious singing of some kind, was alive and well in the Byzantine half of Europe in at least the third and fourth centuries, because something of it even survives in a written-down form. In the papyrology collection of the Sackler Library at the University of Oxford is the world's oldest surviving Christian hymn, featuring a form of now undecipherable notation. It was excavated by Oxford archaeologists at the partially buried city of Oxyrhynchus in Egypt in the late nineteenth century. Thanks to these excavations and others, the Sackler Library contains the largest collection of ancient classical manuscripts on earth. The Oxyrhynchus hymn, written in Ancient Greek, dates from the late third century, making it nearly two thousand years old.

Meanwhile, in northern and western Europe, the waning of Roman influence provoked a wave of local wars as tribes fought for territorial supremacy – but these tribes were not all 'barbarian', in the generic sense that they were illiterate, marauding hooligans. At the burial site of the early seventh-century Anglo-Saxon king Rædwald in Sutton Hoo in Suffolk, for example, along with all manner of cultural treasures, clothes, jewellery, weapons and so on, are the remains of a large six-stringed lyre, a form of hand-held harp that is comparable to those of the Ancient World. Of course, we don't know what the music played on this lyre sounded like, even though we can strum its strings and admire its crafts-manship. We don't know whether it occurred to its strummers to play more than one string simultaneously, like a chord, or whether they only picked out one-note-at-a-time tunes. Likewise, even though we know that in early seventh-century China 'orchestras' of instruments played together, *what* they played is guesswork.

It is possible, though, to reconstruct, to some extent, the chants that were being sung in churches and abbeys from around the fourth century onwards, from manuscripts of various kinds. Even where the primitive notation used was crude or unclear, the same chants continued to be sung without significant alteration into the period when reliable notation *did* exist. The incredible thing is that, for the first few hundred years of the first millennium AD, before a universal notation system emerged, all of the chant that monks and nuns sang was memorised. It was passed on aurally, monk by monk, nun by nun, painstakingly, patiently, for century after century. This chant, also called plainchant or plainsong, has by default often been described as 'Gregorian' chant, after Gregory the Great, who was Pope at the end of the sixth century. It is beautiful, ancient, mysterious and – in its incredible test of human memory – miraculous. What it is *not*, we now know, is anything to do with Pope Gregory.

Indeed, plainsong developed gradually and separately all over Christian Europe according to local tastes and traditions. There was Gallican chant in France, Ambrosian chant in northern Italy, Beneventan chant in southern Italy, Mozarabic chant in Spain and Sarum chant in the British Isles (Roman Sarum becoming in the thirteenth century the modern English city of Salisbury). But what all this chant had in common was that it was one memorised, meandering tune with no accompaniment and no harmonising, the Greek term for which is *monophonic*: one voice.

Plainchant is our only audible link with the musicians of the first thousand years AD. Its survival into the modern era we owe to two gigantic musical discoveries that began to make their presence felt in the two centuries before AD 1000. To grasp the significance of these two discoveries, we need to transport ourselves back to the sound world of that period, one thousand five hundred years ago.

It is a Sunday morning service in an abbey or cathedral. Some monks are singing a section of plainchant, together, in *unison*. After a couple of lifetimes, someone thinks it would be a good idea to add some young lads to the choir, to feed and clothe them and keep them out of mischief, and to begin the long, slow process of teaching them from memory the entire plainsong repertoire for the Church year.

The musical effect of adding the boys is that there are now two parallel lines of music, not just one, since the boys' voices are higher than those of the men. The higher version the boys sing is made up of identical notes to the men's, but at a higher register; so there is a fixed, natural distance between the two identical lines of music. This fixed distance between a note and its higher self is something that occurs in nature – we humans didn't invent it, we just found it to be lurking behind all musical sounds.

I can tease out this 'secret' natural relationship between a note and its higher self by illustrating the magic of musical pitch. If I pluck any string on a guitar, or blow across the end of any piece of tubing, the length of the string or the length of the column of air will determine how high or low my note will be. We can call that note anything we like but we may as well call it 'A', and when we talk about how high or low 'A' sounds, we are talking about its 'pitch'. If you twang a rubber band it will make one pitch, if you stretch it so that it is longer and tighter, the pitch of the note will have changed. In ancient music-making, pitch was fixed – defined – *only* by the length of your string or pipe, hence the need for a label like 'A' to denote the same sound made on different-shaped instruments. Nowadays we are able to fix pitch using an electronic measurement, Hertz, which gives each pitch a numerical value, though we have stuck with the alphabetical names for ease of use. (As an aside, the 'A' that modern orchestras use as a reference to tune to – usually played by the oboe – was set at a sound-wave frequency of 440 Hz by international agreement in the 1930s, having previously been standardised in some countries at the slightly lower 435 Hz. Before electricity made any of this possible, 'A' could be different pitches not just in different countries but also from town to town or even from instrument to instrument. Surviving organs and other instruments from Bach's time indicate that the average pitch was lower then than it is today, so his music is mostly performed at A = 415 Hz. Likewise the music of Mozart and Haydn is sometimes played at the 'historically authentic' frequency of A = 430 Hz.)

Here's the magical bit. If I pluck my guitar string again, but this time ever so gently resting my finger halfway down its length, it plays a higher version of note A: let's call it Little A. If I fill half my pipe or tube with water, effectively halving the instrument's length, the new note that sounds when I blow across its top will also be Little A. Little A and Big A were both there all the time, but it just took a bit of teasing to get Little A to reveal itself. In fact, every time you hear Big A you are also hearing Little A hidden within it, as it is part of Big A's rainbow spectrum of sound.

In musical terms, we say that Little A is an *octave* higher than Big A and that Big A is an octave lower than Little A. This natural distance was originally named octave, meaning eight, because in the medieval church there were only eight notes to choose from, with one of these octave notes at either end of the eight. From the Ancient Greeks to the Reformation, it was believed that certain musical notes had a dangerously seductive effect and needed to be outlawed by authority; this eight-note restriction was driven by the medieval Church's desire to simplify and order the potential musical free-for-all. Later, octave came to mean a choice of twelve notes, not eight, and we got saddled with the wrong descriptor for ever, but I'll explain that development when it arrives. For now, in the early Middle Ages, octave meaning eight is a fair definition of the relationship between Big A and Little A.

Men monks and boy choristers sang together, an octave apart, for a very long time. But this idea, having two notes for one, prompted a further revolutionary thought: what if we had two notes together that *weren't* an octave apart? Not just Big A and Little A but Big A and Big E, for example?

Believe it or not, this possibility didn't occur to medieval musicians for *centuries*. It was as if they'd discovered black and white, then maybe brown, but never thought to look for further colours. Indeed, the process of eking out those new notes took so long that we don't even know in which century it happened. Some time before 800 is all I can tell you. This was a really major breakthrough: layering two lines of voices singing at the same time, but singing slightly different notes. And yet, when the musical monks finally started doing it, their caution was staggering.

They took the original plainchant and added a second line that ran exactly in parallel to it, at a slight distance, like two train tracks. Usually it was the note pitched five steps higher up the ladder (of eight) that they used for the new tracks. The reason for the singers' attraction to the pitch five steps up the scale (or four down, if you are going in the descending direction) is that this pitch, like the octave, has a natural resonance in all sounds. We created Little A by halving the length of our stretched guitar string. If we had divided the length of the string by a third instead of a half, we would produce this very pitch; if we had started at A, we would now have E. These resonances are caused by a phenomenon known as the *harmonic series*, which we will encounter in a later chapter. For now, it is enough to know that the notes at the fourth and fifth rung of the medieval musical ladder were derived from what were deemed 'perfect' mathematical ratios and were therefore the monks' first choice for their additional pitch. Medieval church musicians called the technique of running two notes in parallel – which they improvised on the spot – 'organum', because to their ears it sounded like an organ. Which it does. The Greek term for more than one voice line singing together is *polyphonic*: many voices.

Organum became very popular across Europe – and, dare I say

it, formulaic to the point of tedium. In around 800, you'd probably have heard it in any abbey you stumbled upon from Italy to Northumbria. But the heady excitement of turning one tune into two at no extra cost had another spin-off: organum where one voice stood still instead. This version has the basic plainchant as normal, but instead of adding another line following its contours like the parallel train tracks, the new additional line stays put. It just holds one long note throughout, a sound that is known as a *drone*. Holding the drone, however, turned out to be unusually boring to perform, not to mention quite tiring, so more often than not it was played on an instrument instead: an organ, perhaps, or now almost forgotten instruments such as the *crwth*, the *psaltery*, the *hurdy-gurdy* or the *symphony*. These instruments shared the ability to regenerate a held note seemingly endlessly, without a break for breath or a change in fingering. A bow drawn backwards and forwards across a string, or a handle mechanism that turned the edge of a wheel against a string, were the most common solutions. An organ could keep going indefinitely as long as you had someone, or a team of people, to pump its bellows.

The point of adding a drone to a chant melody was that new combinations of notes were created as the melody line moved closer or further away from the drone. If we imagine parallel organum as a train track winding across the landscape, the drone style looked more like a graph in which one line moves and the other stays constant.

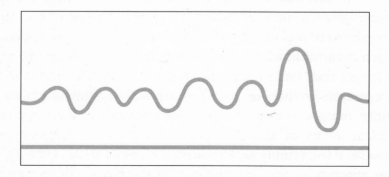

It is a concept that survives to this day in the music of the bagpipe. The instrument's ancient (and surprising) connection to plainsong is preserved in the naming of its parts: the perforated tube you play the melody on is still called the 'chanter'.

As time went on, more adventurous musicians, such as the ninth-century Byzantine composer Kassia of Constantinople, began mixing the parallel organum style with the drone style. Kassia's haunting music has recently been recorded for the first time in a thousand years, and it rather gracefully refutes the assumption that the development of early music is exclusively the handiwork of men.

These new layered sound effects, built on plainsong tunes, were edging very close to what today we would call 'harmony' – that is, the existence and exploitation of simultaneous clusters of notes. This was the first giant step our medieval ancestors took as the year 1000 loomed.

The other was to alter the course of music history dramatically. It was the invention of a reliable, universally adopted musical notation. It took an Italian monk, immortalised as Guido of Arezzo, to crack the code in around AD 1000 and give Western music its unique system of notation, still in use today. His system was an iteration of an earlier attempt at transcribing melody, and it is worth tracing the journey from the wholly aural approach to the written-down approach.

What singers of plainchant had in front of them in the centuries before about AD 800 was the text, in Latin, of what they were singing. Just the text. They had to *memorise* the melody. There were, for example, one hundred and fifty psalms in the standard church repertoire, all of which had their own melodies. Some of the longer ones had multiple melodies in sequence. Added to this were prayers, responses, canticles, hymns and the words of the various masses: several thousand different tunes for the church calendar, many of them – thanks to the puny eight-note pool available – worryingly similar to one another. This is one of the most spectacular feats of memory in the history of the human race. But it's also a bit mad. So it was deemed highly desirable to find a way of reminding singers what the tune of any given passage might be. Medieval musicians started their quest by adding what looks like shorthand to the text.

The oldest surviving manuscript of two-voice parallel organum in the world can be found in the Bodleian Library, Oxford, as part of a book called the Winchester Troper. It is a thousand years old, roughly contemporaneous with a report of an organ at Winchester Cathedral that boasted an extraordinary four hundred pipes. If you thought that the departure of the Romans caused the British Isles to descend into mindless savagery that would not be reversed until the Norman Conquest in 1066, think again. Winchester's Troper of two-voice *organa* manuscripts and its mighty four-hundred-voice pipe organ were the work of Anglo-Saxon Christians.

The Winchester Troper shows Latin text that was intended to be sung, with various accents and inflexions above it and in the margin, to indicate to the monk or nun what kind of melody they were supposed to be chanting. The Troper is not unique, though: between about 650 and 1000, an ad hoc system of small, above-the-text markings became more common in chant books all over Western Europe. The markings were called *neumes* (from the Greek word *pneuma* meaning 'breath') and they were probably inspired by similar markings in the Masoretic Hebrew texts of the Old Testament, which were transcribed between the seventh and tenth centuries, and by subsequent archaic Latin translations. Vowel sounds were not written out in Ancient Hebrew, so the accents and markings around the text indicated correct pronunciation and instructions for chanting. Similarly, neumes were there to give some indication of whether the note of the melody went up or down on any given word, and they were certainly a step in the right direction.

Neumes did, though, have one major flaw: they were essentially a way of jogging the singer's memory, reminding him of a tune he already knew. They could not help him sight-read a new tune from scratch. Rather like a road map with all its place names removed, you could see all the features – the musical rivers and roads – but with no clue as to *where* this all was in relation to anything else. Neumes were really just for people who already knew the way.

Various musicians attempted to formulate ways of improving the neumes, including a ninth-century French monk called Hucbald, who suggested giving specific note pitches an alphabetical name – ABCDE and so on – as we still do today. To be fair, Hucbald merely experimented with this concept rather than invented it; it had been circulating in musical theories since antiquity, as indeed it had in Indian and Chinese musical systems. He also toyed with the idea of having the words move up and down with the shape of the tune. Perhaps not surprisingly, this did not catch on.

Enter, at last, Guido of Arezzo and his remarkable breakthrough. His job at the cathedral in Arezzo was to train the young choristers, and he'd calculated that teaching them the whole of the Church's plainsong repertoire by ear, parrot-fashion, would take over ten years. What he desperately needed was a method of notation that you could read and turn into singing *at sight*, and he set about developing this miraculous time-saving device. His methods were simple and clear. First he gave the neumes a standardised, easy-to-read form. Each note had its own identifiable blob, a mark on the page, and they were placed in the order, from left to right, in which they were meant to be sung.

He then drew four straight lines on to which the notes would be placed, so that it was instantly possible to see the relative positions of every note:

These days we call the collection of lines a *stave* or *staff*. He coloured the second line from the top red, in order to give each tune an absolute bearing in relation to all other tunes. The position of each note represented its pitch position, that is, whether it was an A, a B, or any other note. If the tune went up, the notes went up. If it went down, the notes went down, step by step. This method has been refined over the years, for example by altering the blob shapes to indicate the duration of a note, or to group notes together in clusters to pick out a rhythm, and in time his four lines became five, but it is essentially the same system for notating music as is used universally in the twenty-first century.

Guido had given music its map at last. From now on – around AD 1000 – you could write down a tune and someone else could sing it back to you, never having seen it or heard it before. It was a revolution. Within a century Guido's notation started popping up in monasteries almost everywhere. Except in the Eastern Orthodox Church, which stuck with its neumes.

One of the most important consequences of the notation revolution was the way it changed *how* music was created. Instead of thinking up a tune and then teaching it to everyone you know and hoping they pass it on without modification to everyone *they* know, generation by generation, down the ages, a composer could now place music, like words, on a page. It would stay unmodified for ever, as long as the paper didn't disintegrate. The ability to do this encouraged a far more ambitious approach to music than anything that had preceded it.

A story that has to be memorised and spoken out loud is necessarily less complex than a novel that can be written down and unfolds over a greater length of time. So it was with the complexity of music following the invention of musical notation. So much so that, not long after notation became generally available, we start seeing the names of composers attached to pieces. This is no coincidence. If you can write something down, you can claim it as yours. Try claiming an idea is yours just because you told it to someone down the pub.

One of the first named composers worth knowing about was a woman – a spectacularly clever and imaginative German woman, Hildegard of Bingen, who was born in 1098. She was also a scientist, nun, poet, visionary and diplomat, and her music is still performed and admired now, nearly a thousand years later.

Hildegard's imaginative, lyrical and reflective music represents a fulcrum between two eras. It still essentially sounds like a colourful variant of plainchant, but she embellished the outline of the tune with touches of her own. Whereas the vast body of church plainchant that existed prior to Hildegard sounds (intentionally) discreet and anonymous, her poetic sacred songs have a character, a style. She was well known in her own time: born of the nobility, she became abbess of a thriving Benedictine community she herself had founded, situated on one of Europe's busiest arteries, the River Rhine, where she was visited by many pilgrims and prestigious guests who subsequently spread word across the continent of her scientific, political and artistic works. She corresponded with the Pope and the Holy Roman Emperor. Significantly for music, she was one of the first composers in a new trend that sought to move away from the conformity and rigid tradition of plainchant by adding ornamentation and melodic detail that lay outside the strict confines of the standard method. Instead of handing on the tried and tested chants, as had been the norm in earlier centuries, Hildegard made up her own chant tunes. This seems to us an obvious thing to do, but in the twelfth century it was both daring and unexpected.

The revolutions in both notation and harmony during this period had been hundreds of years in the making, but once they were in place the pace of innovation accelerated rapidly. The development of layered voices and notation ushered in a period of great experimentation and adventure – particularly with regard to harmony – and because of them Western music, by 1100, was already utterly distinct from every other musical culture that had ever existed.

Within Hildegard's lifetime a group of younger composers working at Notre-Dame in Paris had become known for their radical approach to harmony. The trailblazer of this group was called Léonin, and by the standards of the early twelfth century he was both prolific and admired, regularly combining plainsong chant melodies with a second voice, a technique now known as *organum duplum*. His greatest legacy to music, though, is the inspiration he provided for his young colleague, and possibly pupil, Pérotin.

What Pérotin did was ask a very simple question: what would happen if you had *more* than two voice lines singing at the same time? What would it sound like to hear three or even four notes simultaneously? Such a cluster of notes, known to us as a *chord*, did not even have a name at this time, so novel was its concept. Pérotin strikes us, even today, as an irrepressibly adventurous creative force, a firecracker of a composer who conceived and wrote down the most complex simultaneous note clusters that had ever been heard. In the decades and centuries to come, there would often be fierce debate as to what constituted an appropriate combination of notes, or what cluster was beautiful, or ugly, or seductive, or *dis*cordant. But none of this mattered to Pérotin. He was like a child in a sweet shop, ramming notes together to see what effect they would have. He was truly the first musical radical, referred to in a contemporary record as 'Pérotin the Master'. Harmony made from chords came alive in his four-part vocal music, even if some of his note combinations sound accidental rather than intentional. But there was another key ingredient that Pérotin added to the musical mix, one that he was hearing all around him and which must have seemed extremely daring in the context of his job at Notre-Dame.

Paris in the twelfth century was expanding fast, as was its university, which was beginning to shrug off its ecclesiastical roots and embrace a more secular approach to learning. This was the era of the troubadours and trouvères: skilled, far-travelled poet-singer-songwriters whose fame was built on songs of 'refined' love. For them, Paris was the jewel in any tour programme. At the peak of the troubadour-trouvère craze, several hundred of them plied their trade, with troubadours from Occitania, the southern half of France, then virtually a separate country with its own language and culture, and trouvères from the northern half. It sparked a lively exchange of ideas and tunes between countries, but also between contemporary church music and its secular counterpart. And it was a two-way street: folk songs were made from well-liked passages of sacred music and popular tunes found themselves layered on to existing religious plainchant, an exchange so beloved that it continued for the next three hundred years.

The troubadour phenomenon had been inspired by the example of professional singers in the courts of al-Ándalus, Muslim Spain, which had its resplendent capital at Córdoba. As Christian armies of the *reconquista* began to sweep south in the eleventh and twelfth centuries, seizing province after province from the collapsing Caliphate, they plundered the libraries of Muslim cities, ransacked the palaces and villas of the fleeing Moors and pillaged the treasures of their culture. As a result, European musicians inherited from the Arab world at least three instruments that became central to secular music in the centuries to follow: the *al'Ud* (literally 'strip of wood'), of Persian provenance, which developed into the lute, thence the guitar; the *rebab*, a primitive form of violin; and the *qanun*, a variant of the Ancient Greek *psalterion*, which had spawned the psaltery elsewhere in Europe.

The poetic songs of the Caliph's court, sometimes called *ghinā'mutqan* (the perfect singing), came from a long tradition nurtured by both *qaynas*, professional women performers, many of them slaves, and male composer-scholars such as Ibn Bājja (also known as Avenpace). The mingling of musicians with Arabic training with those of a European background in the final, chaotic stages of the al-Ándalus Caliphate gave rise to a form of rhymed song, the *zajal*, which became a key ingredient of the growing troubadour repertoire. These songs were shaped by the poetic metre of their lyrics, and consequently most of the troubadour songs, even the sad ones, have a gentle, foot-tapping pulse.

Which brings us back to our Parisian composer, Pérotin, and his great legacy to Western music. The revolutionary element he introduced into the sacred music he wrote at Notre-Dame was something he'd clearly learnt from the troubadours, who had in turn picked it up from Spain: rhythm.

Before Pérotin the subject of rhythm in sacred music is a thorny one. No one knows for sure if medieval plainchant singing had a pulse or beat of any kind, because there was no way of writing it down. No surviving medieval plainchant reveals to us that a pulse was intended, and books of theory and instruction are ambiguous on the subject. The first we really know about rhythm is that Pérotin found a way of notating it.

These days, guitarists who want to play a well-known pop or folk song can do so simply by reading a chart with the names of the chords. Guitarists familiar with the tune of 'Morning Has Broken', for example, would be able to play the song just by seeing the lyrics alongside the chords:

C   C Dm G   F   C

Morning has broken, like the first morning,

C   Em Am   C   D – G7

Blackbird has spoken, like the first bird

But if, in eight hundred years, musicians come across a piece of paper with just the chord names on it and a few lyrics, with no further information as to the speed, rhythm, mood or groove of the song, they will be in trouble. This is what it's like for us looking at twelfth-century notation.

Pérotin, though, began using an upgraded method of notation that *did* for the first time indicate the rhythmic value of notes. The system he used, while not as flexible or sophisticated as the one used today, relied on the grouping together of notes with horizontal bars called *ligatures*. Every time he grouped notes together with a ligature, he meant that those notes should be shorter than the others. And once you start specifying long and short notes in a chain, you generate a rhythmic pattern.

Pérotin was particularly fond of one rhythmic pattern, one you can easily remember because it is the rhythm of the theme tune to *The Archers*: dum ti dum ti dum ti dum. It is generated by alternating notes long-short-long-short-long-short, and so on. Pérotin made this pattern his own, using it throughout the hymn he composed for Christmas Day 1198, 'Viderunt Omnes'. It is the same rhythmic pattern that drives the only popular non-religious song of the early thirteenth century still known today: 'Sumer is icumen in'. It is not known who wrote this catchy English song – it may have been a man from Herefordshire known mysteriously just as 'W de Wycombe' – but as a piece for six simultaneous voices that ingeniously interlock, it sounds as if the composer took Pérotin's style, made it more accessible, gave it bawdy rustic words and expected folk to dance to it. A delightfully clear original manuscript of 'Sumer is icumen in', possibly in W's own hand, survives at the British Library. It features a simpler version of rhythmic (sometimes called 'mensural') notation than Pérotin's ligatures, but nonetheless it does the trick.

Without question, the ability to write down rhythms fired the imaginations of composers. In fact, for the whole of the thirteenth and fourteenth centuries, composers thought of little else than how to construct ever more complex layers of sound with their four voices, singing simultaneously but at different speeds and with different rhythms. Now they had the building blocks with which to construct long pieces of music that you didn't have to memorise, they set about creating the equivalent of musical labyrinths – mathematical and geometrical structures embedded in the texture of the music. Which isn't really surprising, I suppose; this was also the age of ecclesiastical mazes – which may have served as metaphors for pilgrimages to Jerusalem – such as those at Chartres and Lucca Cathedrals.

Examples of musical labyrinths can be found in abundance in the choral music of Guillaume de Machaut, a composer-poet working in northern France in the mid-fourteenth century. One is a Mass he wrote for Reims Cathedral, newly rebuilt but subsequently destroyed in the French Revolution, and which, as it happens, had a complex maze set into its nave. The score of this Notre-Dame Mass has four lines of music, each of them representing one of the voices singing. This is more or less how all choral music is laid out to this day: one line of music for each singing part, running alongside each other on the page. So what was so special about Machaut's mass setting?

This is the thing. Machaut and his fellow fourteenth-century composers thought of the notes to be sung as units in a vast mathematical game, so the duration values of the notes (that is, how many beats) were treated as a long string of numbers. The top voice, for example, begins the first part of the mass, the Kyrie Eleison, with duration values that make up the following number sequence: 6, 2, 2, 2, 4, 1, 1, 2, 2, 2, 4. The sequence runs along for a while and then repeats itself. Each of the four singing parts had its own duration-value sequence that started and ended at a different point, creating an overlapping lattice of notes of different lengths. And alongside each singing part's duration-value sequence, Machaut added a repeating pitch-value sequence: A, A, B, G, A, F, E, D, E, F, G.

Making things even more complex, the pitch-value sequence would normally be of a different length to the duration-value sequence, so the two sequences would repeat at different rates. Sometimes Machaut would double or halve the sequences in his compositions, or run them in reverse order, or invert the pitch pattern, or use a mathematical formula like the Golden

Section – much exploited in architecture and painting in the late Middle Ages and Renaissance – to configure the sequence of numbers.

But all of this intricate structuring was hidden. It is not possible, by listening to the music, to perceive the underlying design, although a skilled score reader may be able to plot its workings by studying the music on the page. The musical term for the secret guiding sequences in fourteenth-century composition is *isorhythm*, and the pieces that employed it are among the most complex musical structures ever attempted. Indeed polyphony, the interweaving of separate vocal lines, had become so complicated by the time of Pope John XXII that he actually issued a decree in 1325 ordering church music to be made more simple. No one took any notice.

What makes the achievements of Machaut and his contemporaries even more incredible was that they were composing at a time when a third of the population of Europe was being wiped out by the Black Death. How on earth did they find the inspiration to create such bafflingly intricate music? The answer, surely, is that they had recently acquired these extraordinary new gifts – the notation of music and the multiple layering of voices – and they were flexing their intellectual muscles. Alongside death and despair, this was also the period of astounding Gothic architecture, with the most extraordinary cathedrals, abbeys and churches being built all over Europe. To sing a note in one of these cavernous spaces is to hear its sound echo and reverberate, returning to its source modified by the building itself. Composers of Machaut's time were undoubtedly playing with the acoustics of the cathedrals they worked in, creating vocal manifestations of them, building layer upon layer of sound on a mathematically plotted foundation of isorhythm – and all of it to glorify (or impress) God.

Much like the Gothic architecture that shaped the buildings for which it was written, isorhythm did not last as a tool in the organisation of music. Guillaume de Machaut was its champion and its paragon.

Before leaving isorhythm, there is a footnote to be added about the way it is organised as strings of note values. There is a strik-ingly comparable procedure in the practice of *tala* in Hindustani and Carnatic classical music, whereby cycles of note values in the rhythm pattern may operate independently of a sequential melodic cycle, known as *raga*. That the Indian technique pre-dates European isorhythm by a considerable period is incontrovertible: *tala* (literally 'clap') is described in the text version of the eleventh-century *Ramayana*, a Sanskrit epic whose oral version is thought to have existed as early as the fifth century BC. It may be mere coincidence, but the fourteenth-century term for the rhythmic cycles in isorhythmic compositions by Machaut and others was *talea* (from the Latin for 'stick' or 'cutting').

By the end of the fourteenth century, nearly all of music's vital components had been discovered: notation, both melodic and rhythmic; structural organisation; and polyphony, the layering of voices on top of one another. But one final piece of the jigsaw still needed to click into position. When it did, in England in around 1400, it took musical harmony on to a radical new plane, and altered the way music sounded for ever.

From Pérotin in 1200 to Machaut in 1350, composers had enjoyed the resonant, sonorous effect of simultaneous notes in clusters, or chords. Although Pérotin's use of chords would have to be described as eccentric bordering on haphazard, by the time of Machaut the general menu of approved-of chords was in fact extremely limited. This was partly due to ecclesiastical interference – priests, bishops and cardinals knowing better than composers which sounds were godly, pure and appropriate – and partly due, I suppose, to fear of the unknown.

To understand the musical revolution that occurred in around 1400, at the hands of a composer and astrologer named John Dunstaple, we need to play with some notes. In the century leading up to Dunstaple's time, composers layered notes on top of each other but chose only from a very limited number of possible combinations. These revolved around the basic 'octave' – Big A and Little A, Big C and Little C – and what they called diatessaron and diapente (from Greek: 'through four' and 'through five'). Nowadays known as the 'perfect fourth' and 'perfect fifth', these are the pleasing-sounding combination of a note and the one four or five rungs above it, which we encountered earlier in the chapter. What makes them 'perfect' is that both have a mathematically pure 'pitch ratio'; dividing a taut plucked string by exactly two-thirds, for instance, will produce a perfect fifth. Where the 'pitch ratio' of two identical pitches is 1:1 and that of an octave 2:1, the ratio of a perfect fifth is 3:2 and a perfect fourth is 4:3.

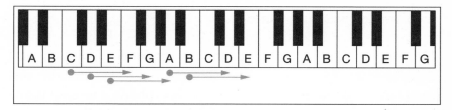

Perfect fourths on a keyboard

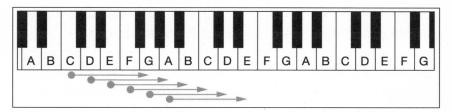

Perfect fifths on a keyboard

You will notice that I have not included F to B in the possible menu of perfect fourths. This is because F to B is not perfect: to achieve the desired pitch ratio of 4:3 we would need to pair F with B-flat (B♭), or F-sharp (F#) with B – the *flats* and *sharps* are the black notes on a keyboard. F to B was considered so unpleasant that it was given the names 'the devil in music' and the 'wolf tone', and disallowed from the list of perfect fourths. The 'diabolical' sound produced by F and B, a distance known as a *tritone*, is likewise produced by pairing B♭ and E, E and A#, C and G♭, and all the other possible tritones. (This has more to do with traditional keyboard layout than the logic of the 'four steps' idea. In the sound world of the period AD 300–1600, more or less, the allowable perfect fourth ran, in fact, from F to B♭ – that is, the black note just to the left of B. It is only a black note on a keyboard: a voice, or any other instrument, does not discriminate between 'black' and 'white' notes – and nor, aurally, does a keyboard – but the *look* of the arrangement of notes makes one think of the two types differently. It is a psychological rather than a musical problem.)

Where we are in history at this moment, 1400, you can safely ignore the black notes, even though in theory and occasionally in practice they were fully operational.

So in fourteenth-century polyphony, the perfect fifth, the perfect fourth and the octave comprised the vast majority of note combinations, or chords, on offer. Two features of this sound immediately spring to mind when you listen to it. One is that it sounds quite bare compared to later harmony. The other is that no piece ever really sounds as though it has ended properly. There's a reason for this. To our ears, accustomed to the subsequent six hundred years of harmony, there's something missing that accounts for the bareness of sound. What's missing is any sense of logic in the use of these chords. When we listen to the music of Bach, or Gershwin, or Sting, or Alicia Keys, we are being taken on a journey of chords, a 'progression'. We are guided towards the all-important end of the phrase, called the 'cadence'.

Imagine, if you will, the spiritual song, 'Amazing Grace'. In the first phrase of the song, the words 'Amazing grace' share one chord, our 'home' chord. Let's call it Chord I. Then, as the tune moves towards the word 'sweet', the chord shifts to what we will call Chord IV – because, as it happens, we have moved up a perfect fourth in the bass. At the end of the first line, as we land on the word 'sound', the harmony moves back to where we started, Chord I:

'*Amazing grace* how *sweet* the *sound*'
  CHORD I   IV   I

Everything feels 'right' about that little journey of chords. We felt good falling back to where we had started. This was our first little cadence – a term that has its origin in the Italian *cadere*, to fall.

In the second phrase we go on another short chord journey:

'*That saved a wretch* like *me*'
    CHORD I   V

This time, we travel to a new chord on the word 'me'. This is Chord V because, yes, it is a perfect fifth. Again, this progression feels logical and satisfying. We are being led from one place to another and then back again.

The verse completes itself by making two further mini-moves, from I to IV and back, and then from I to V and back:

'*I once was lost*, but *now* I'm *found*/*Was blind*, but *now* I *see*'
    CHORD I   IV   I   I   V   I

You can quite clearly hear that there's nothing haphazard about the choice of chords accompanying this tune. What is at work here is a logic in the progression of the chords. They are obeying strict laws, rather like the laws of gravity or of planets in orbit, whereby some chords exert more power than others.

The laws that chords obey, like the chain in 'Amazing Grace', were first teased out in the music of our English composer-astrologer John Dunstaple in the early 1400s, by the unveiling of a powerful new chord combination. It was neither a perfect fourth nor a perfect fifth. It was the mighty, but *im*perfect, third.

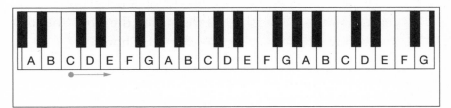

Back at the keyboard, if you count three white notes up from your starting point, C, you arrive at E. It sounds quite pleasant, so why isn't this third a *perfect* distance? The reason is that the third, unlike perfect fourths and fifths, has both a *major* and a *minor* version. It is Mr Ambiguous. If I count three white notes from D, for example, I come to F, creating a *minor* third.

Ditto E to G:

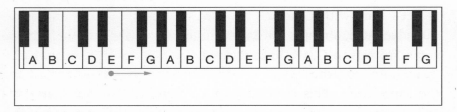

But F to A, like C to E, is a *major* third:

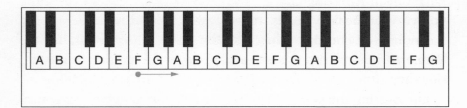

We can turn major thirds into minor thirds, and vice versa, by using the black notes to shorten or lengthen the distance between our two notes. To hear the minor third starting on C, for instance, we would land on E♭ instead of E, and to hear the minor third starting on F we would land on A♭ instead of A. Similarly, to hear the major third starting on D we just carry on past F to F#, and to hear the major third starting on E we continue past G to G#.

All the way up the ladder of notes, the third can either be major or minor, and the pivot between the major third and the minor third is the pivot upon which all Western music balances. In very crude terms one sounds happy and one sounds sad, but it's much more intriguing than that; allowing the third into note clusters had one other big by-product: the *triad*.

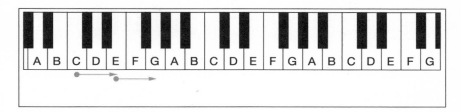

Let's start with C again. We'll count up three steps and find ourselves at E, a major third. But if we carry on up another three steps, from E to G, we have created a minor third. If we play all three notes together we hear both a major and a minor chord at the same time. This combination of major and minor thirds is called a triad, and triads are the bread and butter of all music with harmony. Triads are what create the logic and the power of the harmony in 'Amazing Grace', and in pretty much every other tune you've ever heard. Triads are the chords around which every harmonic, or chordal, journey is structured, in virtually all the Western music written between the early fifteenth century and our own time.

Discovering the power of triads was like discovering a chemical reaction or a miracle cure. Composers immediately sensed that something transformative had happened; all of a sudden their harmony started obeying laws of attraction and repulsion, whether they liked it or not. The most popular triad progressions have been used over and over again, century after century.

John Dunstaple used triads abundantly in his music, and his fame spread rapidly across Europe after he travelled to France with Henry V's army. Dunstaple was a composer with a new and enchanting style that everyone wanted to emulate, and musicians fell over themselves praising the startling new sound of English triads. Dunstaple was dubbed the *fons et origo* of the triadic craze, the 'fount and origin' of what the French called 'the English countenance'. Just as we might call Dunstaple's contemporary Geoffrey Chaucer the father of English literature, so we should call John Dunstaple the father of the triad, and therefore of the Western harmonic system.

As the fifteenth century drew on, the various Franco-Flemish courts of the Dukes of Burgundy became the artistic powerhouses of northern Europe, and it was here that Dunstaple's new cocktail of chords really took off. Its best-known champion was Guillaume Dufay (c. 1397–1474), by far the most celebrated composer of the fifteenth century – more so than the pioneer Dunstaple – in both sacred and secular music. It is in Dufay's body of work, from his rabble-rousing Crusader song and spin-off Mass, *L'Homme armé* (The Armed Man), to his humblest, most heart-melting ballads such as 'Se la face ay pale', that we see laid out the essential ingredients that characterise the great sweep of Western music that followed. Dufay builds an identifiable melody, nestled among harmonious chords that lead along the arc of a phrase towards a satisfying cadence. He has a metrically organised rhythmic structure, able to support the shape of the words of a poem, successfully allowing important stress syllables or rhymes to fall at the appropriate point in the music.

Most of all, Dufay's music sounds, at last, familiar to us. It doesn't sound distant, antique, exotically quirky, with strange tuning and asymmetrical, jerky rhythms. It doesn't sound as if someone's making it up on the spot. It is carefully designed and proportioned, and yet it flows with graceful ease. It aspires to be both a work of art and something instantly accessible to anyone's ear, for the sheer pleasure of it. Unsurprisingly, Dufay's songs spread from city to city even before the ready availability of printing; although he composed for noblemen and the Church, his work suggested a more democratic, accessible future for music than had ever been envisaged before.

By the mid-fifteenth century, Western music was a dynamic, confident art form. Armed with harmony, rhythm, a large palette of chords, and most importantly the ability to write all of these down, its most innovative sounds expanded rapidly throughout Europe. But this period of hectic experiment was under threat: a religious storm was whipping up across the continent and music was in its path. In the century following the death of Dufay, life for composers whose livelihoods depended on the Church was to become both dangerous and unpredictable.

2

The Age of Penitence
1450–1650

When we consider Europe in the period 1450 to 1650 from the distance of our own century, it looks like an age of rampant intolerance – of religious bigotry, state-sponsored terror, continuous war and bloodshed, famine, slavery, population displacement and, for most people, unrelenting misery. Even the discovery of new worlds, to the east and to the west, which one would imagine to be both positive and mind-broadening, was accompanied by genocide of the most sickening kind. Cortés's arrival in Mexico in 1519 with a few boatloads of priests and soldiers, for instance, was the cue for the deaths of between ten and twenty million Aztecs within fifty years, thanks to religion-endorsed slaughter, and the unwitting introduction of African smallpox and European influenza.

All that stands in the way of our assessment of our sixteenth- and seventeenth-century ancestors as cruel, barbaric monsters is what they produced in art, poetry, architecture and music. And the beauty and delicacy of the cultural riches of those bloodthirsty centuries are nothing short of miraculous.

In music, composers tried to come to terms with their times by imagining a compassionate and suffering God, despite precious little evidence for his presence in their world, by aspiring to capture the elation and sadness of human love, and by trying to create in their music a sanctuary of beauty and sensitivity. Perhaps more than ever, musicians felt compelled to offer humanity a better vision of itself. The music we have inherited from the years 1450 to 1650, therefore, gives us an emotional subtext to a period of history that otherwise looks rather like the high-water mark of Europe's deadly experiment with religious fundamentalism.

The year 1450 is best remembered for one of the most important technological breakthroughs of human civilisation: Johannes Gutenberg's development of a moveable-type printing press in the German town of Mainz. Without it, it is inconceivable that the next most important event of the period, Martin Luther's reforming challenge to the Roman Catholic Church in 1517, would have taken off with quite the same dramatic speed and effect. Both these epoch-changing events were to have huge implications for the dissemination and transformation of music.

Gutenberg's printing press coincided with and gave impetus to the general artistic, literary and scientific movement called the Renaissance, which had its origins in the fourteenth century but which blossomed in the fifteenth and sixteenth centuries. It is best to use the term very cautiously when applying it to music, however. There are several reasons for this. One is that music followed its own timetable, a timetable that does not fit neatly with developments in art, architecture, design, philosophy and science. Another is that, whereas in those other fields, the balmy political hotchpotch of Italy was without doubt the epicentre and dynamo of the renewed interest in antiquity, especially the culture of Ancient Greece, it was the Franco-Flemish and English spheres of influence in the chilly north of Europe that dominated fifteenth-century music. While the Fall of Constantinople in 1453 had a major impact on literature and architecture, as Christian Greek scholars laden with Ancient Greek manuscripts and artefacts fled their Ottoman conquerors and arrived in Italy, this cultural relocation seems to have had very little effect on music. More important to Italy's musical enrichment than the cultural salvage from Constantinople was the importing, at vast expense, of skilled and celebrated Flemish composers.

One such well-paid immigrant was Josquin des Prez, born in Burgundy in 1450 on what is now the Franco-Belgian border, who was tempted away to the Italian city of Ferrara, where he spent

most of his adult life. In terms of pure sound, Josquin could not
be described as a radical. He simply carried on where Dufay left
off, thickening and embellishing the polyphonic choral style that
you would have heard almost anywhere across Europe in the
later fifteenth century. But in one vital respect Josquin made a
departure, and one that was to become a hallmark of the music
of the age.

Josquin was the first composer in history for whom the meaning
of the words being sung was paramount. He was the first to bring
out and express that meaning in the way in which he set words
to music. Small wonder that the majority of pieces he composed
for the Church were called 'motets', a word derived from the
French *mot* (word). Small wonder, too, that this period saw a new-
found interest in words: thanks to the invention of the printing
press, books of all kinds were appearing everywhere, stimulating
an appetite both for poetry and for greater personal analysis and
understanding of the Bible.

Josquin's motet *Miserere mei, Deus* composed in about 1503, shows
us how far the musical treatment of texts had come since the
death of Dufay. The motet had been commissioned by the Duke
of Ferrara, Josquin's employer, who was grieving the recent loss
of a man close to him. Josquin was asked to compose something
in this friend's memory, to be performed by the Ferrara Chapel
Choir and quite possibly the duke himself in the role of tenor. It
might have been a straightforward job if the deceased had been
anyone else, but he was in fact an incredibly controversial character
named Girolamo Savonarola. This Dominican friar from Ferrara
had sought to challenge what he saw as the moral bankruptcy of
the Catholic Church, launching a bloody crusade in Florence –
where he was for a while the city's self-proclaimed spiritual and
political leader – in opposition to its supposed decadence. It was
Savonarola who instigated the Bonfire of the Vanities in Florence
in 1497, in which books, pictures, cosmetics, sculptures, mirrors,
and indeed anything encouraging or depicting sensuous pleasure,
were thrown on to a huge fire. His uncompromising crusade

brought him into direct confrontation with the Vatican. He was arrested and tortured on the order of Pope Alexander VI and finally burnt alive in May 1498, on the very same site in Florence where he had lit his infamous Bonfire.

During his imprisonment and lengthy torture he wrote a prayer of contrition to God, *Infelix ego* (I am desolate), the text of which spread rapidly, and subversively, across Europe. This prayer, which asks God's forgiveness for having confessed under torture to crimes he did not commit, was based on Psalm 51, *Miserere mei, Deus*. Its tone of both remorse and defiance was to be an inspiration to the Humanist theologian and scholar Erasmus and the soon-to-be founder of Protestantism, Martin Luther.

This was the politically sensitive text Josquin was asked to set to music, in tribute to the Duke of Ferrara's friend. There would be no way of disguising its meaning. Setting aside the fact that Pope Alexander VI was his former employer, Josquin threw himself into the commission. His first task was to make sure that the words were always clearly audible. This meant abandoning the centuries-old trend of writing whimsically long stretches of melody attached to just one syllable of text, the so-called 'melismatic' style (from the Greek *melos*, melody) that underpins most plainsong and indeed much soulful singing of the modern era, as exemplified by Mariah Carey.

In the first few bars of Josquin's motet, therefore, each voice utters the simple phrase, *Miserere mei, Deus*, (Have mercy on me, Lord), one by one, a note for each syllable. Josquin repeats this phrase throughout the piece in two equally effective ways, either as a cascading figure, like falling tears, voice overlapping voice as they descend, or by stopping all individual activity (counterpoint) and having the voices sing in block chords together.

Slowing down the movement or arresting the vocal parts were not the only ways in which Josquin manipulated his motet to draw attention to its meaning. There was another process at work in the block-chord sections that would have sounded attractively new to people of the day. He was beginning to use harmony as a way of 'locking down' the music's centre of gravity, creating a sense of 'home' in the music via a method we nowadays call a system of *keys*.

The term 'key' in music is a misleading one. The best way of describing musical keys is as *families* of notes.

All the world's music systems have gradually grouped notes into families, finding (or possibly imagining) that certain associations of notes, if used as the basis for melodies, evoked different moods. In Indian Classical music, for example, this process resulted in the establishing of ragas, of which there are different kinds for different times of day, for different seasons, for special occasions or for particular emotional states. In Western music, the grouping of notes into families began with the Ancient Greeks, who gave each of the note-families, which they called *tonoi* or *harmoniai*, the name of a certain tribe or locality. Thus, the Phrygian *tonos* was named after the Phrygian area of Anatolia, in modern Turkey. (Ironically, even the greatest Greek theorists could not agree on how the Phrygians' character was reflected in the mood, sound or effect of this *tonos*. Aristotle associated it with excitement, enthusiasm and hedonism, whereas Plato proposed that the ethos of the Phrygian *tonos* might help soldiers make wise, sober decisions.)

The medieval Church sought to bring order to the great body of plainchant across Christendom in around the eighth century by borrowing from the Greek idea of *tonoi*, laying down 'modes' that confusingly appropriated the outdated Greek regional names but applied them to new note-families – so the Ancient Greek Phrygian *tonoi* and the medieval Church Phrygian *tonus* (mode) are made up of different notes. One possible explanation for this may be that the Western branch of Christianity took certain elements of its note-family system from the Eastern Byzantine system of modes, called *Oktōēchos*. The church modes, like their Greek forerunners, were ascribed certain moods, and a great deal of theoretical energy was expended over hundreds of years describing their effect and their best possible application.

Modes persisted as a system of organising notes into families well beyond the medieval period, only yielding to the newer definition of 'keys' in the late seventeenth century, as we shall see when we get there. For now, it is enough to know that modes in Western sacred music, for all their supposed characteristics, were far more ambiguous than the modern key system; the sense of 'home' in a piece of chant was not particularly reinforced. Sixteenth-century composers like Josquin were the agents of change, as they began to weaken the modal system. The introduction of harmony also played a vital role here, since the modes of the Ancient Greeks, the Indian ragas, the Byzantine Church and the Roman Church had primarily been designed for solo, unaccompanied melodies; harmony invited notes from outside the family group to infiltrate the texture of a piece.

But for Josquin, chordal harmony was too useful a tool in illuminating the text to worry about its effect on the modes. As he started to emphasise the feeling of stability and home in his harmony, he was (albeit unwittingly) ushering in their replacement: keys. In *Miserere mei* he repeatedly causes the flow of the music to come to rest on cadences, affirming its centre of gravity. This motet is a reasonably long one for the period, and so he also moves the 'home' of the music to new places during the piece, returning at the very end to where he started. But despite its hints at the shift from modes to keys, *Miserere mei* is still framed within the medieval Phrygian mode, often noted for its air of melancholy. It would fall to later composers to take more daring liberties with harmony.

The pervading atmosphere of sorrowfulness in much of Josquin's music, whether applied to sacred music or secular songs of unhappy love, is typical of his strife-filled time. His best-known secular song was 'Mille regretz' (A thousand regrets), which is full of self-pity at having abandoned his beloved. Similarly mournful love songs were cropping up all over Europe during this period, their woeful lyrics gaining popularity in courts, noble houses, and

other places where a sheet of printed music could be afforded.
(The first printed music we know about had appeared in 1476 – a
piece of plainsong printed by the Roman Ulrich Han – but in
around 1500 a Venetian printer named Ottaviano Petrucci began
publishing songbooks using moveable type, which accelerated the
dissemination of printed music throughout the continent, expensive though it was.)

Meanwhile, in the England of Henrys VII and VIII, both the
songs of the nobility and those of ordinary lads and lasses shared
many of the same preoccupations: courting (the great difficulties
of); and nature (how best used to describe the great difficulties
of courting). A list of the most popular English songs of the Tudor
period reads like a litany of love-gone-wrong plaints:

'That was my woe'
'Woefully arrayed'
'Absent I am'
'Adew, adew, my hartis lust'
'I love unloved'
'I love, loved, and loved wolde I be'

But it was not all misery and heartbreak at the turn of the sixteenth
century. Henry VIII's own composition 'Pastyme with good
companye' was a favourite, and there were other jaunty numbers
to enjoy alongside it, such as 'Hey Trolly Lolly Lo!', 'Hoyda Hoyda',
'Jolly Rutterkin', 'Mannerly Margery', 'Milk and Ale' and 'Be Peace!
Ye Make Me Spill My Ale!' (a prelude to violence, I fear). Despite
the popular story, however, 'Greensleeves' was definitely not written
by Henry, serial wife-dispatcher and part-time musician; indeed, it
is likely to have become well known in England long after his death.
A more likely candidate for its authorship is composer-poet William
Cornysh (1465–1523), who wrote regularly for Henry's court and
for state occasions, including the strange mix of fashion and politics that was the Field of the Cloth of Gold (1520). Cornysh's other
songs make remarkably similar use of chords and exude the same

plaintive air as 'Greensleeves', his most famous being 'Ah, Robyn, Gentle Robyn', in which the forlorn singer asks an unusually intelligent and communicative robin for advice on the constancy of women.

Unsurprisingly, church music was a rather more sombre affair, and the ordinary churchgoer prior to the Protestant Reformation is likely to have found singing in church a miserable, largely non-participatory activity. To ask forgiveness, repeatedly, was what congregations were mostly expected to do, all the while listening to choirs and priests singing at great length about the same sentiment.

The only time in the year when the religious misery lifted was Christmas, whose relatively frivolous-seeming contribution to Western music – the Christmas carol – was to have a transformative effect on the development of both melody and communal music-making.

The first printed collection of Christmas carols was published in 1521 by William Caxton's appropriately named apprentice and successor, Wynkyn de Worde. The surge in carol composition around this time, notably in northern Europe, was partly inspired by an earlier Italian tradition of tuneful sacred songs welcoming the Christ-child's nativity. These *lauda* (praises) or *cantiones* (songs) were designed with the whole community in mind – even the peasantry – and they emerged at roughly the same time as the concept of the model manger, which was the brainchild of Franciscan friars trying to lure local shepherds down from the hills into church. Other origins of the Christmas carol include dancing songs ('carol' derives from the Old Greek *choros* and Latin *choraula* or *caraula*, meaning a circling, singing dance), the pagan celebration of the winter solstice, and some fragments of Advent plainsong. The northern European carols 'Personent hodie' and 'Gaudete', as well as the tune of 'Good King Wenceslas', all have their origins in earlier plainchant melodies.

'In dulci jubilo' enjoyed wide circulation in the fifteenth and early sixteenth centuries; as well as boasting an irresistibly catchy tune, it has two of the distinctive hallmarks of the early Christmas carol: a repeating final two lines, known as a 'burden' or 'refrain' ('Oh that we were there, Oh that we were there'); and the mixing of Latin words with – in our case – English words. This technique – the mixing of languages – was immensely popular in the fifteenth and sixteenth centuries, producing what are known as *macaronic* lyrics (which may derive from the Italian *maccare*, to crush or knead, as does the sweet cake made from crushed almonds, *macaroon*).

In countries with a very cold winter, two decidedly *non*-Christian elements tended to be intermingled, somewhat perplexingly, with the carol form. One was the barely disguised pagan roots of the winter and spring solstice celebrations, as seen in 'The Holly and the Ivy', with its talk of evergreen shrubs, the bark, the blossom, the horns, the berries, the rising of the sun and the running of the deer alongside one solitary grafted-in holy line, 'and Mary bore Sweet Jesus Christ to be our sweet Saviour'. The other was the notion that seasonal binge-drinking, or wassailing (Anglo-Saxon for 'saying cheers'), was somehow an appropriate way to praise the Lord, summed up hilariously in the early Tudor carol 'Bryng us in good ale':

> Bryng us in good ale, and bryng us in good ale;
> Fore owr blyssyd Lady sak, bryng us in good ale.
> Bryng us in no befe, for ther is many bonys,
> But bryng us in good ale, for that goth downe at onys.
> And bryng us in good ale.
> Bryng us in no mutton, for that is often lene,
> Nor bryng us in no trypys, for thei be syldom clene
> But bryng us in good ale.
> Bryng us in no eggys, for ther ar many schelles.
> But bryng us in good ale, and gyfe us nothyng ellys.

On it goes, offering up every known foodstuff as inferior to good ale. After the briefest of mentions right at the beginning, 'Our Lady' makes way for the true purpose of the carol: a Tudor booze-up. The Tudor period witnessed a boom in food/drink/Baby Jesus-related carols, surpassed in enthusiasm only by the Victorian era. The once-popular 'Boar's Head Carol', for example, began life as a medieval tribute to a carnivorously excessive banquet at an Oxford college but was at some point refocused to mark the Christian Nativity. In some versions, Christ's later sacrifice on the cross is likened – not very subtly – to that of the wild boar on a spit.

The 'Boar's Head Carol' is not alone among nativity songs in anticipating the Crucifixion. When they weren't thinly disguised drinking songs or pagan-inspired descriptions of northern European forests, fifteenth- and sixteenth-century carols tended, rather morbidly, to emphasise the fact that the new-born baby Jesus was going to die a horrible death and atone for the sins of all mankind. This trend suggests that the songs of Christmas and the songs of Passiontide, or Easter, were once linked, narratively, as in the ancient and still-cherished 'Coventry Carol', a lullaby that originated in a Passiontide community play, or 'Mystery' Play, for performance during Holy Week.

All these carols and songs – whether it's the 'Coventry Carol', 'In dulci jubilo' or 'Ah, Robyn, Gentle Robyn' – are part of a significant shift in texture that was happening across all forms of music during this period. It is to do with where the melody sits.

When, in around AD 900, chanting monks started adding extra voices with new notes to plainsong melodies and beginning the process that became *polyphony* – the layering of many voices – it was always assumed that the principal tune was the bottom one and the accompaniment sat on top of it. Gradually, in the centuries between 900 and 1500, as two-voice parts became three, and then four, this principal melody got left behind *inside* the texture, surrounded by the other voices. This is how the third line down in any four-part piece of choral music came to be known as the *tenor*; not because it had anything to do with the range of the singer's voice, but because this was the part that *held* the main tune, *tenir* being the French verb 'to hold', from the Latin verb *teneo*. This sounds odd to us, since we take it for granted that the tune of a piece of music sits on top of its chordal accompaniment.

This change in position, from the middle to the top, had begun sporadically in the hundred years or so before the sixteenth century, but it was during this period that the tune – particularly in choral music – drifted to the top and stayed there for good. The only style of singing where the tune is still consistently buried within the texture is in the Barbershop close-harmony tradition, where it is generally placed in the second-highest line.

Why did this shift occur? First, the rage for songs of courtly love gave people an appetite for songs that were memorable – which they were less likely to be if the tune was hidden away. And second, singing was becoming less constrained by the three- or four-part structure. While polyphonic singing, rather like a modern close-harmony group, was still a popular pastime for aristocratic types with time on their hands, a new generation of singers had learnt to provide an evening's entertainment by accompanying themselves on one of a number of recently expanded and significantly improved instruments.

By 1500 the main instrument families were all up and running: sounds made by blowing across the top of a tube of air (recorders and flutes); sounds made by blowing across two pieces of reed (the *shawm*, the *crumhorn* and the bagpipes); by operating finger-keys that caused air to feed into pipes (the organ); by drumming taut skin (the nakers – twin drums – from the Arabic *naqqara*); by striking lengths of metal (glockenspiel); by shaking things (timbrel); by drawing a bow across gut (the *rebec* and the *fiddle*); and by plucking cords, or strings. This last category in particular had thrived over the centuries. We have already encountered the al'Ud, which came from Persia via Arabic North Africa and was introduced to Spain during the al-Ándalus Caliphate (711–1492). The al'Ud and its cousin the *oud* were both variants of the earlier Central Asian *barbat* or *barbud*, belonging to the *rud* (stringed instrument) family.

Seeking out common ancestors for similar types of instruments is in many cases complicated by the abundant exchange of commodities via trading routes that ran between Europe, North Africa and Asia. Taking as an example the notion of a resonating piece of long-necked carved wood with tense gut (or, later, wire) strapped along it, there were by 1500 a huge variety of related models: the Greek *kithara* and *pandoura*, the Eastern European and Russian *gusli*, the Welsh *crwth*, the German *rotta*, the Turkic *kopuz*, the Mongolian *morin khuur*, or the Indian *rudra veena*, to name just a handful. But we do know that the oud and al'Ud gave birth to the lute and its kindred *vilhuela*, prolifically – but not exclusively – in Spain. An angel on horseback playing a lute is embroidered on to the so-called Steeple Aston Cope (religious mantle), now at the Victoria and Albert Museum in London, which reveals that the lute was familiar as far afield as England by the early fourteenth century at least.

From these plucked instruments, rested on the lap and nestled against the body, with as few as six and as many as thirty-five strings, would grow innumerable further offshoots. In the second half of the fifteenth century, musicians began using a horse-hair bow against the vilhuela's strings as an alternative to plucking, which meant it could now be played in three different ways: *vilhuela de mano* (plucked by 'hand' or finger), *vilhuela de penola* (plucked with a plectrum), and *vilhuela de arco* (played with a bow). This new third method led to the family of the bowed *viol*, also known as *viola da gamba* (played between the legs, as opposed to the *viola da braccio*, played on the arm, which also described the fiddle or, later, the violin). This same family formed its own distinct sub-species in the late fifteenth century and quickly became popular among the better-off, who might hire three or four violists (a 'consort') to play viols of different sizes rather like a choir: treble (soprano), alto, tenor, bass. Many aristocrats and wealthy merchants themselves played viols at home, too, sometimes combined in a duet with a plucked lute.

The vilhuela de mano and vilhuela de penola were expensive, complicated instruments, and a much simpler, cheaper, plucked alternative had developed alongside them: it had fewer strings and was variously known as the *gittern* in England and Germany, in France as the *gitere* or *guiterne*, in Italy as the *chitarra*, and in Spain as the *guitarra*. Lest you are lulled into a false sense of security at seeing, at last, a name that relates to an instrument that thrives in the modern world, I should point out that the *gittern/guitarra* of the sixteenth century resembles not so much a modern guitar as the delicate, shimmering *mandolin*, to which it is in fact closely related. It did indeed turn into the trusty guitar in due course, but not before it had cross-fertilised with another medieval instrument, the *citole*, whose chief successor in England was unhelpfully called the *cittern*. This last instrument was a common sight in Tudor barber-surgeons' shops, hanging on the wall for customers or resident entertainers to while away the time.

What all of these stringed instruments have in common – more so than the other families of instruments available during this period – was that they made solo musical performances both possible and enjoyable, and the sixteenth century saw a boom in this pastime. Although the majority of professional musicians were men, contemporary paintings show that a huge number of amateur musicians were women. Indeed, if the anonymous song 'And I were a maiden', the sixteenth-century equivalent of Rihanna's 'Good Girl Gone Bad', is anything to go by, female singer-songwriters of the Tudor period were not afraid of expressing themselves with bawdy candour.

> And I were a maiden,
> As many one is,
> For all the gold in England
> I would not do amiss.
>
> When I was a wanton wench
> Of twelve years of age,
> These courtiers with their amours
> They kindled my corage.

When I was come to
The age of fifteen year
In all this lond, neither free not bond,
Methought I had no peer.

When late-fifteenth-century European musicians came up with the idea of taking a bow of stretched hair to their vilhuelas and lutes, producing viola da gambas and viols, they set in train a series of innovations that would ultimately generate one of the most important instruments of subsequent centuries: the violin.

But the idea was not a new one. Bowed instruments had been around for centuries in other continents, notably Asia. In China, there is written evidence of the *xiqin* – a couple of lengths of cord, animal gut or taut silk attached to a wooden stick and stretched across a resonating box – dating from the Tang dynasty (618–907). More elaborate versions featured a spike on the bottom to root it to the ground and a carved horse's head on the top, the latter being a popular detail, not surprisingly, for horse-riding players from the nomadic communities of Central Asia. Early forms of the xiqin could be bowed with a strip of bamboo but horsehair had become the preferred material by the Song dynasty (960–1279). The Arabic rebab or rabab, which, like the al'Ud, came to Europe via Muslim Spain during what is known as the Islamic Golden Age – the Abbasid era of 750–1258 – shares so many characteristics with the xiqin that it is tempting to conclude that its basic design was brought from the East by traders, but the reverse hypothesis has also been advanced. The contemporaneous Byzantine Empire, which fell in 1453, had its own stringed archetype, the *lyra*, which initially had two strings, a pear-shaped wooden body with holes in it, for resonance, and adjustable pegs to grip and tune the strings – not unlike those on later violins and guitars. A Persian scholar of the early tenth century, Ibn Khurradadhbih, reported the lyra to be in widespread use throughout the empire, along with organs and bagpipes. A detailed picture of one, from around the eleventh century, survives on a casket in the Palazzo del Podesta in Florence, and the remains of two early-twelfth-century Byzantine lyras have been dug up in the Russian city of Novgorod.

The Byzantine lyra and the Arabic rebab gave us the specifically European rebec – which to modern eyes looks like a smaller, flatter violin with between one and five gut strings – and the *vielle* and fiddle (probably derived from the Latin *vitulari*, to celebrate or be joyful). The popularity of these precursors of the violin is especially evident in religious paintings of the early sixteenth century onwards, in which musical angels play rebecs, viola da braccias and fiddles of various shapes and sizes in a happy confusion. Matthias Grünewald's panelled Isenheim altarpiece, *Concert of Angels* (c. 1515), is a good example, as is the less menacing ceiling frieze of the same name (1535) by Gaudenzio Ferrari at the church of Santa Maria dei Miracoli in Saronno. This astonishing fresco depicts a heavenly ensemble playing a colourful assortment of stringed instruments – lyra, rebec, viola da gamba, viola da braccia, miniature ('pocket') vielle/fiddle, lute, hurdy-gurdy and psaltery – as well as wind, brass and percussion instruments, an organ and a rare Indian reed instrument, the *Nyâstaranga*.

It is around this time that the violin finally makes its first appearance. Painstaking research by musicologist Peter Holman in the 1990s uncovered evidence for the birth of the violin and its deeper-toned siblings – which became the viola and the cello – at the behest of Isabella d'Este, Marchesa of Mantua, greatest of all early-sixteenth-century patrons of the arts and daughter of Ercole I, Duke of Ferrara, who commissioned Josquin's *Miserere mei*. In December 1511 she made an order for a set of stringed instruments for the Ferrara court which, Holman convincingly suggests, were 'new design' violins, invoiced to a maestro Sebastian of Verona. If they were, this is by far the earliest record of the new instrument; and although no violins from the first fifty years of the sixteenth century survive, there is considerable circumstantial evidence of sets of violins in use in courts in northern Italy, Austria, Lorraine, Germany and France during these decades.

The oldest surviving violin made according to the design we recognise today is generally agreed to be one constructed by Andrea Amati of Cremona for Charles IX, King of France, in 1564. It is now in the Ashmolean Museum in Oxford. Since Charles was only thirteen at the time, it is reasonable to assume the order was placed by his Italian mother, Florentine patron and lover of all the arts in the Isabella d'Este mould, Catherine de Medici. Cremona blossomed as a violin-making hub after Amati set up shop there in the 1560s, although his own enterprise was almost certainly pre-empted by those of *maestri di violini* Gasparo di Bertolotti in Salò ('Gasparo da Salò'), Francesco Linarol in Venice, and Zanetto Micheli and others in Brescia. Amati's family workshop was subsequently imitated by two other now legendary violin-making families of Cremona, the Stradivari and the Guarneri, in whose hands the town swiftly eclipsed the earlier reputation of Brescia. (What maestro Antonio Stradivari would have made of the news that one of his 1721 violins, the 'Lady Blunt' – named after its former owner, Lord Byron's granddaughter – sold at auction in June 2011 for £9.8m [$15m], with proceeds going to earthquake relief in Japan, is anybody's guess.)

The new Ferrara–Brescia–Cremona model of the violin had a stronger, brighter sound than its smaller predecessors, and was capable of greater expression and versatility on account of the way the strings were arched over the bridge, instead of lying flat in a row as on a guitar or lute. The arching allowed for greater pressure to be exerted on the string by the bow without fear of accidentally catching the adjacent string(s). The violin's absence of frets, which had been a feature of the viola da gamba family and the lute, also allowed its player greater freedom in the tuning and individuality of phrasing. What has emerged from study of the sixteenth-century violin, though, is that, for the first few decades of its existence, it was intended as a member of a group (consort), not primarily as a solo instrument. Typically, a batch of four might have been commissioned, with two or even three of the four calibrated to a lower pitch to make a fuller, self-contained chordal sound.

Class as well as fashion shaped the violin's rapid dissemination across Europe. In the fifteenth century, the ruling elite had favoured consorts of genteel viols (viola da gambas) when listening to purely instrumental music, or to accompany singers; stringed instruments were associated with refinement, poise and virtue. For rowdier evenings of dancing, however, they had preferred noisier wind (and sometimes brass) instruments, which were considered rather coarse, licentious and – their assessment not mine – phallic. Anyone who was anyone in Europe had a wind band, or *piffari*, often imported from Germany, at their court. Despite the superiority of stringed instruments, the medieval fiddle or vielle had not been deemed fit for decent society: too common for the well-to-do, it belonged instead to the wandering street musician, suitable for the drunken rollicking of the peasantry but not a lot more. It was Isabella d'Este's idea to commission stringed instruments for dancing that would replace the rude Teutonic wind bands but make a bigger, livelier sound than the viols – an instrument, she hoped, with the upmarket cachet of a lute. The (expensively made) violin was the solution, and the Marchesa of Mantua's preference for it would probably have ensured its instant status as a must-have accessory for the progressive Renaissance court. Whatever the spur, the lure of the violin proved irresistible, and predominantly German *piffari* wind bands were soon surpassed by predominantly Italian violin consorts.

In late 1539, Henry VIII's representative in the Venetian Republic, Edmond Harvel, engaged four members of the same family, the Bassanos, to travel to England to establish a royal consort there on the instructions of chief minister Thomas Cromwell. The brothers duly took up their posts the following spring (on 2s.4d. each a day), joined by another brother already resident. The experiment was clearly successful enough to encourage Henry to invite a second group from Venice (or possibly Milan) to add to the ensemble later in 1540. These multi-instrumentalist musicians are likely to have had sets of both violins and viols with them even at the outset of their lifelong careers at the Tudor court, but certainly by 1545 official documents record them as having violins. Henry's Venetian immigrants are noteworthy for the influence they brought to bear on the home-grown composers Thomas Tallis and William Byrd – of whom more shortly – but their invigorating effect on English music is nothing compared to the long-term consequences of the arrival, in the same period, of Italian violinists at the French court.

Italian fashion dominated the reign of King Henry II of France, thanks to his wife, Catherine de Medici, whose role in the arts of sixteenth-century France is hard to exaggerate. Crowned queen a year after purchasing the 1546 Amati violins, she introduced to the French court what amounted to a complete lifestyle after the Italian fashion. She imported Italian furniture, artefacts, couture, jewellery, paintings, sculpture and architecture. She wore the world's first high-heeled shoes, the first 'designer' perfumes, and owned the first side-saddle to allow women to ride as adeptly as men. Her personal library contained thousands of rare manuscripts. Unusually for a woman of the period, she was as knowledgeable about the sciences as she was the arts: she was the patron of Nostradamus, had observatories constructed to read the stars, and one of her closest confidants was the Florentine astrologer Cosimo Ruggeri. She more or less invented the concept of table etiquette and manners; her Italian chefs gave the French a taste for complicated, fine cuisine, presenting them with hundreds of new dishes, sauces and delicacies: veal, guinea fowl, truffles, artichokes, broccoli, green beans, peas, melons, macaroons, sorbet, zabaglione and ice cream. Most important for our purposes, she staged spectacular pageants at Fontainebleau, Chenonceau and other grand châteaux she had had constructed along Italian lines.

The aim of Catherine de Medici's pageants was undoubtedly political: to impress upon the warring nobility the God-granted power of the Valois monarchy, to distract them from scheming, and to use them as platforms for her relentless diplomacy. The 'magnificences' she oversaw at the French court had many components, from jousting tournaments and firework displays to water fêtes and mock battles. Above all, though, she adored dance, believing it would teach her courtiers elegance, decorum and a respect for order. To this end she recruited Italian dancers, choreographers and a band of violinists, playing on the very instruments she had ordered for her son from Cremona. The director of her violin band was the Italian-born choreographer, composer, conductor and violinist Balthasar de Beaujoyeulx. With Beaujoyeulx, Catherine conceived what have come to be accepted as the world's first formal ballets. The most famous of these, the *Ballet Comique de la Reine*, staged in Paris in September 1581 as part of royal wedding festivities, lasted from ten in the evening till three the next morning and interwove geometric dance patterns involving representations of Mercury, Pan, Minerva, Jupiter and the evil sorceress Circe from Homer's *Odyssey*, an ensemble of water and wood nymphs, recited verse, singing and instrumental music by Lambert de Beaulieu, and sensational scenic effects and transformations.

The choreographed steps themselves were adapted versions of the social court dances of the sixteenth century, typically grouped in pairs such as the French pavane and galliard or the Italian passamezzo and saltarello, as well as the popular allemandes and courantes. Such grouping together of dance movements, accompanied by a string ensemble, was to play an important part in the evolution of the Suite and its successors the Sonata, the Concerto and even the Symphony, as we shall see in the next chapter. Thus the *Ballet Comique de la Reine* can be viewed as a significant landmark not just in the history of ballet, but also in that of instrumental music.

Around the same time that the violin began its conquest of Europe, keyboard technology was also undergoing rapid advancement. This is no coincidence: keyboard instruments of this period used a keyboard layout borrowed from the organ to pluck the strings of, ideally, some kind of lute or a harp lying on its side in a box. This kind of mechanism, known as a harpsichord by the sixteenth century, was first mentioned in a court document from Padua in

1397 and first depicted in a 1425 altarpiece in Minden, Germany, but the oldest surviving example of an actual instrument – lacking its important inner workings – is in the Royal College of Music in London and dates from the late fifteenth century. The harpsichord's heyday lasted from this period until the piano gained popularity in the mid-eighteenth century. The oldest surviving complete harpsichord dates from 1521 and is Italian, the sophistication of its mechanism suggesting that the techniques for making harpsichords were already extremely well advanced by then.

At home, in England, Holland or France, those of considerable means might own a smaller relative of the harpsichord, a *virginal* – or, rather, a *pair of virginals*, since it was played with two hands, even if it clearly looked like one piece of furniture. Henry VIII, who knew an exciting new gadget when he saw one, ordered five in 1530. As with the many-stringed lute – which is so challenging to play that it developed its own unique musical notation, tablature, a graphic representation of the strings and frets that is still in use today – the beauty of this keyboard instrument was that, with practice, you could play relatively complex interweaving lines of music at the same time. But the harpsichord allowed greater flexibility and ease of movement than the lute, so it should not surprise us that the sixteenth century saw the emergence of bespoke music *intended* just for instruments, rather than for instruments as an accompaniment to voices. Likewise the keyboard music of sixteenth-century English composers Thomas Tallis, William Byrd and John Redford, which was originally intended to be sung, was soon adapted, by them and others, into music tailor-made for the virginals. Instrument-specific music seems commonplace to us now, but it was a real novelty during this period, and one which was rapidly taken up by composers on mainland Europe. This new style of music was often wilfully difficult so as to show off the dexterous virtuosity of the player – a habit that became an epidemic in the following centuries, especially when the composer and player were one and the same awe-inspiring artist.

For sheer technological complexity, though, no sixteenth-century instrument comes near the organ. As we have already seen, the earliest organs were invented by the Ancient Greeks, but it is nonetheless often (rightly) claimed that, before the Industrial Revolution, the clock and the organ were mankind's two most complicated machines. The world's oldest playable organ, in the basilica of Valère in the canton of Valais in Switzerland, was built some time between 1390 and 1435. To put that in context, this ultra-sophisticated mechanism was up and running two hundred years before the invention of the thermometer, a hundred and fifty years before the invention of the pencil, and a hundred years before the invention of the first watch.

There is no doubt that the presence of these extraordinary musical machines in most cathedrals and large churches since around the thirteenth century encouraged the composing of keyboard music targeted at the unique qualities and capabilities of the organ. Very little survives of what may have been written especially for the organ before the widespread availability of printing, but the evidence we do have provides us with precious clues as to how this repertoire was developing. Of particular interest is a collection of some two hundred and fifty pieces for organ, compiled between 1450 and 1470 – possibly with the help of Conrad Paumann, a well-known blind organist of the time – and found in the library of the small Bavarian town of Buxheim.

Something very significant can be found both in the Buxheim organ book and on the instrument at the basilica of Valère: the indication to play a line of music on the pedals, with the feet. Why is this so important? It's important because the organ, with its lower, deeper pedal notes, led the way in the innovation of a *bass line* in music.

We have already witnessed the early-sixteenth-century shift in the position occupied by the principal melody in a piece of four- or three-part vocal music, moving from the middle of the texture to the top. Gradually the performing range of the tune-carrying top line was extended upwards and higher, a process accelerated by the use of boys with high voices and even – heaven forfend!

– women in some vocal groups. Around the same time, the lowest line started to take on greater responsibility for the foundation of the harmony: it became more substantial, and instruments started to adapt to give it more depth – such as the introduction of deeper-pitched stringed instruments and indeed organ pedals.

While musicians and instrument-makers were finding ways of expanding the expressive range of what they could play, historical destiny was going to hand the bass line an unexpected boost. Destiny, that is, in the shape of Martin Luther.

The early sixteenth century was a bad time for the Roman Catholic Church and its allied heads of state in Europe. On its eastern doorstep the Muslim Ottoman Empire was expanding in size and military ambition – between 1500 and 1520 it tripled in size and by 1529 controlled the Mediterranean and all of south-east Europe, and had begun its first siege of Vienna with an avowed aim of replacing Catholicism with Islam. As if that weren't enough, Martin Luther's challenge to the Vatican, begun in Wittenberg in Saxony in October 1517 with the publication of his '95 Theses on the Power and Efficacy of Indulgences', tore into the heart of the Catholic Church's authority. He didn't mean to start a breakaway church, but within a few decades swathes of Europe had switched to one form of Protestantism or another.

What has all this to do with bass lines in music?

Luther, as well as being a theologian, scholar, writer and preacher, was a composer. He believed that the congregations in his churches should be able to join in hymn-singing with confidence and enthusiasm, and this meant having easy-to-pick-up tunes to sing. Luther accordingly had collected numerous popular contemporary folk tunes, given them holy words, and encouraged these hymns, or chorales, to be sung in Lutheran churches. One of his own compositions was 'Ein' feste Burg ist unser Gott' (A Mighty Fortress is our God), but he also inspired other composers to provide new tunes for the purpose.

What is immediately noticeable about 'Ein' feste Burg' and the other Lutheran chorales of the sixteenth century is that they move along, syllable by syllable, with the words: the tune is clearly sitting on top of the sound, and the bottom line, the bass, is now in a dedicated supporting role, underpinning the movement of chords. This is what hymns were to sound like until around the mid-twentieth century. And the newly defined role of the bass line altered how composers viewed the shape of harmony for hundreds of years, too. It is as fundamental a structural change to the way music sounded as was the contemporaneous decision to start using timber frames and bricks in the building of houses.

Lutheranism encouraged the growth of church music and its effect was infectious, despite the more radical branches of Protestantism viewing music – like saints, relics, incense, statues, stained-glass windows – as a superfluous distraction from the proper job of communal worship: reading, analysing and drawing conclusions from the Bible. Even Catholic composers were affected by Luther's emphasis on congregational participation, as the Catholic Church's reaction to the spread of Protestantism was to instigate a series of reforms known as the Counter-Reformation, as part of which it largely followed Luther's lead on music. (If you were being mischievous, you might say the Counter-Reformation was the Vatican's way of rebranding Lutheranism as its own idea.)

What Protestant and Counter-Reformation reforms meant, more or less whoever you were, was a simplifying of church music so that the words could be heard more clearly. It meant a retreat from the very florid and ornate polyphony that had obsessed composers for a hundred years. The interweaving, flowing lines of equal voices began to make way for a new and fashionable triumvirate in music: tune, accompanying chords, and supporting bass. The dramatic effect of this simplification can be seen particularly starkly in the work of the Rome-based composer Giovanni Pierluigi da Palestrina (1525?–94), who was forced into a switch of style mid-career. A distinctly non-ornate style is introduced to his music after the Catholic Church's Council of Trent (sitting from 1545 to 1563) laid down strict new rules on the simplification of music.

But it is in non-Catholic countries that a mid-sixteenth-century change in style, according to the mood of the ruling religious elite, is most clearly demonstrated. In England, notably, Catholic composers who had been working for the Catholic Church at the start of the century had to change their style to comply with the country's gradual adoption of Protestantism during the reigns of Henry VIII and Edward VI. These religious reforms were put into reverse under Mary Tudor in the 1550s, but Elizabeth I's resumption of Protestantism, albeit in a watered-down form compared to the Calvinism of Scotland or Holland, confirmed the general trend towards a simpler, clearer, text-dominated choral style.

As a result, the contrast between musical styles in around 1500 and those of fifty years later, at the height of the European religious reforms, is dramatic. At the turn of the century, Thomas Ashwell was writing the kind of sacred polyphony you'd have heard anywhere in Europe: his *Missa Jesu Christe* of around 1500 has the voice parts running all over the place, in and out of each other, and long phrases run on and on with just one open syllable – the 'melismatic' style that Josquin notably rebelled against just a few years later with his *Miserere mei, Deus*. It is a lovely sound, but it is practically impossible to make out where the individual words begin and end, even if you are fluent in Latin. The purpose of this music is to create a sense of glorious beauty and ethereal godliness, to show off how rich the blending of choral voices could be. In sharp contrast, take 'If ye love me', composed by Thomas Tallis for the Chapel Royal of Edward VI when Protestant reforms were in the ascendancy. It is immediately apparent that Latin has been replaced with English, that the voices are singing together so that the words are clearly audible, and that meandering, interweaving voices have turned into blocks of sound that move as one. The process that Josquin had prophetically anticipated, namely the change of musical texture to make the meaning of the text clear and transparent, had by mid-century turned – in effect – into state law throughout Europe.

Although English music outwardly toed the religious line, it is important to stress its one great anomaly during the Reformation period. Elsewhere on the continent, bloody wars, the threat of torture and the clampdown of liberties that accompanied the Counter-Reformation were making the choices composers made a matter of life and death. (One example is the fate of Portuguese composer Damião de Góis, who in 1545 was denounced, interrogated, tried and imprisoned by the Inquisition for, among other things, 'playing unfamiliar music in his house on the Sabbath'.) In England, however, after Henry VIII's split with Rome and especially under his daughter Elizabeth I, a blind eye was turned to the fact that Thomas Tallis and William Byrd, the two most celebrated and revered composers of the day, were privately still Catholic – and indeed that they continued secretly to write sacred music in Latin, in the older style, alongside what they provided for the reformed Church of England. Elizabeth even granted them a monopoly on the printing of sheet music, such was the favour she showed towards them.

It is one of the exquisite ironies of that acrimonious century, stained with the blood of religious conflict, that some of the most beautiful and heartfelt sacred music for the Catholic rite was composed in Elizabeth's Protestant kingdom.

Byrd's 1591 setting of *Infelix ego*, the prison-cell prayer of Girolamo Savonarola, originally set by Josquin over eighty years earlier, catches the mood – through stripped-back, imitative, mournful phrases – that pervades both the sacred and secular music of so much of the sixteenth century: penitence and remorse. It sounds as if artists like Byrd are being crushed by the weight of the world around them; their music is a cry of anguish, a lamentation. Byrd's published collection of 1588, the year of the Spanish Armada, was entitled *Psalms & Sonets of Sadnes and Pietie*, which is as good a description as any of most of the music of the previous hundred years. Never before had humanity so badly needed its music to share the burden of anxiety, and composers everywhere answered this plaint. Settings of the Lamentations of Jeremiah, the Penitential Psalms, the agony of the Crucifixion and the Mass for the Dead abound, from Thomas Tallis in England, Tomás Luis de Victoria in Spain, Giovanni da Palestrina in Italy and Orlande de Lassus in Flanders and Germany.

But although great church music continued to be written, and religious wars continued to rage, the 1570s and '80s saw a new wave of music sweep up like a warm summer wind from Italy through France to England, which seemed to provide an alternative way of looking at the world. While the Catholic Church continued to see menace and conspiracy on every corner, from Jews and Protestants to the scientific challenges of Galilei Galileo, and to oppress its followers by taking so much of the joy out of art and music, it was as if ordinary people sensed that any improvement in the quality of their lives on earth would have to be home-made. This new, irrepressible sound was the still, small voice of secular humanism.

Reflected in the work of Cervantes in Spain, and of John Donne, Francis Bacon and William Shakespeare in England – music lovers all – humanism began a fightback for reason and compassion, qualities in short supply during the preceding century of religious strife. Summed up in one perfect sentence by Donne – 'Any man's death diminishes me, because I am involved in Mankinde' – the movement was a ray of sunshine peeping out from behind storm clouds. And not for the last time in musical history, 'art music', the music of the wealthy, educated and privileged, was to be saved from itself by popular, or folk song, traditions.

Caravaggio's 1596 painting *The Lute Player* shows a musician playing from a score by a Franco-Flemish composer called Jacques Arcadelt, who spent the first half of his life in Italy, where he was a contemporary of and sometime collaborator with Michelangelo, and the second half of his life in France. Arcadelt's great gift to music during one of its darkest hours was his unashamedly life-affirming madrigals – published in Venice in 1539, and probably the music shown in Caravaggio's painting – and his cheerful *chanson* collections, published in Paris in the 1560s.

Arcadelt's first book of madrigals was the most widely reprinted songbook in Europe in the second half of the sixteenth century. Every professional and amateur musician of the age would have known the songs in this bestseller, especially the erotic 'Il bianco e dolce cigno' (The white and gentle swan), which, like the other madrigals in the collection, is concerned with human pleasures and full of sensuous imagery and sexual allusion: dying, in the case of 'The white and gentle swan', for example, is code for orgasm.

When Arcadelt moved to France he did the same for the chanson as he had done for the Italian madrigal, publishing nine books of sweet, uplifting songs that anyone who could sing or play a guitar, lute or theorbo – a sort of oversized lute – could easily learn and enjoy. Typical of the chansons was the jolly, catchy 'Margot, labourez les vignes', though its lyrics spin an odd yarn: Margot, tend the vines, it exhorts repeatedly, going on to recount that the singer of the song met three captains on the road home from Lorraine 'to whom I was the pox'. No further information is given.

Unusually for their time, Arcadelt's madrigals and chansons were intended for performance by men *and* women, and their success inspired many other composers. Chief among these were an Englishman and an Italian whose experiments with the form as the new century unfolded were to give to music what Shakespeare gave poetry and drama: a compassionate eloquence that, in place of intimidation, sought to dignify humanity.

The Englishman was John Dowland, a Londoner and exact contemporary of Shakespeare who spent some of his most fruitfully creative years as the extravagantly paid official lutenist to King Christian IV of Denmark. Quite apart from their haunting beauty, Dowland's hugely influential *First Book of Songs*, published in 1597, are the first outstanding examples of the kind of solo song that – structurally and stylistically – has since thrived more or less continuously in Western music. While a four-part chanson by Arcadelt still sounds to us like music from another epoch, almost any composer from 1600 to the present day would have been proud to come up with Dowland's 'Flow, my tears'; if, for example, Sting were to release it on CD, it wouldn't sound out of place in our own time. Which is exactly what he did in 2006, as it happens.

This makes Dowland's contribution, like Shakespeare's, something very different from what had gone before: his work has a universal appeal that transcends its age. It is an overused word, but this is what makes him a genius.

Although Dowland used 'Flow, my tears' as the basis for a set of purely instrumental pieces called *Lachrimae, or Seaven Teares* for strings and lute, songs remained, by and large, his format of choice. Meanwhile, over in Italy, one of Dowland's masterful contemporaries – one of the most influential musicians of all time – was taking the concept of song in the most extraordinary new direction. The composer was Claudio Monteverdi and the new style of singing gave birth to opera.

Born in Cremona, adopted home of the violin, Monteverdi worked for a time at the court of Duke Vincenzo of Gonzaga in Mantua before taking Europe's most prestigious musical post in 1613: director of music at St Mark's basilica in Venice. He published nine volumes of madrigals between 1587 and 1651, which were themselves so revolutionary that – even forgetting for a moment the issue of opera – we would still be ranking him as among the most experimental and daring composers of all time.

What Monteverdi did in his madrigals was to take the idea of triads and chords, and start to mess with their chemistry. Like all sixteenth-century composers, he knew that some chords felt especially close and comfortable next to one another: the C major triad, for example, contains two of the same notes as the E minor triad and is therefore closely related to it; likewise the E minor triad shares two of its notes with the G major triad and they too are closely related. Monteverdi knew that blending these related chords in one piece of music would create something tranquil, reassuring and ethereal. A prime example of this technique is the *Missa Papae Marcelli* by Giovanni Palestrina, probably composed in 1562 and considered one of the most treasured masterpieces of all sacred music. Palestrina uses closely related chords throughout, moving from one to another slowly and gradually, and the overall impression is one of stability. But it is this sense of stability that Monteverdi wanted to undermine. He was the Galilei Galileo of music, challenging the status quo.

In his madrigals, Monteverdi dips in and out of all kinds of chords, many of them startlingly unrelated, in order to create ear-catching effects. He wants his listener to feel disorientated, or surprised, or intrigued, especially if it fits or enhances the words of the poem. So in his 1605 madrigal, 'O Mirtillo, Mirtillo anima mia' (O Myrtle, Myrtle my soul), for instance, on the words, 'che chiami crudelissima Amarilli' (the one you call cruellest Amaryllis), he creates a series of deliberate clashes of chord, called a 'dissonance' or 'suspension'. These discords, though relatively tame by modern standards, would have sounded shocking to Monteverdi's contemporaries. Dissonance was just one of the effects he employed to 'paint' the lyrics in sound. As his career progressed, his music became more and more about aural effect and emotional manipulation.

Nor was it just in his madrigals that Monteverdi started shifting chords around for the sheer surprise and delight of it. By a strange quirk of fate, this ambitious choral composer found himself working in the one building in the world which, by dint of its architecture, was responsible for a new style of choral music. St Mark's basilica revealed to Monteverdi a new world of possibility; as far as I know, this is the only example in Western music of a building changing the course of history.

The basilica is a vast, cavernous, echoing space, with all sorts of alcoves, balconies, domes, cupolas and arches affecting its acoustics. Any sound you make ricochets around, bouncing against all these different-shaped stone, mosaic and tiled surfaces. But what you cannot do in the basilica is speak or sing quickly: it would come out as gobbledegook. The composers who worked at St Mark's in the late sixteenth century – particularly uncle and nephew Andrea and Giovanni Gabrieli – recognised this, and they pioneered a form of choral music in which huge blocks of sound, chord after chord, were sung in short, dramatic bursts, accompanied by bands of instruments, particularly brass – and then there'd be a pause to let the sound reverberate awe-inspiringly around the space. The Gabrielis also experimented with placing clusters of singers and instrumentalists in different pockets of the building, a technique known as *antiphony*, meaning 'voices against each other', or *polychoral*, 'many choirs'. An anthem like Giovanni Gabrieli's 'Omnes Gentes plaudite manibus', a setting of Psalm 46, 'All people clap your hands', published in 1597, is the kind of polychoral work that would have sounded spectacular in St Mark's when it was first heard. It may be church music but it is also theatrical and grandiose, and when Monteverdi applied for the music director's post at St Mark's in 1610 he attempted to out-Gabrieli Gabrieli in one fell swoop: his audition composition was an epic setting of the Vespers, the Catholic Evening Service, rightly considered one of the landmarks of choral music.

It was only a matter of time before all these ingredients – the daring chord progressions and intimacy of the madrigals, and the polychoral grandeur of the St Mark's style – were put together into an extraordinary, unforgettable cocktail: opera. It had all started when a group of humanist Florentine intellectuals known as the Florentine Camerata came up with the notion that they would try to recreate or reimagine what they claimed was Ancient Greek sung drama. In 1597, their first semi-collaborative attempt at this new form, which they called 'drama through music', was a piece called *Dafne*, with music by one of their number, Jacopo Peri. He followed with another offering, *Euridice*, in 1600. The manuscript of *Dafne* has not survived, although a fair amount was written about its preparation and performance, making *Euridice* the world's oldest surviving opera. If you launch a new musical form, though, what you need is a composer of such stature and brilliance that there is a decent chance of someone taking your new art form seriously. Peri was not such a man. Luckily, fate handed that baton to Monteverdi, whose 'musical fable' for the Mantuan court, *Orfeo*, premièred in 1607.

Monteverdi brought all the tricks he was learning composing madrigals and sacred choral music into his telling of Orpheus's descent into the Underworld to rescue his recently lost lover, Euridice. He was aiming for maximum emotional effect, maximum narrative clarity, maximum impact, even shock, and wasn't going to obey anyone's rules about what he could or could not do. The result – to people of the time – was stunning. He invented an orchestra for the occasion, a combination of instruments never before gathered under one roof. It included brass and wind instruments, percussion, and a whole gallimaufry of types of strings: plucked, stroked, strummed, keyed and bowed. He had instrumental fanfares, solos, duets, choruses. He borrowed old and new styles wherever he felt it appropriate and requisitioned the St Mark's-style choral music for the big moments. (Indeed, the exciting opening phrase of *Orfeo* was recycled for his 1610 *Vespers*, so interchangeable was the style.) He told the story through characters directly expressing themselves and their feelings to the audience, always and only singing, something that had never been tried before. Almost everything about it was a novelty. It was – by the standards of the day – loud, long, and modern.

Orfeo played twice at the palace in Mantua to an audience of fewer than a hundred invited guests. It was quite a different sight a year later when Monteverdi's new opera, *Arianna*, premièred. Mantua, celebrating a royal wedding, laid on an open-air stadium into which were crammed several thousand people a night. He subsequently moved to Venice, which soon became as obsessed with opera as it had traditionally been with carnivals, and the world's first public opera house, San Cassiano, opened there in 1637. While in Venice Monteverdi composed at least half a dozen other operas, all but two of which are now lost.

Incredibly, it is Monteverdi's last opera, *The Coronation of Poppea*, composed in 1642, his seventy-fourth and final year, that has gone down as one of the most radical dramas, never mind musical dramas, in history. What makes *Poppea* so radical is that, to put it simply, it is about real people and their complicated, messy

emotions. Monteverdi's music explores the real-life passions of
two real historical figures: the emperor Nero and his mistress,
Poppea; there is no sign here of the usual allegorical characters
from myth or ancient legend, and the only gods we meet are
merely symbolic. Crucially, *Poppea* shows how far music's social
function had come since Guido of Arezzo put notation on the
map. Music was still used for great occasions of state and it was
still central to religious ritual – but now it was also addressing
people's intimate emotional exchanges. It was adopting the role
that it plays for us, in the twenty-first century: it was becoming
the soundtrack to the affairs of our hearts.

On the surface of it, *Poppea* is about lust and ambition conquering
all, with poor old virtue, decency and good governance being
jettisoned in the process. Nero and Poppea fall for each other and
the consequences for everyone around them are catastrophic. The
pursuit of carnal pleasure sweeps all before it. We are as far from
the ideals and arguments of the previous century as it is possible
to be. The religious disputes of the Reformation and Counter-
Reformation have all been abandoned – issues of moral authority,
piety, remorse, sacrifice, obedience to God, spirituality and the
afterlife are all swept aside as *Poppea*'s lovers seek and find physical
gratification above all else. The opera's climax, and I choose that
word deliberately, appears to reward them for their selfishness.

It ends with a duet for Nero and Poppea of unabashed sensuality
– probably composed or revised by one of Monteverdi's assistants,
Francesco Sacrati – called 'Pur ti miro, pur ti godo'. The passion
that oozes out of this duet, 'I adore you, I embrace you, I desire
you, I enchain you', is so frank and sensual it almost turns its
audience – remember they are in the room too – into voyeurs,
awkwardly witnessing the private interchange of two weirdly
uninhibited strangers. This was new territory indeed.

But beware of first impressions. The Venetians of 1642 to whom
The Coronation of Poppea was directed knew this historical story,
and they knew what happened next, after the curtain fell – that
is, after the apparently triumphant ending of the opera. Nero

killed his new empress Poppea, their unborn child, then himself, and his regime collapsed disastrously, with Rome in flames. What Monteverdi's Venetian audience understood was that this was a satire. They would have seen the opera's ending for what it was: a savage attack on Venice's arch-rival state: Rome. In the light of this, *The Coronation of Poppea* can be seen as a damning, deliberately shocking critique on corruption and the excesses of Roman power, and the pressing need for self-restraint.

It was a cry that fell on deaf ears as far as Rome was concerned – or, for that matter, in France, where Louis XIV was about to embark on a reign that would give new meaning to the word 'excess'. For sure, the age of penitence, remorse and piety was well and truly over.

3

The Age of Invention
1650–1750

The spirit of musical invention heralded by Monteverdi was enthusiastically taken up by his successors over the following century. While the first half of this new musical age, from around 1650 to 1700, was totally dominated by Italians – both at home and working across Europe – the irrepressible urge to create, improve and challenge gradually spread further north to Germany, France and especially, in the genius of George Frideric Handel, England. Above all, the music of this period was characterised – as were the contemporary sciences – by a powerful marriage of imagination and ambition.

This was an era in which the Church's unquestioned supremacy truly began to crumble and mere mortals took on the responsibility of creating the world around them. From Pascal's mechanical calculator (1642), Otto von Guericke's machine-generation of electricity (1672) and Leibniz's calculating wheel (1673) to Newton's *Principia* (1687), Hadley's octant (1730) and Harrison's marine chronometer (1736), restless ingenuity was directed at a myriad ways of measuring, understanding and exploiting the dimensions of the natural world. Little wonder, then, that this period is sometimes called the Scientific Revolution – although advances in science would also offer the artistic community a series of technological breakthroughs. Indeed, as we shall shortly see, every note of music subsequently written and played would be shaped by the spirit of the age.

The link between science and music had never been far from composers' minds – from the Ancient Greek belief in the 'music of the spheres' to Monteverdi's exploitation of the echoing architecture of St Mark's basilica – but in the seventeenth century this relationship took on a less celestial nature. One of the great leaps forward was the invention of the world's first pendulum clock in 1656, which finally transformed Galileo Galilei's groundbreaking research into the physics of pendulums in the 1580s into a practical tool. The clock was designed by Dutch scientist Christiaan Huygens – who incidentally had published essays on the physics of music – and built by clockmaker Salomon Coster. It goes without saying that the development of a totally accurate timekeeping device was an enormous breakthrough in an age of feverish navigation and exploration, but Huygens's beautiful pendulum clock also neatly epitomised the central obsessions of the era: the intricate workings of machines, the interplay of cog and wheel, the laws of motion and gravity, and the dimension of time itself.

It should not surprise us, then, that the notion of keeping time in music became a subject of some debate during this same clock-making epoch – nor indeed that its music has a mechanical regularity about it that delights in repetition, jaunty imitation and an unwavering, foot-tapping pulse, all characteristics shared by the other great motivator of seventeenth-century musical style: dance music.

Yet there is a great irony to the relationship between horological time and musical time, since music is the only art form that follows its own, independent time scheme, obeying its own internal clock and seemingly suspending the normal division of seconds, minutes and hours, according to the whims of the composer. As if to underline this ambivalent relationship, the technical term in music for 'speed' is the Italian word *tempo*, meaning, literally, time – not, as would be logical, *velocità* (velocity). It was not until the arrival of electrical metronomes in the twentieth century that musical speeds obeyed absolute relationships with seconds and minutes; earlier definitions of musical speeds were always relative, subjective instructions that differed from place to place, composer to composer, decade to decade. Modern-day attempts to estimate what a composer of a previous era meant by the terms *allegro* (quickly), *andante* (moderately) or *largo* (very slowly) have been hampered by this lack of an absolute relationship with everyday measurements of time. (One deceptively simple method of establishing the lower limit of musical speed has been to use reproduction seventeenth- or eighteenth-century wind instruments and measure how long a player could hold his breath while holding a single note. By comparing this to the longest-lasting *written* notes of the period, researchers have painstakingly teased out what composers might have expected from slower directions such as *largo* and *adagio*. These kinds of experiments are somewhat approximate, as you would imagine, but before them there was no way of knowing what, say, Monteverdi's speeds sounded like *to him*.)

In 1676, Thomas Mace, who had been one of Oliver Cromwell's favourite composers, outlined the possibility of measuring musical pulse against a pendulum in his ambitious, florid and comprehensive tome, *Musick's Monument* (*'A remembrancer of the best practical musick, both divine, and civil, that has ever been known, to have been in the world'*). Mace was probably aware of Galileo's research, which included the design – not made in his lifetime – of a pendulum clock that pre-dates Huygens by fourteen years. Subsequent efforts to align musical pace with horological time, however, failed to ignite general enthusiasm; indeed, others were still attempting to match musical pulse with less scientific external sources. The Venetian theorist Ludovico Zacconi had proffered the idea of using the human pulse as a guide as early as 1592, in his essay *Prattica di musica*, and this notion was still popular in 1752, when Johann Joachim Quantz, flautist to Frederick the Great of Prussia, published his biblical guide to playing the flute. It is, however, worth mentioning Parisian composer Étienne Loulié's startlingly forward-looking collaborative studies with the 'father' of the science of acoustics, Joseph Sauveur, in the 1690s. The two colleagues, who were funded by Philippe II, Duke of Orléans, and had certainly read Galileo's findings on pendulums, developed not just a *chronomètre* for the semi-accurate setting of musical pulse, but also a mechanical tuning device, the *sonomètre* – this was a good decade before John Shore's much less sophisticated invention of the tuning fork – and the *échomètre*, for calculating the duration of sounds. It is an extraordinary fact about Joseph Sauveur that, as the meticulous, indefatigable founder of acoustics, he should have been partially – later severely – deaf, with a lifelong, relentlessly lampooned speech impediment resulting from childhood mutism.

The first practical, accurate musical chronometer was invented in 1814, over a hundred and fifty years after Galileo's pendulum clock design, by Dutchman Dietrich Winkel, but his mechanism was shamelessly pirated, renamed and repatented by German engineer Johann Maelzel two years later, becoming Maelzel's Metronome. Despite his losing a court battle to rectify the wrong, posterity rewarded the scoundrel Maelzel and it was his device that was embraced by composers from Beethoven onwards to give more accurate indications of their compositions' ideal speeds.

While Galileo Galilei's calculations relating to the pendulum undoubtedly enabled composers to be more specific, for the first time, about the tempo of their music, *what* they composed was thanks in large part to Galileo's father (and music teacher), Vincenzo. This composer, theorist and lutenist had been a leading member of the Florentine Camerata, the humanist group of the late-sixteenth century that had developed the earliest concept and idiom of opera, inspiring Jacopo Peri but more importantly Monteverdi. His published discourses on the physics of music and on the proper use of dissonance – deliberately clashing discords of various kinds – influenced many, if not all, Italian composers of the seventeenth century.

Indeed, by the middle of the century Italian artistic pre-eminence was a phenomenon across Europe, especially in music. Anecdotal evidence of this lies in the quaint tale of English composer-lutenist John Cooper, who changed his name to Giovanni Coprario in the hope of it improving his career – which it did, judging from his subsequent patronage by the future Charles I. More compelling evidence still of the Italians' dominion over music at this time is the legacy they left, for better or worse, in the descriptive language developed in this period. To this day the international musical lexicon includes the names of Italy's newly invented forms: *concerto, sonata, oratorio, sinfonia, opera*; definitions of speed: *tempo, presto, allegro, andante, largo*; techniques for playing: *legato, staccato, arpeggio, rubato, pizzicato, forte, piano, crescendo, diminuendo*, and so on – and a host of other terms, from *a capella* ('in the chapel style', since appropriated – inaccurately – to mean unaccompanied voices) to *segue* (following swiftly on without pausing). Likewise opera, or *dramma per musica* as it was known in its first, Italian century, spread from its power base in Venice to Naples and Rome, and thence north into Germany. The first operas seen at the French court were Italian, including *Orfeo* (1647) by Luigi Rossi, and *Xerse* (1660) by the wildly successful Venetian Francesco Cavalli, which was brought to Paris for the wedding celebrations of Louis XIV. This was followed by the première two years later of Cavalli's *Ercole amante* in the Salle des Machines in the Tuileries, but the French had by this time developed a preference for ballet. Ironically they saw ballet as more patriotic, even though the first formal ballets as developed in France, among them the *Ballet Comique de la Reine* of 1581, had been the brainchild of the Italian Catherine de Medici and her Italian choreographer. And the composer who was responsible for the spectacular popularity of ballet at the French court in the second half of the seventeenth century, Jean-Baptiste Lully, was none other than Giovanni Battista Lulli, an Italian.

Florence-born Lully had been musical supervisor (and often composer) of the French court's ballet productions since 1653, when Louis XIV himself, aged fifteen, had appeared in five different roles including Apollo, the Sun King, in *Le Ballet de la nuit*. Lully's contribution to this event, held in the Salle du Petit Bourbon in the Louvre, was rewarded by his being offered a permanent post as one of the court's resident composers; he was promoted to royal musical director in 1661, the year he became a naturalised French citizen.

Both music and the colourful ritual of ballet thrived at the French court under Lully and Louis XIV, who built upon the musical patronage of his predecessors. His father, Louis XIII, had in 1626 established an innovative twenty-four-piece violin band, a string orchestra in all but name, called *Les vingt-quatre violons du roy*, which comprised six four-stringed violins, tuned as modern violins; twelve violas of three sizes, though tuned identically; and six cello-like instruments. In 1656 Louis XIV expanded the violin band further and renamed it *La grande bande*. By now Lully was in charge and for some ballet (and opera) performances, he supplemented the resident string band with the wind, brass and percussion instruments of the king's so-called *Grande Ecurie*, a pool of about forty players attached to the ceremonial cavalry, who normally played for outdoor pageants and military events. This bringing together of string, wind, brass and percussion ensembles for the accompaniment of ballet can be seen as the prototype of the orchestra, whose birth, therefore, is intrinsically linked to the invention of the violin – the instrument for accompanying dance – in the early sixteenth century.

Dancing at the French court, though, was not merely a way of passing a pleasant evening. It became under the Bourbons a highly political endeavour, and the ballet spectaculars put on at Versailles were above all thinly disguised allegories designed to give prestige, power and glory to *le Roi Soleil*, the Sun King. To emphasise the intended awe and majesty of the occasion, Louis XIV's long, mythological ballets would begin with a self-contained instrumental introduction, or opening. Though it has a French name, this *ouverture* (or overture) was essentially, in its musical format, the *sinfonia* that had featured quite prominently in Italian music of the late-sixteenth and early-seventeenth centuries. The sinfonia (from the Greek *syn*, together or with, and *phōnē*, sound) was a mood-setting prelude that might consist of two short sections, one solemn and the other lively, and it was certainly popular by at least 1589, when it featured in a pageant mounted for the wedding of Ferdinando I de Medici to Christina of Lorraine at the recently completed Uffizi Palace theatre. Members of the Florentine Camerata, including opera pioneer Jacopo Peri, are known to have contributed to this festive occasion, which included a performance of the comic diversion *La Pellegrina*, with the sinfonia acting as a musical prelude to a recitation or dance, or to cover scene-changing. Around the same time, sinfonias had also started appearing as short instrumental introductions to more substantial choral works in a non-theatrical setting, and in the chamber works and dances for (usually two) violins, cello and harpsichord by composers such as Salamone Rossi, Jewish colleague of Monteverdi in Mantua. (Rossi is highly likely to have played or sung in the première in 1607 of the latter's *Orfeo*.) Rossi's publication of books of *Sinfonie e gagliarde* in 1607 and 1608 are among the earliest printed references to the sinfonia as a distinct form.

For Lully, back in Paris, the idea of the overture or sinfonia was carried over from his court ballets into the operas he composed with playwright Molière in the 1670s and '80s – a switch encouraged by Louis XIV, who was tiring of ballet as he aged. Very soon, in any case, a new Italian sound was to dominate European music once again, leaving both the French opera and ballet styles in its wake. For the next half-century, the concerto reigned supreme, and its godfather, or archangel perhaps, was composer-violinist Arcangelo Corelli.

In 1672, aged nineteen, Arcangelo Corelli left his home in Fusignano, south of Venice, in order to visit Paris. As a violinist of some distinction it is inconceivable that he did not brush shoulders with Lully's *Grande bande*, nor fail to take in the dance-orientated music it played, full of quick and sprightly rhythms and titillating switches of speed and metre. But he spent most of his life in his native Italy, becoming one of the foremost cultural figures of the century, dying rich and revered, and being honoured with a burial, in 1713, in the Pantheon in Rome. While this was partly due to his status as the first famous violin virtuoso in a country in love with the instrument, it was also a recognition of the fact that the style he perfected for stringed ensembles was the definitive sound of the time. Indeed, an otherwise unremarkable German composer called Georg Muffat travelled to Rome in the 1680s for a study break and wrote enthusiastically about some intriguing modern music he had heard: 'concertos for violins and other instruments called sinfonie' by Corelli. But what was it about Corelli's 'concerto' style that so caught the imaginations of other musicians?

Corelli's instantly noticeable hallmark – heard, for example, in his delicately attractive *Christmas* concerto (opus 6, no. 8), which features prominently in the 2003 film *Master and Commander* – is, appropriately for the period, the regular ticking of a clock, the chugging, pulsating, perfectly calibrated whirring and spinning of cogs, and the pleasingly equal balancing of energies. Simple melodies are passed back and forth between the violins in playful repetition, rather like the push and pull of a pendulum. Part of the satisfaction of the Corelli style is that there is a predictability about its internal movement, and yet it is never tedious. In an age when the rich danced obsessively, you would be forgiven for assuming that Corelli's clockwork rhythms were, like Lully's ballets, destined for the stage or the courtly dance floor – but the surprising truth is that his chamber sonatas for just a few instruments, and in due course his concertos for a small string orchestra, were composed to be heard during church services.

But what Corelli perfected, above all, was a form of musical contrast, an internal drama in the texture that was fresh, surprising and – for the time – highly original. To appreciate how radical his approach must have seemed, we should remind ourselves that the prevailing instrumental style of the first half of the seventeenth century had been consort music – that is, four- or five-strong ensembles playing gently soothing, mellifluous pieces, rather like an instrumental version of a choir, or what Shakespeare called 'still musick'. Indeed, consorts were generally made up of 'choirs'

– soprano, alto, tenor and bass – of the same instrument, typically viols or recorders, or later the violin family. Occasionally these consorts were mixed, so that a lute might join in, or a recorder with some viols, but composers on the whole did not specify which instruments they expected to hear, or even whether the parts were vocal; they merely wrote generic consort music and whoever was around joined in. It was, in effect, a modular approach to music-making. Appealing though this laissez-faire undoubtedly was, especially for amateur musicians, it resulted in instrumental music that did not make great demands on players, their instruments, or indeed composers. There was no point in writing an exciting solo for a violin if the chances were that the part was going to be played on, say, a shawm, a wind instrument of sweet tone but dangerously limited range.

Gradually this attitude changed. Prompted in part by the dexterity and showmanship of celebrated virginals and lute players, string and wind members of consorts began to liven up the texture of the music with ornaments, fast runs, trills, fast repeated notes and fancy rhythmic figures. The jaunty patterns of popular dances were put together into contrasting groups of three to provide variation – slow-fast-slow or fast-slow-fast – even when the consorts were not accompanying actual dancing. The graceful early-seventeenth-century 'Consort Setts' of Charles I's in-house composer William Lawes, for example, create a triptych from the dances 'Fantazy', 'Paven' and an 'Almaine', where the first and last are jovial and the middle reflective and sad.

One great shift in consort music made by Corelli and his imitators from the 1680s onwards was to strip back its traditionally *contrapuntal* texture. That is, to replace its interweaving but independent voices with a more unified, streamlined sound, with the keyboard and cello locked together supportively, underpinning the sparring interplay of the two violins above them. But arguably the greatest aspect of Corelli's revolution was his approach to dynamics: the manipulation of loud and soft passages in music.

In the seventeenth century, the concept of music *gradually* becoming softer or louder was technically difficult to achieve for many instruments, and in any case it was not a trick it had occurred to composers to incorporate in their scores. A seventeenth-century trumpet, for instance, was incapable of playing softly – it was more or less a case of 'on' or 'off' – whereas a pair of seventeenth-century virginals was all but inaudible to anyone standing six or more yards away. Keyboard instruments were quite unique in that they had soft and loud settings – but no way of moving smoothly between the two. You could jump from a loud sound on one organ keyboard (or 'manual') to a softer sound on another manual – to create the impression of an echo, for instance – but it was virtually impossible to do so gradually. What composers could impose instead of incremental change were more abrupt contrasts of loud and soft, like the juxtaposition of light and shade, *chiaroscuro*, in painting.

What Corelli did was create a musical version of chiaroscuro by contrasting a big-sounding band of stringed instruments with a small group, switching between the big and the small throughout the piece. The larger ensemble was called the *concerto grosso* (and sometimes the *ripieno*, the Italian for 'stuffing') and the smaller group was the *concertino* (little consort). They would play phrases in succession, one after another, three players alternating with, say, twenty. The pieces in which Corelli developed this light-and-shade technique came to be known by the name of the larger group, *concerto grosso*, and subsequently the generic term 'concerto'. Corelli's typical concerto grosso was divided into three sections of contrasting speeds – slow-fast-slow or fast-slow-fast – after the fashion of the earlier consort suites or setts.

Not fatigued by his radicalisation of both musical texture and technique, Corelli added another flourish to his work: a musical shorthand called *figured bass*, or thorough bass, inherited from Monteverdi and universally adopted after him. Though it was intended merely as a time-saving tool, its use began to change the way composers and keyboard players manipulated chords, changing the sound of harmony along the way. It was as if text-messaging shorthand as used on mobile phones were to shape the way language was written in books.

Figured bass allowed composers to jot down a minimum of information on their scores, assuming that their players already knew what the jottings meant, and to dash off their compositions much more quickly and succinctly than ever before. Music copyists, printers and engravers had much less to squeeze on to each expensive page and, as an added bonus, it gave the players quite a lot of artistic freedom to do a bit of on-the-spot improvisation.

In this ten-note example from Corelli, all the keyboard player has in front of him or her is the bass line notes, borrowed from the cello player, and those extra numbers above it. That's all. And yet this shorthand translates into a fully realised, harmonised (that is, with chords for every note) keyboard part for both hands.

When I, the keyboard player, read the first note, G, I know I am meant to play the straightforward chord of G: the notes G-B-D. If the G had had a '6' written above it, though, I would shift the top note, D (known as the fifth note due to the distance between it and our starting point, G), up one step of the keyboard scale to the so-called sixth note: E. Thus I would play a slightly different chord: G-B-E rather than G-B-D. The third and fourth notes have two numbers above them: '76'. This means that on each I would replace the fifth note, first with a seventh then with a sixth, making two different chords, one after another. In the next bar, the figure '7' is accompanied by what has been known for centuries in music as the 'sharp' sign. This tells me that, of the two possible chords allowed on this note, B – B major and B minor – I should choose the one with a sharp (B major) rather than the one without. (The '#' here clears up any ambiguity between the two: the distinction is offered wherever the default option for the chord might be unclear, according to the key of the piece.)

This system of figures, which prevailed until the music of Haydn and Mozart in the late eighteenth century, when composers began specifying the exact notes they wanted played, allowed composers to give their players a string of chords, out of hundreds of possible combinations, in quick succession. *How* the players chose to play those chords could alter from performance to performance; it is a rather non-prescriptive, jazz-like system in that respect. Indeed, figured bass was a style that every trained musician in Europe and the colonised New World understood and imitated, rather as every modern-day guitarist knows what is meant by 'G7' or 'Blues in E'.

If you shape your music around a bass line with a series of chords, though, there is a hefty knock-on effect in terms of the sound you create, and the advent of figured bass marked a significant – and clearly audible, even in Corelli's earliest works – break with the past. The progression from one chord to another became much more purposeful, and chords began to take on a life of their own. Since placing one chord after another in a random succession is not very appealing in any form of music, composers now needed to become much more aware of how to string chords together in a way that was neither haphazard nor ugly. The solution was *harmonic progression*.

We have already witnessed the fifteenth-century composer Josquin des Prez beginning to harness a sense of 'home', or cadence, in his choice of chords, and that this 'home' could be moved around within a piece, within reason, to provide variation and movement. But while Josquin lived at a time when very few chords were considered wholesome and acceptable, the permitted harmonies had increased considerably for our seventeenth-century composers. Vincenzo Galilei's guidelines for the approved use of dissonance, *Discorso intorno all'uso delle dissonanze* (1588–91), had introduced combinations of notes that would have sounded shocking and disturbing to Josquin, yet even Galilei was considered outdated within twenty years. The chords in Monteverdi's madrigals likewise shocked contemporary listeners, but his experiments in harmony showed how rewarding and expressive the interplay of chords could be. His successors pushed the boundaries of chordal harmony yet further, revealing powerful gravitational forces at work in the relationship between chords, and it is by experimenting with the juxtaposing of certain chords that they stumbled across harmonic progression. It could just as easily be described as 'musical gravity', and it is one of the most rewarding gifts in all music.

Musical notes, as we have seen, are grouped in families called 'keys'. Within these families certain notes have more prominence than others, a hierarchy evolved from the natural properties of sounds in all resonant materials. In the sixteenth and seventeenth centuries, composers increasingly found that chords had a hierarchy, too: certain chords exert an influence over other chords. If, for example, we are in the family or key of G, the chord of G – the triad G-B-D – is 'home'. The chord B minor (B-D-F#) is a close relation to G because it shares two of G major's three notes; it has two-thirds of its DNA, if you like. As we saw with Palestrina's use of closely related chords to create a soothing, ethereal sound, and Monteverdi's mischievous use of more distantly related chords to intrigue or surprise the ear, these relationships between chords could be potent elements in any composition. Composers discovered that some chords were drawn magnetically to others: adding an F to the G major triad, G-B-D, made it yearn to move towards the C major triad, for example – of which more shortly. Others changed their character with the addition of an unexpected bass note beneath them.

As well as a general drift towards more adventurous combinations of notes than before, composers of the seventeenth century
now had figured bass to work with, and this encouraged them
to experiment with the *roots* of chords. The root of the G major
triad, G-B-D, is G, because it lies at the bottom – but if you add
a low bass note playing the note E, for example, the root of the
chord shifts to E and the chord changes its sound. All triads are
transformed in some way if the root in the bass line is not the
same as the bottom note of the triad. This seemingly simple
device hugely increased the chordal nuances available to
composers, and they began constructing sequences of chords
whose position was dictated by the gravitational pull exerted on
them by the behaviour of the root note in the bass line. These
sequences, once discovered, became bread and butter to the music
of the late-seventeenth and early-eighteenth centuries and are
still in use today in popular songwriting – particularly, as it
happens, by songwriters who play the bass, such as Paul McCartney
or Sting. Like that which cycles through Pachelbel's 'Canon', these
sequences were driven by the direction of travel of the bass line,
giving forward momentum to the music, hence the name
'harmonic progression'.

Composers became so fond of certain chord progressions in
the seventeenth and early eighteenth centuries that it was even
possible for them to create the *impression* of chords when there
was only one solo instrument playing a melody and no apparent
'accompaniment' at all. What might be described as 'virtual' or
'invisible' harmony was conjured up by skimming up and down
the constituent notes of a chord, for example on a solo violin, so
that listeners assembled the chord in their heads. It was a kind of
aural trompe l'oeil.

A brilliant example of this occurs as the epilogue of Heinrich
Biber's devotional cycle of sixteen solo violin sonatas known as
the 'Rosary' or 'Mystery' sonatas, composed in 1676. Each sonata
portrays an aspect of the Virgin Mary's or Christ's life – the
Annunciation, the Nativity, the Crucifixion, and so on – and it

ends with a piece for solo violin, called simply 'The Guardian Angel'. Although there are a few moments in this sonata where the player is in fact able to play two notes simultaneously by drawing the bow against more than one string at once, mostly we only hear one note at a time. Our ears, though, *believe* we have heard full chords, a whole accompaniment, from this one solitary instrument. It is partly a trick and partly the conditioning of our ears: thanks to the vast musical catalogue that has used these same chord sequences time and again since the seventeenth century, we complete the sequence in our heads without it being spelt out.

Biber's 'Guardian Angel' is an especially interesting piece because it is constructed in a format known as a 'Passacaglia', which divided moral opinion in the seventeenth century but continues to influence music today. The Passacaglia structure involves a short sequence of four or eight chords repeated many times, which act as the springboard for a series of unfolding melodic explorations or improvisations. It is a template that would describe a vast amount of twentieth-century jazz, too, although the term Passacaglia has rarely, if ever, been used in that context. It derives from the Spanish prototype, *Pasacalle*, meaning 'street steps' – another example of the fashionable Italian term being universally adopted – which, coupled with the fact that it has a repeating bass line, suggests the form's origin lay in dance. Indeed, the Passacaglia was also known by the name *Chaconne* in the seventeenth century, and this most certainly was a dance form, referred to by the Spanish writers Miguel de Cervantes and Lope de Vega as a popular dance among servants, slaves and the Amerindians of colonial New Spain. The term 'chaconne' may come from the sound of the Mexican castanets used to accompany the dance.

The Chaconne dance swept Europe in the early 1600s, with a popularity that bordered on a craze. It was deemed so sensuous and irresistible that some supposed it could only have been put on earth by the devil himself to tempt people to behave in a lewd manner. But over the course of the seventeenth century, the

Chaconne lost its wicked reputation and became a courtly dance, its repeated musical pattern increasingly associated with just one sequence of chords (over the descending bass line, for instance G-F-E♭-D). By the time Heinrich Biber incorporated the Chaconne sequence into his sacred devotional pieces in 1676, no one remembered the supposedly Satanic origin of the Chaconne – but they did remember the chord sequence, which is what allowed Biber just to hint at it in order for the listener to hear the full chordal texture. Eventually the dance elements of the Chaconne were abandoned altogether and the chord sequence alone remained in music of all styles and rhythms. The sequence has been among the most persistent in music history, its shape faithfully reproduced, for example, under the chorus of Adele's 'Set Fire to the Rain' (2011).

Though the Rosary/Mystery sonatas weren't published in Biber's lifetime, it seems unthinkable that J. S. Bach did not know them when he composed his own set of Sonatas, Partitas and Suites for solo violin and solo cello forty years later, pulling off exactly the same aural illusion with 'silent' chords. He too held the Chaconne in high regard, composing as the final movement of his Second partita for solo violin a *Ciaccona* lasting an incredible fifteen minutes, possibly written in memory of his late first wife, Maria Barbara Bach. It is one of the undisputed masterpieces of all music for the violin, comprising an astonishing sixty-four continuous variations on a single theme, creating the impression of an orchestra of sound from one single instrument.

In the late seventeenth and early eighteenth centuries there was one sequence of chords that composers loved more than any other. They all used it, in virtually every piece, thousands of times in all. It is still in use today, though not quite so obsessively as back then. We have already witnessed composers beginning to play around with this sequence as they became aware of musical gravity, but in the dusty world of music terminology it has a name: *the Circle of Fifths*.

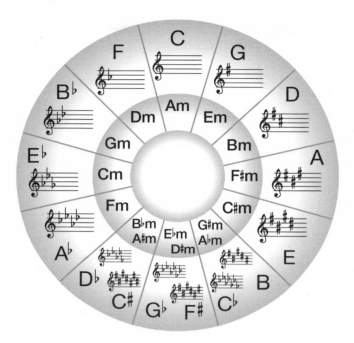

The circle, or cycle, of fifths, works like this: you start with a triad on any note on the keyboard, say B, and you construct a sequence of chords by dropping down five white notes on each step: B-E-A-D-G-C-F-B, and so on. When the sequence first started appearing profusely in the late seventeenth century, the norm was to cycle through just three or four chords rather than the possible chain of twelve. The sequence works by exploiting a weakness in the first of two chords. If you play a triad, for example G, comprising the notes G-B-D, you can make it vulnerable to change by adding the 'seventh' note to it, in this case F: G-B-D-F. Now this triad of G yearns to move to the chord lying a fifth below it, C. Adding a seventh to C will make it yearn to move to F, and so on.

You can find these virtuous circles of three or four (and very occasionally five) chords all over the music of Corelli, Vivaldi, Bach and Handel. What comes across in their work time and again is a relishing of the joys of chords for their own sake, the delicious transition from one to another and the effect it might have. Sometimes they dispensed with melody altogether and simply

allowed a lovely chain of chords to unfold, as Vivaldi does in the
opening *Adagio e spiccato* section of the second concerto in his
collection unashamedly labelled *L'estro armonico* (the inspiration of
harmony).

What may surprise you is that the dozen or so chord sequences
beloved of composers around 1700, including the circle of fifths,
are *still* the top dozen harmonic sequences mined by composers
of all styles today; the chord sequence shared by Bach's 'Air on a
G String' and Procul Harum's 'Whiter Shade of Pale' is just
one of innumerable examples. I can guarantee you that there is
no chord sequence out there, however fresh its apparent sound
or however young and innovative its creator, that hasn't been
thrashed into oblivion many, many times before.

Playing around with musical gravity had one effect that no one
quite expected. Since the time of Josquin des Prez, the growing
reliance on chordal harmony, on locating a sense of home in the
music and on exploiting the chemical reactions between different
chords and different 'homes', had gradually been undermining the
older, medieval system of note-families, the modes, which were
above all ways of organising melodies rather than chords. In the
late-seventeenth century, the modes finally gave way to their
successor: keys.

While the modes adopted by folk music and by the music systems
of other cultures, all melody orientated, had a wide range of note
choices in them – like a palette with fifty colours on it – the plainchant modes established by the European Church were made up
of a very limited diet of available notes. They had a uniformity
and blandness about them, as if our palette now had fewer than a
dozen colours. The limitation of both ethnic and ecclesiastical
modes was that you had to stay in whatever mode you had started
in for the duration of the performance. So in the Church's mode
system, if you were singing a tune in, say, Aeolian mode, your
given notes would be ABCDEFGA – all the white notes on a piano
or organ keyboard. You would stick loyally to just those notes for

the whole piece. This was a cosy, unsophisticated world were you did not wander off mid-song to another 'home' or mode, but it was also a pragmatic measure, since medieval instruments had a limited number of notes and generally only played in one or two modes. A penny whistle, to this day, has the same limitation: to play tunes in a range of mode families you have to buy several penny whistles, each calibrated to a different mode.

But during the seventeenth century, musicians intrigued by the forbidden fruit opened up by chord sequences increasingly sought to be able to move from one mode to another. If, for instance, you follow the logic of the circle of fifths sequence, you are forced to move into new modes whether you like it or not. Gradually, then, the restrictive modes were replaced by the more flexible system of keys, which allowed for a larger number of notes to be available at any given time. This was because, through the mechanism of the minor and major third that we encountered in John Dunstaple's music at the turn of the fifteenth century, keys included in their dual scale (palette) notes that would, under the mode system, have belonged to separate modes. Thus the key of E minor embraces nine notes – E, F#, G, A, B, C, C#, D, D# – and the key of E major adds a tenth note, G#, in contrast to the ecclesiastical Phrygian mode's modest seven. What's more, the overlap of notes belonging to closely related keys made moving from one key to another easy.

While it is not, strictly speaking, accurate to say that a minor version of any given key is sad and its major version happy, since there are notable exceptions, the ability to switch from one mood to another, instantaneously and at will, was a very big advantage of the key system over the older modes. Modes were one thing or another, the Ionian and Lydian being sunnier, like modern 'major' keys, and the Dorian and Phrygian being darker, like modern 'minor' keys, but a key could change its mind about its mood whenever it liked.

The modal sound did not disappear completely after it had been supplanted by the major and minor keys. It lingered at the edges of art music, popping up one moment in Chopin, or another in Debussy. It never went away in folk music, so whenever composers were trying to sound rustic, earthy or homesick for their native countryside, you could expect them to dip back into the modal well for inspiration. But for a trend-setting composer like Corelli, with his well-integrated string ensembles and his radical musical style, the modal sound would have seemed, I suspect, rather old-fashioned and like something better suited to street music. His music, joyfully and abundantly at ease with the new major and minor key palette, was a gateway to the extraordinary creative possibilities opening up with the new system.

Corelli's influence in creating the new concerto style from the innovative musical ingredients of his day is hard to overestimate, not least because of the effect he had on a red-haired Venetian twenty-five years his junior: Antonio Vivaldi, whose *L'estro Armonico* concerti grossi of 1711 immediately established him as a genius of the first order. (Its success also marked the moment when Italian-led moveable-type printing for music was replaced by the faster, more accurate, plate-engraving technique.) Compared to the clockwork finesse and gentle charm of Corelli, Vivaldi introduced a sense of drama and virtuosity that took his contemporaries' breath away. In effect, he was turning his violinists and cellists into divas to rival the opera stars of the day – of whom he knew a thing or two, claiming to have composed ninety-four operas of which only about twenty survive.

It is estimated that Vivaldi composed in excess of five hundred concertos for a variety of instruments, taking Corelli's big group-little group idea one step further by pitting a charismatic solo violin against the whole ensemble. This dynamic new style of solo concerto announced its arrival on the musical stage in 1714, with a set of concertos Vivaldi proudly unveiled as *La Stravaganza* (The Extravagance), followed in 1723 by a set of pieces that were to become deservedly, utterly ubiquitous by the twentieth century. The first four concertos, of twelve, were called *Le Quattro stagioni*

(The Four Seasons), but the umbrella title of the collection perfectly captures the spirit of Italy's monumental contribution to seventeenth-century music: *Il cimento dell'armonia e dell'invenzione* (The Contest between Harmony and Invention).

The Four Seasons, as well as showing off the virtuoso capabilities of the solo violin, also explored the notion that purely instrumental music could be pictorial, or at least descriptive, in this case of non-musical features in the natural world. Vivaldi came up with musical effects to depict dogs, mosquitoes, a variety of birds, the hunters and the hunted, winter and summer landscapes, rivers, storms and an assortment of rustic characters at play, all of them the imaginative result of experimenting with the various violin-playing techniques pioneered by Corelli, Biber and indeed Vivaldi himself at the end of the seventeenth century. Thus chilly raindrops in winter are evoked by high violin notes being plucked (*pizzicato*), the chattering of teeth is the high strings playing ultra-fast repeated notes (*tremolando*), and so on.

Incredibly, the popularity Vivaldi enjoyed during his middle age did not last. After living most of his life in Venice, he moved to Vienna in his sixties and died there lonely and impoverished. For the next two hundred years his prolific body of music would stay silent, his career forgotten.

Almost. Vivaldi's legacy survived in the somewhat surprising influence he had on another, very different, composer. Vivaldi's Italian innovations, honed to sensuous perfection in the carnival city of Venice, travelled north across the Alps and found a fan in Lutheran north-east Germany: Johann Sebastian Bach. But it was not just Vivaldi who, musically speaking, migrated from the bustling Arcadia of Italy to the spiritual lucidity of the Protestant north. This phenomenon can be seen almost everywhere you look when it comes to the music of the early eighteenth century, and there is no neater demonstration of this process than in a subject close to Bach's heart: the invention of new keyboard instruments.

★

What we now call simply 'the piano' was invented in around 1700 by a Florentine instrument builder and restorer called Bartolomeo Cristofori. The unique selling point of the new instrument, distinguishing it from all the harpsichords, clavichords, spinets and virginals that went before it, was its ability to play 'soft and loud' – or, in Italian, *'piano e il forte'*.

Its main predecessor, the harpsichord, plucked its strings, like a harp on its side in a box, and the mechanism only allowed for a single pluck of uniform strength, thereby creating a sound that was always one volume. No matter how hard you pressed the keys, the sound had the same power. The only way of making a harpsichord louder was to have a double (or triple) set of strings that were plucked simultaneously, a mechanism that was, once again, either all on or all off. The only way of making it softer was to lay felt against the strings – also either on or off – and there was no way of moving gradually from one state to the other.

Cristofori's invention, instead of plucking the strings, tapped them with a gentle hammer tipped with deerskin. Crucially, the harder you hit the key the harder the hammer hit the string, resulting potentially in different levels of volume for every note. The piano was a musical revolution, but despite its ingenuity and novelty it did not catch on in Italy, whose intense relationship with stringed instruments – among them the harpsichord – was second only to its passion for opera. (The piano, which, like the harpsichord, operated via an arrangement of tightened strings, was from the outset treated as a new species, an outsider to the string family of instruments.) It took a German organ builder and friend of J. S. Bach, Gottfried Silbermann, to see the piano's potential and – with help and advice from Bach – to begin manufacturing pianos. Indeed, it was thought for many decades outside Italy that Silbermann had actually invented the piano, such was the oblivion into which Cristofori's effort had fallen.

It was around the same time that the piano's close relative the organ also mastered the art of volume control, thanks to a device called a 'ratchet swell pedal'. This mechanism opened or closed shutters on a box containing the pipes, thus allowing organ sounds to get progressively louder or softer. In 1711 an organ was installed at the church of St Magnus-the-Martyr at London Bridge with such a pedal, thought to be the first of its kind.

Although Bach played on a few of Silbermann's prototype pianos, he never expressed any great enthusiasm for them. It was his son, Johann Christian, living in London, who was to be the champion of the new instrument thirty or so years later, paving the way for the young Mozart and others to follow his lead. But Bach *père* was involved in a keyboard innovation that proved equally important to the history of music as the invention of the piano. It could in fact be the single most important invention in all Western music. Like nuclear fusion, it's not easy to explain but it had an enormous effect. It was called *Equal Temperament*.

It all started with a problem. The problem was that composers were outgrowing not just the old modes and the restrictions placed on them but also the complicated system of tuning that allowed instruments to play in different keys. It was bad enough that many instruments found it difficult to play with each other and stay 'in tune', which was partly because they were not designed to be able to play in lots of different modes, or keys, and partly because the materials they were made of – animal gut, treated soft woods, lightweight metals – made them, by modern standards, unstable in variable temperatures. (In the 1970s, when the movement to reproduce 'authentic' replicas of pre-1800 instruments was enjoying its early boom, orchestras discovered that it was virtually impossible for these replicas, or indeed the few originals pressed back into service, to stay in tune with each other for more than a few minutes. Recordings of, say, Bach on these instruments involved hundreds if not thousands of edits, splicing together countless snippets from numerous 'takes' to fake the sound of a tuneful ensemble.) This issue of tuning came to a head with the growing dominance of keyboard instruments in the sixteenth and seventeenth centuries.

On a modern 'equal-tempered' keyboard, I can play in any or

all of the available twelve key-families – that is, major and minor versions of all the notes that lie between our Western octave – to my heart's content, and I can switch from one to another whenever I like. I can play any piece in any key without worrying that the piano, or organ, will sound out of tune when I move from key to key. I can also play any other instrument I like, for as long as I want, within reason, without succumbing to the same worry. But this was not the case until the growing dominance of keyboard instruments in the sixteenth and seventeenth centuries finally led to a breakthrough in the first few years of the eighteenth: the adoption of Equal Temperament in Western music.

In order to understand the importance and impact of this breakthrough – and indeed to understand what Equal Temperament is – we need to look back at what it swept away, which was, in effect, *nature*'s tuning system. Why would eighteenth-century musicians have wanted to do away with nature's musical laws?

To illustrate nature's musical laws we can use a piece of pipe or tubing. If you blow across the mouth of a length of tubing you can make a musical note. This is the technology behind every flute, whistle, shakuhachi or recorder ever blown in the history of humankind. Obviously each length of tube only plays one main note, so if you want to play more than a one-note tune you'll need to change the length of the column of air; a Swanee whistle demonstrates perfectly that, if you gradually shorten the length of air in the tube, the pitch of your note becomes higher and higher.

As we saw when we first encountered the octave, if your column of air is exactly half the length of where you started, you will get a note that is the same pitch, only higher. If you glide up the octave from bottom to top on a Swanee whistle, however, all sorts of notes are revealed between the two, and every musical system in the world has subdivided the octave into formal, measurable positions along that scale. But not every musical system in the world opted for the same number of subdivisions. Much Asian and Arabian music has a larger number, as a result of which it often sounds exotic and 'out of tune' to Western ears. The Western system had by about 1600 settled on just nineteen subdivisions between one note and its octave, and all of these nineteen pitches were determined by natural, mathematical ratios in the relationship between one string or pipe length and another. These tunings have been called 'Pythagorean' because it was the Ancient Greek philosopher-mathematician-physicist Pythagoras who worked out the ratios for creating notes in music (by dividing a taut cord and plucking it). These nineteen subdivisions were easily singable, or playable on stringed instruments, because tiny differences of pitch can be achieved by allowing your voice to rise by minute degrees, or by sliding your finger ever so slightly up or down the neck of the violin. But for keyboard instruments, on which the pitches of each step are firmly fixed, these nineteen subdivisions were a nightmare. Two solutions were on offer.

One was to build keyboards with the necessary fidgety subdivisions.

This is a picture of a nineteen-note-per-octave keyboard; notice the double-decker nature of the black notes and the extra little black note between the bigger clusters. It is absurdly difficult to play, but not quite as deranged as the thirty-one-note keyboard built by a Venetian called Vito Trasuntino in 1606, involving triple-decker black and white notes. He called it the 'Clavemusicum Omnitonum' (all-tones musical keyboard). It did not catch on. More notes does not mean better music.

The other solution was to reduce the number of divisions from nineteen to a more manageable twelve and to fudge the swallowing up of the pitches that were left out. This meant, for example, the two *separate* notes Gb and F# were combined into one, all-purpose note: one key represented them both.

But this was not quite the brilliant solution it might have seemed, since F# and Gb were still – to stringed instruments, singers and some brass players – separate notes, albeit just a short distance apart. If a keyboard played its Gb while the violin played an F# it produced an unpleasant, headache-inducing dissonance. This grating struggle over where the pitch should fall affected most of the notes of the scale in one way or another. It was a bad state of affairs. All that keyboard tuners could do was plump for one or the other, and squeeze the strings this way or that, so that, for example, key-families using the sharps (edging upwards in pitch) – E major, A major, B major – would be favoured while key-families requiring the flats (edging downwards in pitch) would have to be avoided. Which explains why moving between key-families that had flats to ones with sharps was dangerous and disagreeable. And keyboard tuners were kept incredibly busy in the sixteenth and seventeenth centuries: keyboards of all kinds had to be tuned every day, or at least before every performance, rather as harps or guitars must still be tuned for every performance today.

Clearly this was not satisfactory either for keyboard tuners or composers, who were in practical terms restricted to certain keys. I doubt it was much fun for all the other instrumentalists, either, who would not ordinarily have been bound by such restrictions. But why *did* it matter that Gb and F# carried on being separate notes everywhere other than on a keyboard, or B# and C, or Bb and A#? Why couldn't the violinists and singers forget they ever existed and toe the line?

The reason is that the more precise divisions of the octave into nineteen steps obeys mathematical ratios that occur in nature. Let's say your column of air, your bamboo pipe, is of such a length and thickness that, when you blow across its mouth, the note produced is a pure, lovely-sounding B. Dividing the column of air by the mathematically perfect ratio of 2:1 will produce Little B, an octave higher. Dividing that column of air by the mathematically perfect ratio of 3:2 will produce F#. These relationships, and all the others based on mathematically straightforward ratios, are pure and 'perfect'.

However, if even just this 3:2 ratio is applied to all the notes in the scale – A, B, C, D, E, F, G – and thereafter to all the 'perfect' 3:2 ratio notes they throw up – E, F#, G, A, B, C, D – and thence the 'perfect' 3:2 ratio notes *they* throw up – B, C#, D, E, F#, G#, A – and so on, you eventually end up with too many sharps and too many flats to accommodate, and this is before we worry about all the other perfect ratios. The upshot of all this is that it was generally considered a worthwhile compromise, for the sake of keyboard practicality, to reduce the number of divisions from nineteen to twelve, even though this omitted some of nature's purely produced notes.

The next act in this drama had tuners artificially *moving* the pitch of some of the twelve subdivisions so that, instead of lying where they should according to nature's laws, they were shunted into twelve equally spaced, man-made positions between the two ends of the octave. It would be like re-portioning the days, hours and minutes so that there were exactly twelve months of thirty days in every calendar year. It was this recalibration of pitch that became Equal Temperament – or equal tuning.

Although others had hinted at the possibility of evenly dividing the twelve notes of the octave, the first precise calculations of an equal temperament were made by Vincenzo Galilei in his *Dialogo della musica antica et della moderna* of 1581, and by Zhu Zaiyu, a Ming dynasty prince, in *Lüxue xinshuo* (New Explanation of Musical Pitches) in 1584. Why these two dates are curiously close, given the geographical distance between Europe and China, is a mystery yet to be unravelled, but Galilei's and Zhu Zaiyu's calculations were the same – one worked out using lengths of plucked cord

(Galilei) and the other with thirty-six specially made bamboo pipes (Zhu Zaiyu). The calculations showed that each string or bamboo pipe had to be 94.38744% of the length of the previous one in ascending order; the twelfth rung would thus be exactly 50% the length of the first.

Having the theory, though, did not lead to its immediate adoption as a tuning system in either China or Europe. In the West it took another century of experiment and debate before this evenly spaced solution for twelve, not nineteen, notes emerged as the front-runner solution. Gradually, over the course of the seventeenth century, all instruments were reluctantly persuaded to conform to the twelve-note division of the keyboard, needing to be tuned before every performance to the pitches that best suited the keyboard. Though it was created in defiance of nature's musical laws, the new, interlocking, standardised system came with huge benefits, not least making all twelve key-families compatible. Out of the chaos and confusion, the evenly spaced octave was born and we have lived with that huge shift in Western music ever since.

It was J. S. Bach who presented, in around 1722, the most conclusive evidence that an Equal Temperament system could work. He called his system 'The Well-Tempered Keyboard', landmarked for ever in history by his composing two companion pieces, a prelude and a fugue, for every one of the newly adapted key-families. Its first prelude is now very well known – and incidentally made up entirely of a chord sequence, no melody, exactly as Bach's hero Vivaldi might have done.

Equal temperament, or the 'well-tempered' keyboard, wasn't perfect, but it was a practical solution to what had hitherto seemed intractable problems. It is hard to exaggerate the importance of its arrival and adoption as a standard across the industrialised world. Like the adoption of the Greenwich Meridian, which made everyone perceive the map and their place on it in a new way, for better or worse, Equal Temperament altered the mindset of everyone who enjoyed music. The modern population of the world now hears *all* music through the filter – some would say imperfection – of Equal Temperament. Indeed, all of us alive today have a different impression of what sounds 'in tune' or 'off key' from those alive in, say, 1600.

The sense of order out of chaos that was ushered in by 'well-tempered' keyboards would have appealed to Bach enormously. There is a fundamental logic at work in all he wrote that was not merely the function of a character trait – like people who simply have to order their bookshelves alphabetically – but rather a product of his deeply felt Lutheran faith. All you have to do is compare the atmosphere and architecture of an Italian church of the period, or even the Catholic south of Germany, with the kind of church Bach was familiar with in Saxony to see how profoundly this difference of attitude might have affected every note he composed.

Bach's Lutheran Christianity, unlike the Papal Catholicism with which Galileo Galilei battled, was at ease with scientific investigation and the widening education of its laity – indeed, it positively encouraged it. Though he might not have recognised the label, Bach's faith falls within the movement known as German Pietism, which reached its high-water mark in his lifetime. Pietism laid great store by helping congregations find God themselves, through personal acquaintance and knowledge of the scriptures, through humility, non-confrontation and piety, through an ethos of hard work, and through education. Subsequent scholarship – notably Robert K. Merton's seminal 1936 thesis and 1938 book, *Science, Technology and Society in 17th-Century England* – has helped establish the dynamic link between the Scientific Revolution of the seventeenth and eighteenth centuries on the one hand and Anglican Puritanism and Lutheran Pietism on the other. For our purposes it is enough to note that Bach, an inventive musician par excellence, was actively involved in the search for Equal Temperament, the development of the piano in Germany and the design of state-of-the-art techniques in organ building – and yet saw no contradiction between the scientific and the religious aspects of his music-making. On the contrary, his Pietism embraced the relationship between God and science.

For Lutheran Pietists like Bach, illuminating the Gospel was paramount, as were metaphors of light and transparency. Lutheran (and Reformed) churches were purged of decorative trappings, elaborate altarpieces, art that was potentially distracting, statues of saints and the kind of ornate, gold-leaf trinketry that sprawled across the walls of Catholic churches of the period, a style that is sometimes referred to as 'high Baroque' or 'Rococo'. Lutheran congregations were expected to be active participants in the service, with communal hymn-singing given high status. A huge amount of what Bach wrote – including virtually all his three-hundred-plus cantatas and his vast output of organ music – is based one way or another on hymn tunes, or 'chorales', as he would have called them. He would weave a tapestry of sound around a hymn being sung or played slowly through the centre of the work, as he does to majestic effect in 'Jesu, Joy of Man's Desiring', in which what appears to be a lilting dance theme is transformed by the stately progression across it of a German hymn-chorale.

To Bach, the *point* of music was to glorify God, to reflect upon, interpret and celebrate the meaning and mystery of the scriptures. Because the Protestant reformation had grown out of a sense of disillusionment with the corruption of the Roman Church, central to Lutheran attitudes was the importance and sanctity of law, uprightness and thrift, and Bach's way of expressing this priority in music was through a technique we have already touched upon but of which he was the undisputed master of all time: *counter-point*.

Counterpoint, to Bach, was the ultimate set of laws in music; obeying these laws was for him something beautiful, uplifting and reassuring. The quintessential Bachian form of counterpoint was the fugue. A fugue, which means 'flight' in Italian, is a complicated form of canon, or round, such as 'London's Burning', in which, as in any canon or round, the same tune is sung by different groups at different points, each new entry fitting on top of the others. A fugue is an extremely clever and essentially more grown-up version of the same thing. In a typical Bach fugue, such as the 'Gigue Fugue', the tune to be imitated would be much longer than the four notes that begin 'London's Burning'. In the 'Gigue Fugue', the first part (or 'voice', though it is all played by one organist, with the help of his or her extremely athletic feet) is then joined by three others, also carrying this tune. Some of the entries in the 'Gigue Fugue' are in new keys – it starts in G major, but there are versions in D major, B minor, briefly A major and also E minor – and some are upside-down: that is, the tune leaps upwards in one version and downwards in the variant. Another fugal trick is 'retrograde' motion, whereby the tune is played backwards against its forward-playing self. In some fugues Bach introduces the incoming imitation at half or double the speed of the original, and sometimes he uses a number of these techniques at the same time in the same fugue, in different 'voices'. He truly was a master of the counterpoint form.

As if to underline this, Bach created (but did not complete) a collection of mind-bogglingly complex fugues, *Die Kunst der Fuge* (The Art of the Fugue) towards the end of his life. The fourteen fugues he did finish all start with the same relatively straightforward tune but then explore different options and techniques. As a whole it is a vast, miraculous musical jigsaw, never since matched by any composer. Bach could layer three, four, five or even six simultaneous parts on top of each other, all using variants of the basic theme. *Die Kunst der Fuge* includes such showpieces as 'mirror' fugues, which invert their first-half laws during the second half of the piece, and which could operate on up to six different levels: the original *melody* (which Bach called *rectus* – 'straight') would have its backwards variant (*inversus*) laid on top of it in the second half; the *home* of the melody would reverse the relationship between its voices, so that five notes higher became five notes lower; the *key movements* would likewise switch, so that a modulation (change of key) in the first half moved in the opposite direction in the second; the order of *voice entry* would be reversed, from, say, bass – tenor – alto – soprano to soprano – alto – tenor – bass; the *chord sequences* would run in the opposite direction during the second half; and finally the *cadences* (coming-to-a-rest chords) would be approached from opposite directions in the reflected mirror of the piece.

Constructing musical scaffolding as complex as these fugues would be hard enough to achieve with the whole map of it laid out in front of the composer on the manuscript page, like an empty crossword to be slowly and painstakingly filled in. The staggering fact is that Bach could *improvise* fugues like this at the keyboard, and often did. There's a story about Bach as an old man being summoned to the court of the young King Frederick the Great of Prussia, a major patron of the arts and a trained musician himself, to show off his skill at counterpoint, by then deemed an old-fashioned and largely redundant skill. The king had his court musicians, one of whom was Bach's son Carl Philipp Emanuel, devise a tune specially, one they mischievously knew was practically impossible to turn into a fugue without creating horrible dissonances.

Bach sat down at the keyboard (one of Frederick's brand-new Silbermann pianos) and improvised, on the spot, a three-voice fugue to this apparently impossible theme. The king, his guests (including the music-loving Russian ambassador), and his in-house musicians were flabbergasted. But not as amazed as when the king received, a few weeks later, a written-out fugue, or *ricercar*, based on the supposedly impossible theme, this time in six parts. The Italian term *ricercar* means, appropriately, 'to seek again', and Bach even titled his *Musical Offering* (*Das musikalische Opfer*) with an acrostic: *Regis Iussu Cantio Et Reliqua Canonica Arte Resoluta* (Theme Issued by the King, with Additions, Resolved in the Canonic Style). This six-part *ricercar* is still, to this day, considered by musicians and composers the greatest, most complex feat of counterpoint of all time.

Bach's interest in counterpoint, though, was not about putting haughty monarchs in their place, nor about solving puzzles and codes for the sake of it. He believed what he was doing was the musical embodiment of God's master plan for humankind, a recognition of the intricate mathematical beauty of the natural order as ordained by the Almighty. Counterpoint was a manifestation of Lutheran Pietism in music. In the towering achievements of his career – his sacred settings of the trial, crucifixion and resurrection of Jesus of Nazareth – he brought to fruition every piece of the musical toolkit then available to him to address what was to him the deepest and most powerful mystery of all. Two of these epic settings survive: the Passions according to St John (1724) and St Matthew (1729).

The *St Matthew Passion*, a work divided into sixty-eight movements, for orchestra, choir and soloists, and which lasts over three hours (probably four hours in Bach's time), is one of the crowning creative achievements in all European culture. At its heart lies one supreme government: the Lutheran hymn-chorale, with its simple, memorable tunes for the congregation – another of the central pillars of Pietist doctrine. At the climax of its monumental opening chorus, with two adult choirs and a double-sized orchestra already in full sway, Bach introduces a new, majestically slower tune on top of the entire structure. Like a phalanx of trumpets announcing the arrival of a mighty ruler, it is a children's choir, singing a hymn-chorale, 'O Lamm Gottes, unschuldig' (O innocent lamb of God). There are few moments in all music as dramatic, as unexpected and as moving. For Bach, this breathtaking moment of musical shock and awe is not music for music's sake; it is a manifestation of divine intervention.

But for all this, Bach's Passions do not feel like the beginning of some new movement. He was no pioneer, despite his brilliance; that mantle fell to his sons, Carl Philipp Emanuel and Johann Christian, who broke new ground and paved the way for Mozart's generation. Bach senior instead synthesised all the musical styles around him to create his huge cathedrals of sound – from the music of Lully and François Couperin at Louis XIV's court in

France, to Italian concertos and oratorios, and the church music of his north German predecessors, such as Heinrich Schütz and Dietrich Buxtehude. Composers at the very cutting-edge of change are rarely the ones whose music lasts longest. Posterity eventually rewards those, like Bach and Handel, who can absorb and repackage the currents and fashions of their times, giving the resulting collage a distinctive voice of their own along the way.

For the first hundred years after his death, though, Bach was a forgotten, unperformed composer. If he had written operas rather than church music, it might have been a different story. Opera composers have always attracted more immediate fame (or notoriety) than church composers. Luckily for his great contemporary George Frideric Handel, opera *was* his thing – to start with, at least.

Bach and Handel, the two musical giants of the eighteenth century, were born just eighty miles and four weeks apart and yet they never met. Though there are similarities in their idioms, particularly when it came to sacred music, they chose quite different career paths, which inevitably transformed their styles. Bach stayed firmly grounded, throughout his life, within the Lutheran tradition and the region of Thuringia-Saxony where he had grown up. Handel was the more adventurous pan-European traveller, learning his craft in Italy and then, in his twenties, settling for good in England, where he was to create the great body of his masterpieces. Indeed, his arrival in London in 1710 coincided with the completion of Christopher Wren's St Paul's Cathedral and Thomas Newcomen's invention of the steam engine in Dartmouth, potent omens of Britain's coming status as a world power.

That a recently arrived talent like Handel should find himself plunged into composing for royal occasions of great pomp and prestige was impressive enough. His birthday ode for Queen Anne, 'Eternal Source of Light Divine' (1713), manages to sound regal, ethereal and gracious all at once, whereas the utterly thrilling coronation anthem 'Zadok the Priest', fourteen years later, cracked superpower pomp in one master stroke, proving Handel had adapted to the indigenous choral style, as epitomised by Henry Purcell, as if he had been born, like Purcell, under the very shadow of Westminster Abbey.

Handel's significance in music history is that he was the first composer we can call truly international. Whereas Bach undoubtedly absorbed Italian and French flavours of style, he was nevertheless inescapably a north German composer whose music would take a century to be reintroduced into the mainstream. (By Mendelssohn, incidentally, who in 1829 conducted and arranged – from a manuscript copy – the first performance of Bach's *St Matthew Passion* since its composer's death, triggering a widespread reassessment of his music.) Likewise, his formidable French contemporary Jean-Philippe Rameau, for all his understanding of Italian opera, carved out a reputation through his determination to put French opera and French musical pedagogy on the map, which he did with great flair. In England, the tragically short career of Henry Purcell (1659–95) was – though brilliant – a local success story, remaining so until the twentieth century. Over in Italy, the composers who followed Vivaldi were fixated on the lucrative but non-progressive business of Italian opera, both at home and abroad. Handel, though, not only represented a musical amalgam of European styles during his lifetime; he also bequeathed to the next generation of composers a non-parochial, universal idiom that was venerated and built upon. Thus Mozart, an Austrian writing largely Italian-flavoured music, thought of himself as a natural successor to Handel, a German trained in Italy who settled in Britain. To this day, Handel's music is cherished with unqualified, familial warmth by all Western musicians, belonging not to one nation's musical history but to all.

He had two reasons for coming to the newly unified kingdom of Great Britain. One was to promote his brand of Italian-style operas on the London stage, which he did with considerable success, at least initially, and the other was as resident composer for his former employer, George, Elector of Hanover, who acceded to the British throne as George I in 1714. Though never accorded any official title, Handel contributed grand anthems and orchestral suites for the Hanover Georges, from the *Water Music* to the *Music for the Royal Fireworks*, for the rest of his life.

Handel composed thirty-nine operas for the London stage between 1711 and 1741, cashing in on a Europe-wide hysteria for Italian opera among the nobility and richer merchant classes that raged throughout the seventeenth and eighteenth centuries. The form that Monteverdi had nursed to life in the early 1600s had settled into a format, thanks to his pupil Cavalli, Vivaldi and others, that took stories from classical legend and ancient history and manipulated them to provide as many opportunities as possible for solo arias with big tunes for star singers. You cannot describe this style, dubbed *bel canto* (lovely singing), as edge-of-the-seat drama, even if it was often tragic, emotionally charged and full of pathos. But an aria like Handel's 'Lascia ch'io pianga' from *Rinaldo* could leave an audience hoarse with cheering as well as weak with emotion, depending on which heart-throb singer was delivering it.

The biggest stars of the day, paid outrageous fees and treated like royalty, were *castrati*. The practice of castrating young boys so that they could continue to sing soprano for the rest of their adult lives was promoted in the sixteenth century by the Vatican, envious of Protestant church choirs that had young women singing a soaring top line. Women were forbidden to sing in Catholic churches so the competitive cardinals chose instead to mutilate children. It is estimated that, by Handel's time, around four thousand boys a year were being castrated in Italy in the hope of singing stardom – a procedure undertaken without any form of sterilisation – often while being administered near-fatal doses of narcotics or being strangled to restrict blood flow and render them unconscious.

In Handel's London, the vogue for adult soloist castrati was short-lived, and Italian-style opera itself soon came up against stiff competition in the shape of what we would today call jukebox musicals. John Gay's *Beggar's Opera* of 1728 was one of a crop of satirical pseudo-operas in which popular and familiar tunes, sixty-nine of them, including a couple by Handel, were given new words to fit a bawdy story lampooning the injustices of contemporary society. It was the musical-theatre equivalent of the satirical engravings of William Hogarth (who painted its leading actors, as it happens), set in a grubby Soho underworld of losers, dodgers and ne'er-do-wells. Songs like 'How happy could I be with either' and 'At the Tree I shall suffer' would have been known to every Londoner of the day, absolutely regardless of status or wealth. Gay's *Beggar's Opera* was produced by the impresario John Rich, so the saying around town was that the venture had 'made Rich gay and Gay rich'.

That there was a thriving theatre audience of Londoners of lower rank is in itself a significant fact. Audiences had first started paying for tickets and enjoying live performances of opera in Venice, in the 1630s, but at that time only a tiny percentage of people, the super wealthy, could afford such a night out. When the first commercial public concerts started taking place in London the net widened to include merchants and tradespeople, a development in which England very much led the way. The first known concerts for a paying audience were presented by violinist John Banister on Fleet Street in 1672 and the world's first purpose-built concert hall was built eight years later at York Buildings on Villiers Street in London. The oldest surviving purpose-built concert hall in Europe is the Holywell Music Room in Oxford, built in 1748. To put England's advance in context, it would be *over a century* before music-mad Vienna had similarly open-to-all, ticketed public concerts.

Notwithstanding the novelty of public concert-going, music-making in the British Isles had had a more democratic profile since the temporary fall of the monarchy during the 1650s, at the end of the Civil War. Far and away the most successful musical publication of the age was John Playford's compendium of dancing tunes, *The English Dancing Master* (1651). The popularity of Playford's collection of dance tunes for fiddlers and dancers the length and breadth of Oliver Cromwell's Commonwealth was all about short, catchy numbers that anyone could join in, most of the contents being regional folk songs and dances collated together in one, later two, volumes. It is still in print today.

The rise of a middle class – and a growing, wage-earning working class, as London's industry expanded – was to have a greater effect on changing musical tastes in Britain than the whims of aristocratic patrons. The populist ballad-operas that came in the wake of *The Beggar's Opera* had an impact throughout British culture – *The Beggar's Opera* undoubtedly influenced Hogarth's *A Harlot's Progress*, for example – leading even the 'proper' opera audiences to wonder why the operas they attended at enormous expense were not also written in English, or why they didn't have fully developed men and women playing leading roles. (One of the leading actresses of the day was Lavinia Fenton, who as Polly Peachum in *The Beggar's Opera* was the focus of the song 'Our Polly is a sad slut'. Fenton became the most desired woman in London, and the Duchess of Bolton as a result, so it is hardly surprising that castrated Italians were finding it hard to attract the same degree of public attention.)

In the 1730s, in some part because of John Gay's anti-opera, Handel's golden touch with Italian opera seemed to desert him; semi-bankrupt, he abandoned opera in 1741, along with most of his fellow Britons. Luckily, he had another ace up his sleeve.

As well as banning women from singing in church, the Church authorities in Rome in the early seventeenth century had issued a prohibition on opera. In some years it was a total ban while in others it was just during Lent. Opera, the Vatican thought, was likely to incite immoral behaviour. So seventeenth-century Roman composers, led by the Jesuit Priest Giacomo Carissimi, had concocted a form of opera that did without costumes, or women, or lewd plots, or comedy, or scenery, or acted-out action, and drew its subject matter from the venerated Old Testament. Performers just stood there and sang it.

Carissimi's oratorios, particularly *Jephta*, which was composed some time in the 1640s, attracted great fame among European musicians. Carissimi was probably the most respected composer of the century in his own time, and the great English oratorios that Handel created when his luck with Italian opera began to ebb owe a huge debt to his style. Handel even quotes from Carissimi's *Rorate Filii, Israel* in his own oratorio *Samson*, composed a hundred years later. Before long, Handel's English-language oratorios even featured home-grown English singer-soloists, too, fulfilling contemporary actor-playwright and Poet Laureate Colley Cibber's aspiration to 'reconcile Musick to the English Tongue'. It was an inspired move.

Handel's first English oratorio was *Esther* in 1732, performed in the King's Theatre in London's Haymarket. The public immediately took to his new form; indeed, he hurriedly produced two more within twelve months and performances of all three at the Sheldonian Theatre in Oxford in 1633 prompted some students there to sell their furniture in order to afford the precious five-shilling tickets. The musical fame of the Sheldonian Theatre (completed in 1668) can be attributed in large part to the early attention drawn to it by Handel performances.

After *Esther* Handel presented a further twenty-one oratorios in London. His iconic *Messiah*, though, was uniquely premièred in Dublin – then Britain's second-largest city – in 1742. It was to be the one most applauded by posterity, justifiably so, although it was not the most enthusiastically received at the time; there are at least half a dozen other, equally top-drawer masterpieces among the collection, including *Saul, Solomon, Judas Maccabaeus, Theodora* and the magnificent *Israel in Egypt*, which has the distinction of being the oldest (surviving) piece of recorded classical music, from a performance at the Crystal Palace in London in June 1888, on to a paraffin cylinder recording disc.

There are a number of reasons why Handel's mostly Old

Testament musical stories should be such a perfect fit with the public of the 1740s and '50s, who greeted the oratorios with immediate and sustained rapture. The significance of audience approval is paramount in assessing Handel's oratorios since, unlike Carissimi or, for that matter, his contemporary Bach, who composed for congregations who would have been in church anyway, Handel had to court his public: they were expected to choose to come to the theatre and then pay for the privilege of hearing his work.

First, Handel brought together in a wholly accessible way all the musical idioms of the previous fifty years, with dramatic and stirring choruses evoking the grand state occasions at Westminster Abbey, moving and tuneful solos borrowed from opera style, and an orchestral bedrock based on the concerto style he and Bach had inherited from Vivaldi. Second, these were richly allegorical stories with plenty of incident and emotional impact but without extravagant, over-egged operatic acting to embarrass the English. And third, after the failure of the Jacobite Rebellions and the decisive victory for the Protestant-Hanover side in the Battle of Culloden in April 1746, stability began to transform the United Kingdom, and its growing wealth and military prowess found their celebration in Handel's patriotic choruses, in which God and the King were more or less interchangeable objects of praise. When, in *Messiah*'s famous 'Hallelujah' chorus, the choir sing '. . . and He shall reign for ever and ever', two kings are being celebrated: one in heaven, the other at St James's Palace. The immigrant Handel, a naturalised British citizen from 1727, demonstrated more successfully than any other composer before the nineteenth century how music could become the collective voice of nationhood. He may not have composed 'Rule, Britannia!' – the Catholic Freemason Thomas Arne did in 1740, as well as the adopted version of 'God Save the King' in 1745 – but Handel's was the template Arne followed, having been among the rhapsodic throng at the Oxford oratorios in 1733.

As Great Britain's self-confidence grew, its people began more and more to identify with God's chosen people, the Israelites of the Old Testament, whose destiny the British were more than happy to appropriate. Handel's oratorios, like *Israel in Egypt, Saul, Samson* and *Solomon*, extolled the virtues of wisdom, strength and patrician fairness – the hallmarks felt to lie at the heart of British self-esteem as it began to build its huge empire. As if to underline the association, the British Parliament passed a Jewish Naturalisation Act in 1753, which was not to be emulated in any other European country for half a century.

Handel's adopted countrymen and women knew a compliment when they saw it and returned it handsomely. He died rich and famous, and was the subject, a few years after his death, of the first ever book-length biography of a musician. Until Elgar, Vaughan Williams and perhaps Parry in the twentieth century, no composer commanded as much respect, pride or admiration among Britons. Indeed, when Josef Haydn arrived in London for a series of concerts in January 1791, he was struck by the continued reverence accorded Handel, a reverence with which he wisely chose, in PR terms, to associate himself. The international prestige of Handel was unmatched among British composers until Lennon and McCartney in the 1960s. (It is possible that Handel's legacy was ever so slightly double-edged, though, in that he unwittingly prompted a tendency for Britain's musical elite to believe that his native Germany was an inherently more musical country, a tendency that persists to this day. In 1905, Edward Elgar, a fervent admirer of German music, described the British music scene as 'vulgar, mediocre, chaotic and insipid'. Over a century later, in January 2012, the Liverpool-born conductor of the Berlin Philharmonic Orchestra, Sir Simon Rattle, remarked at the launch of the 2013 Baden-Baden Easter Festival, 'We British have every reason to be modest about our music.' It was best heard, he quipped, 'in homeopathic doses'.)

The hundred years of music from 1650 to 1750, a period of feverish invention and technical ingenuity, began in Italy, found momentum in France and Germany, and reached some kind of apotheosis in

Britain with Handel's sublime English oratorios, which, with Bach's cantatas and Passions, embedded in music a profoundly moral dimension. Indeed, against the backdrop of scientific endeavour and machine-like precision there was a very human emotion that enriched every note of Handel's solo arias in opera and oratorio: compassion.

In his maturity, Handel converted this artistic response into action, becoming one of the founding sponsors, alongside artists Hogarth, Reynolds and Gainsborough, of Thomas Coram's Foundling Hospital in London. Not strictly speaking an orphanage, the Foundling Hospital was a place of refuge to which poor or destitute mothers could bring their children to be sheltered and educated. Thought to be the world's first incorporated charity, it continues as a foundation, museum, garden sanctuary and philanthropic cause to this day. Handel's *Messiah* was as linked with Thomas Coram's enterprise as J. M. Barrie's *Peter Pan* was with Great Ormond Street Children's Hospital, which stands virtually adjacent to the site of the Foundling Hospital. Even for its first performance in the unfamiliar setting of the 'New Musick Hall in Fishamble Street' in Dublin, Handel made arrangements for a portion of his earnings to be diverted to three Irish charities, including the Charitable Musical Society for the Relief of Imprisoned Debtors, which had built the six-hundred-seat hall for its meetings. Though *Messiah* was a sacred work, its frequent performances given in secular settings, and its relationship to the very real social issues of the time, place it firmly in a Lutheran-Anglican ethos of community and pragmatism, and reveal a changing attitude to the function and reception of music. It would not exist as a work in the form that we know today were it not for the engagement and approval of a broader public in Handel's lifetime. Like the scientific inventions that were sparking into life all around him, heralding the beginning of the Industrial Revolution, this music was intended, primarily, to benefit and enlighten all.

One of his final oratorios, *Solomon*, contains towards its end an aria for the Queen of Sheba, who is bidding a longing farewell to

King Solomon, whom she will never see again, as he returns to Jerusalem. 'Will the sun forget to streak?' is no hysterical outburst of operatic tragedy, nor is it a plaint of sentimental, self-indulgent misery. It is the mature voice of rueful acceptance. As we listen to it, it is as if the centuries have melted away and we are left with Handel's simple, humane message: time does not stand still, so cherish every moment of joy with gratitude.

> Will the sun forget to streak
> Eastern skies with amber ray,
> When the dusky shades to break
> He unbars the gates of day?
> Then demand if Sheba's queen
> E'er can banish from her thought
> All the splendour she has seen,
> All the knowledge thou hast taught?

4

The Age of Elegance and Sentiment
1750–1850

As with rosy steps the morn,
Advancing, drives the shades of night,
So from virtuous toil well-borne,
Raise Thou our hopes of endless light.

(from Handel's and Morell's oratorio *Theodora*)

Handel's first eighteen oratorios in London theatres were packed-house affairs. Then, in 1750, he premièred a controversial new work that was a box-office flop. The offending piece was *Theodora*, a setting of a libretto by his friend Thomas Morell, which itself was based on an account of the early Christian martyr by Robert Boyle, the founder of modern chemistry.

Even before the première Handel had a premonition that *Theodora*, with its uncompromisingly tragic ending involving the eponymous princess choosing virtue over life, might unsettle his regular audience, telling Morell, 'The Jews will not come to it because it is a Christian story; and the ladies will not come because it is a virtuous one.' But the real reason why *Theodora*, with its ravishing music and Handel's name above the title, opened to a near empty theatre in March 1750 was altogether more unexpected. Two earthquakes had hit London that month and the well-to-do had heeded fire-and-brimstone sermons, Charles Wesley's among them, about the quakes being God's punishment for wickedness, and had fled to their estates in the more godly countryside. (An ill-conceived escape plan, as it turned out: the subsequent tremors shook rural Lincolnshire.)

Though the tremors injured some Londoners and caused stones to tumble off the top of Westminster Abbey's new spire, they were as nothing to a quake, five years later, along Europe's Atlantic seaboard that really did seem, to some, to signal the end of civilisation. Indeed, the coming age of cultural change – including new trends in music – was ushered in by a widely held belief that the world was on the brink of catastrophe.

As if to confirm people's biblical fears, the earthquake and tsunami that devastated Lisbon in 1755 struck on 1 November: All Saints' Day. What was left standing of the Imperial city after the initial shocks was then razed to the ground by uncontrollable fires. It is thought as many as sixty thousand people perished. Similar scenes were played out along the coasts of western Europe and northern Africa, with Galway City's walls partially swept away and a tidal wave reaching as far west as Barbados. Across Europe, prophets and priests portrayed it as the wrath of God and a foretaste of an imminent Armageddon. Voltaire composed a poem on the disaster that had considerable cultural impact, opening a floodgate of intellectual challenge and debate. What is perhaps most striking about 'Poème sur le désastre de Lisbonne' is its astonishing challenge to the prevailing seventeenth- and eighteenth-century concept of, and faith in, God. Nothing could be further from the omnipotent, benevolent creative force of Handel's oratorios or Bach's cantatas and Passions – yet Handel was still alive, just, and Bach had only died five years earlier. In a direct riposte to post-tsunami Portuguese Jesuits, like the immensely powerful Gabriel Malagrida, who declared unequivocally that the catastrophe was God's anger at the population's immoral behaviour, Voltaire rejected a compassionate deity and the notion of providence, divine or otherwise, asking what sin babies had committed to deserve such a punishment.

> *Quel crime, quelle faute ont commis ces enfants*
> *Sur le sein maternel écrasés et sanglants?*

The great change in attitude of which Voltaire was a supreme philosophical weathervane coincided with a rapid reshaping of music after the deaths of Bach and Handel. Two of Bach's sons, Johann Christian in London and Carl Philipp Emanuel in Berlin, were pioneers of the new sound. This sound was stripped of the multiple layers and intricacies of counterpoint, and designed for clarity and instant sensual impact. It wasn't just a new sound, though, that could be heard in the 1760s and '70s, but a new approach to music altogether. Faith and morality, the watchwords of the previous generation, gave way to the Pleasure Principle. Instead of trying to *improve* their listeners, musicians started pampering them. In politics, science, philosophy and literature this was the period of the Enlightenment. For composers and musicians, it might just as well have been called the Enjoyment.

Throughout the history of music, periods of complication and innovation are followed by periods of simplicity and consolidation, which are then in time followed by more complication again. It is something to do with the younger generation contradicting the efforts of their elders, the perennial parent-child dynamic of human civilisation: 'whatever they did, we will do the opposite.' As far as Bach *père*, Johann Sebastian, was concerned, the point of music was to glorify God and reflect upon the great mysteries of creation through music of unabashed seriousness. What his sons and their contemporaries undertook, instead, was a massive spring clean of musical style and a project to celebrate not earnestness but wit, not inventiveness but elegance, not piety but beauty. The young brothers Bach, though, did not have the kind of natural genius required to lead a new movement out of its initial rebellious stage into the mainstream. They were musicians' musicians. This task would belong to a group of composers whose lives overlapped and found focus within the walls of one great city: Vienna. They were Haydn, Mozart and Beethoven.

Just eight weeks after the 1755 Lisbon earthquake, as if to provide Voltaire with a new god to replace the discredited old one, a boy

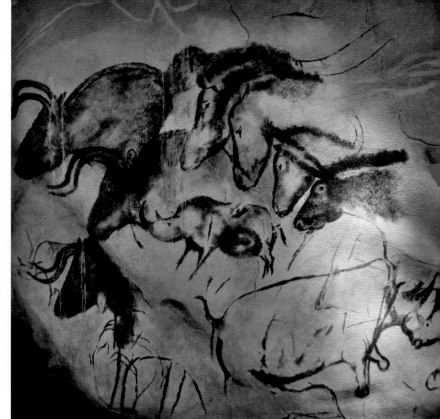

The famous rock paintings at Chauvet, France, are located at the points of greatest resonance in the pitch-black cave network. It is thought that Palaeolithic cave-dwellers would sing here not only as part of communal ritual, but also to find their bearings.

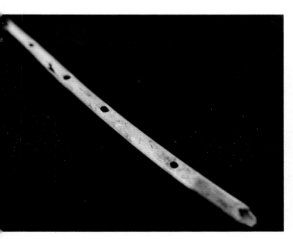

This flute made from bone was found at the Stone-Age Hohle Fels cave in southern Germany and is thought to be 35,000 years old.

The *lur*, a curved brass horn, was a popular instrument in Bronze-Age Denmark. One of the country's most famous modern-day exports – Lurpak butter – features the horn both in its name and on its packaging.

This clay tablet from Mesopotamia (modern Iraq) dates from 2600 BC and is the oldest list of musical instruments ever discovered.

Egyptian art is rife with depictions of musicians and their instruments, suggesting that music was an important feature of public and private life.

The *kithara* –
a form of lyre –
appears prominently
on artefacts from
Ancient Greece,
such as this vase
from the fifth
century BC.

The Ancient Greeks
invented one of the most
influential instruments
of all time: the organ.
This early model was
known as a hydraulis
organ because it used a
tank of water to pressurise
the air for the pipes.

One of the earliest forms of musical notation involved *neumes* – markings above a song's text – but they were only useful to someone already familiar with the song.

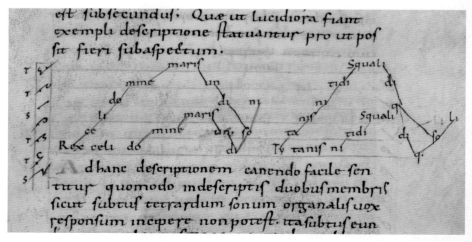

This imaginative but impractical form of early notation, attributed to a ninth-century French monk called Hucbald, had the words rise and fall according to the shape of the tune.

Composers of the fourteenth century were inspired by the aunting acoustics of the astounding cathedrals in which they worked. This is Reims Cathedral in France, for which Guillaume de Machaut composed masses that were unprecedented in heir musical complexity.

Composer Josquin des Prez (*left*) attached new importance to the meaning of the words being sung in sacred music. His *Miserere* of 1503 was a setting of a controversial prayer written by Girolamo Savonarola (*above*).

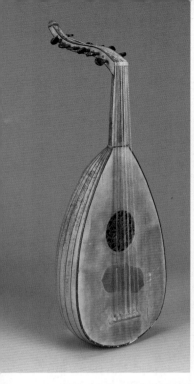

The *al'Ud* (*left*) arrived in Europe from Persia via Muslim Spain over a thousand years ago. It inspired later European instruments such as the lute (*below*); the cittern (*below left*), a predecessor of the guitar; and the violin (*below right*).

This violin was built by the famous Amati family of Cremona, Italy, whose mid-sixteenth-century violins are the world's oldest surviving examples of the instrument.

The world's oldest playable organ, in the basilica of Valère in the canton of Valais in Switzerland, was built some time between 1390 and 1435.

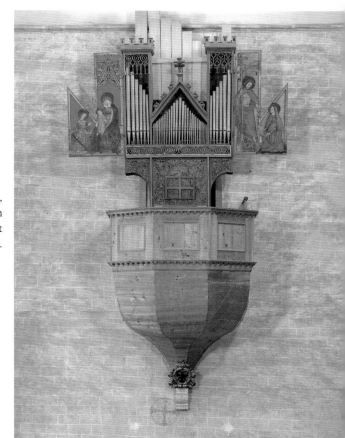

In an attempt to offer keyboard players the greatest range of notes per octave, Vito Trasuntino of Venice built the 'Clavemusicum Omnitonum' in 1606. With thirty-one notes per octave, it was ludicrously difficult to play and did not catch on.

Louis XIV, aged fifteen, as Apollo, the Sun King, in Lully's *Le Ballet de la nuit* of 1653.

The English Dancing Master, John Playford's compendium of catchy regional folk songs and dances, was the most successful musical publication of Oliver Cromwell's Commonwealth. It is still in print today.

was born in Salzburg who would provide an exhilarating focus for the new musical generation: Wolfgang Amadeus Mozart. The new musical style was already well under way by the time Mozart was a young composer, and he grew up in a Europe experiencing a sea change in cultural attitudes. But what had prompted this new wave was far more extraordinary than a straightforward backlash to what had gone before.

In the 1730s and '40s, building work near Naples had accidentally discovered the buried ruins of the first-century Roman towns Herculaneum and Pompeii, in the shadow of Mount Vesuvius. In the decades that followed, extensive excavations revealed to increasingly intrigued eighteenth-century Europeans how sophisticated – and, to their consternation, how saucy – their ancient ancestors had been. The excavation of Pompeii and Herculaneum sparked a major re-evaluation of the Ancient World and a near mania – among the wealthy and educated of the later eighteenth century – for all things connected with it. Ancient Greek and Roman civilisations became something of an ideal to which people might aspire. In contrast to the strict work ethic and emphasis on service to the public good that had governed thought in the previous hundred years, the privileged now took their cue from the perceived sensuality and hedonism of the Ancient World, and sought pleasure without guilt or responsibility.

The significance of the fashion for Ancient Greek and Roman culture is an awkward one for music, leading to possibly the least successful and most confusing of all its labels. In other fields, imitations of Roman and Greek architecture, art and scholarship acquired the name 'classical' or 'neo-classical', but the term is misleading in music, because composers of the eighteenth century had no Ancient World, or 'classical'-era, music to imitate. If you had told Carl Philipp Emanuel Bach or Josef Haydn they were working in a consciously 'classical' style inspired by the period 800 BC–AD 100 they would have been baffled by the comparison. That is because they thought they were being ultra-modern, the cutting edge, the new blood. They thought they were sweeping away the fusty, clickety-clackety music of their elders, a style that has sometimes, equally unhelpfully, been called 'Baroque' – unhelpful in that the musical style of Corelli, Vivaldi, Bach and Handel had very little to do with Baroque architecture, or art, or literature. Their ambitions had no resonance with the streets of Pompeii or the poetry of Ovid; it was targeted on what they saw as an outdated, complicated, rather serious style that needed to be replaced with something simple, clear, emotionally unambiguous, easy on the ear, and ordered. They found the cleverness of their forebears' music, with its fugues, its interweaving counterpoint, its layering upon layer of sounds, too academic and dry, rather like student exercises. We might even rename the new style typified by Bach junior 'minimalist', were it not for the fact that this term was coined by the English composer Michael Nyman to describe his music, and that of some of his peers, in the 1980s.

Carl Philipp Emanuel Bach, who was revered by Haydn, Mozart and Beethoven, invented his own label for his new approach, *Empfindsamer* (sensitive) style, while musicologists of the time came up with the description *galante* for the general shift towards musical simplicity. Unfortunately 'classical' is nonetheless how the music of the late-eighteenth and very-early-nineteenth centuries came to be categorised in musicological terminology from the early-twentieth century, a trend led by Germans who were keen to identify the Viennese trio of Haydn, Mozart and Beethoven as constituting a Golden Age, untouchably perfect and unique, a pantheon of Divine Masters worthy of the Greek and Roman *Classical* era. (To add to the confusion, 'classical' had come to mean *all* music, especially old music, that wasn't 'popular' by the later twentieth century. The icing on the cake of this terminological mess is a sub-genre of 'classical' music known as 'neo-classical', which describes music by composers of the 1920s and '30s who sought inspiration from the seventeenth and eighteenth centuries. This is why I prefer to call the period 1750–1850 'the age of elegance and sentiment', because that at least is what it *is*.)

*

The new-wave composers of the mid-eighteenth century, call them what you like, were encouraged by a new generation of art-loving patrons, such as Frederick the Great of Prussia, and by a growing concert-going public. The concert hall as a dedicated venue was still a novelty outside England, but wealthier members of the bourgeoisie were often invited to hear musical events inside the grand palaces of aristocrats and princes. They could also buy their way into opera houses, most of which were nevertheless built, owned and controlled by rich patrons, chiefly for their own benefit and that of their friends and hangers-on. When, in the time of Haydn, Mozart and Beethoven, we refer to a 'public' concert, it is not in the modern sense of a gathering open to absolutely anyone, for the price of a ticket. It was a luxury for the relatively well-off, often arranged at short notice in an informal manner, as 'public' as a ball at Bath's Assembly Rooms might have been. The nearest thing to the modern concept of a public concert were the outdoor entertainments laid on at London's vast Pleasure Gardens, in particular Ranelagh and Vauxhall, which sprawled competitively across large sites on opposite sides of the Thames. Both Ranelagh and Vauxhall had large permanent performance structures, the Rotunda at Ranelagh being the subject of a particularly striking painting by Canaletto in 1754. Eleven years later, a nine-year-old Mozart played a recital in the packed Rotunda, which had a capacity of two thousand.

The Pleasure Gardens offered much else besides music to entice their huge crowds – food, wine, arrack punch, acrobats, rope-dancers, fire-eaters, mechanical fountains, equestrian displays, battle re-enactments, masked balls and leafy glades in which to make secret (or paid-for) assignations, and so, unlike Bath's Assembly Rooms, they attracted all classes of society. A rehearsal of Handel's *Music for the Royal Fireworks* in 1749 drew an estimated twelve thousand spectators (paying 2s. 6d. each, £17.50 today) and created a gridlock of carriages across the newly built Westminster Bridge, paralysing central London for three hours. Johann Christian Bach composed songs for Vauxhall every season for fifteen years, though even he must have felt upstaged by an Italian gentleman called Rivolta whose novelty act at the Gardens involved his playing eight musical instruments simultaneously: pandean pipes, tabor, Spanish guitar, triangle, harmonica, Chinese crescent, cymbals and bass drum.

Composers adapted quickly to the new conditions, new paymasters and new tastes of the second half of the eighteenth century. While Handel – whose statue greeted visitors to the Vauxhall Gardens until they closed in 1839 – felt able to submit his London theatre audiences to three hours of religious parable and uplifting spiritual instruction, as he did in his Old Testament oratorios, just twenty years later this would have been utterly out of place. Hoping to seduce an audience, his successor composers dropped the rigorous moralising and, wherever expedient, God. And this change of attitude and mood is audible in the musical style of the period, particularly within the harmony that supported melody.

Composers of J. S. Bach's generation, as well as glorying in the satisfying chemistry generated by sequences of chords, loved to suspend notes over unfamiliar territory, to mix up chords unpredictably, to dice with dissonance, to play aural tricks on the listener. They used harmony as an additional layer of subtlety and effect, even by using discords to intensify the meaning of texts conveying suffering, loss or anguish.

By contrast, the pain suggested by dissonance – the clashing of adjacent notes – is almost entirely absent from music written between 1750 and 1800. What's more, even very skilled composers decided there were really far too many chords available and that they needed far fewer for their purposes. Bach's and Handel's rich palette of chords was stripped back to just a handful. This may not be strange to modern ears – after all, dissonance is almost totally absent from the popular music of the twentieth and twenty-first centuries, too, even if there is plenty of it in 'classical' music of the same period. Modern listeners, on the whole, also seek pleasure rather than pain from music, and even the most aggressive of the early punk bands of the 1970s, while yelling angrily over deliberately distorted guitar, bass and drums, were nevertheless adhering to a basic diet of three or four uncomplicated chords and a melody that fitted with them harmoniously. The Sex Pistols' songs are no more discordant than, say, 'Lovely yet ungrateful swain', a Vauxhall Gardens song of Johann Christian Bach.

Indeed, so refined is the music of this period, the era of elegance, that music written for modern-day commercials or film and TV scores often deliberately recalls the style of Mozart and Haydn to convey stability, comfort, class and contentment. Stevie Wonder borrowed this same, stately style in his 1976 masterpiece *Songs in the Key of Life*, to evoke, satirically, an idyll of charming, happy, village life as he sang of the desperation of the African-American underclass in 'Village Ghetto Land'.

Composers of the mid- to late-eighteenth century limited themselves to a small choice of chords partly as a reaction to the harmonic style of their predecessors, but also to emphasise the primacy of the melody. The tune, they felt, should glide unencumbered across the aural landscape, without the listener being too distracted by chordal complexities lurking beneath it. There are three chords in the slimmed-down list that were used obsessively, because they were the three that most brought out the sense of 'home' in the sound, reinforcing the melody's typical journey away from home and back again. Vast swathes of the music written in the sixty or so years after 1750 slavishly hung on these three master chords – the same three, as it happens, that dominate rock and roll and its various twentieth-century offspring. Just as the period's architects designed buildings from the same limited collection of motifs and shapes, Haydn and his contemporaries were designing music from a similarly limited catalogue.

The three chords in question can be expressed as the numbers I, IV and V, because they are the triads that belong to the first, fourth and fifth notes of the major or minor scale. Thus, in C major, they are the C, F and G triads. In G major, they are G, C and D, and so on. These three chords for every key-family can also be described as 'tonic', 'sub-dominant' and 'dominant', terms whose etymology I am not going to elaborate on because they are among the most misleading and ill-conceived of all music's bad terminology. It suffices to know that they appear time and time again across the centuries. But why?

The reason is that, as we saw as part of 'musical gravity' in the last chapter, these three harmonic centres are the most inherently powerful. They are created from the most 'natural' ratios, even taking into account the distorting fix of Equal Temperament. They are music's primary colours.

Two pieces from the era in question – one from 1762 and the other from 1808 – demonstrate the ubiquity of the I, IV and V chords. The first excerpt is from an opera, *Orfeo ed Euridice*, by Bavarian composer Christoph Gluck, a composer credited with having 'reformed' opera by insisting on more natural storytelling, less showing off from the singers and more natural acting, all improvements he had picked up from watching the actor David Garrick in London. Gluck was also music teacher to the Arch-duchess Maria Johanna, later to be Marie-Antoinette, Queen of France, a keen and able musician, and by the 1750s was working in Vienna, where *Orfeo ed Euridice* had its first performance. *Orfeo* has a dance interlude that later came to be called 'The Dance of the Blessed Spirits'. It is a charming, gentle tune that appeals precisely because of its simplicity. Looking at its score we could give each of these three governing chords a colour code: the 'home' chord that begins and ends the piece is chord I. (We are in the key of F, so it is the triad of F.) Whenever this chord I is the basis of the harmony (and tune) I have shaded the score light grey. Light grey is pretty powerful but there are still some areas of the map not yet conquered by its empire. Our next important chord is chord IV, which I have marked with a dotted line. Now there is not a great deal of unoccupied territory left, but there is still room for chord V, which I have marked with a grey line.

So between them, our three chords are all-conquering. There is hardly anything left for all the chords that aren't part of this mighty triumvirate.

The predominance of these three chords was no passing fad. Our second comparison piece, Beethoven's fifth symphony, completed and first performed in 1808, nearly half a century after Gluck's *Orfeo* opera, sounds bigger in every respect, more ambitious and more dramatic, yet it nevertheless shows how dependent he is on those three chords. The opening of the symphony's final movement is entirely harmonised by chords I, IV and V, and indeed the first chord we hear that *isn't* one of those three is in the thirty-sixth bar, roughly forty-eight seconds into the piece.

To be fair to Beethoven, who elsewhere was delving into a far greater palette of chords by 1808, he was obliged to stick to those simple chords if he wanted to have brass instruments (horns, trombones, trumpets) and timpani (kettle drums), because these latter were only able to play a very limited number of notes that belonged to the 'home' chords. By the time he wrote his hefty ninth symphony, completed in 1824, technology in the form of pistons and valves had come to the rescue and provided brass instruments with a much fuller menu of notes and available keys.

But limiting themselves to a small number of chords did not mean that the composers of the second half of the eighteenth century wrote simple music. Beneath the surface of the music of Gluck, Haydn, Mozart and their contemporaries lies an infrastructure every bit as sophisticated as the sacred geometry and sense of divine proportion revered by one of the most influential European movements of the age: the Freemasons. Indeed, it comes as little surprise that a large number of late-eighteenth-century composers were themselves Freemasons: Christoph Gluck was a member of the Parisian Masonic lodge Saint-Jean d'Écosse du Contrat Social, Haydn of the Viennese lodge Zur wahren Eintracht (True Unity or Concord), and Mozart joined Zur Wohltätigkeit (Beneficence) in 1784 and also attended meetings of Zur wahren Eintracht. Other notable eighteenth-century Masonic musicians included Frederick the Great of Prussia, Benjamin Franklin, Johann Hummel, Ignaz Pleyel and, in England, Johann Christian Bach, Thomas Arne, William Boyce, the Thomas Linleys (father and son) and Samuel Wesley.

Composers of the period were as fond of order and formal infrastructure as their architect contemporaries, but with no way of resurrecting the lost music of the Ancient World they had to invent their own ways of building grand, formal structures into the foundations of their pieces. Rather than simply producing nice but random tunes with accompaniment, they framed them according to an underlying logic: every piece they composed was constructed with the help of what amounted to musical maps. An opera, naturally, could follow the route set by its story. A sacred choral work could navigate through the religious texts and order of service as ordained by the Church. (The Catholic and Lutheran mass, or Eucharist, for example, had a strict order of movements whose duration and scale was dictated by the step-by-step progress towards the congregation taking communion.) A song was servant to its lyric.

In the previous two centuries, most if not all instrumental music was either specifically for dancing or had its origin in some form of dance music, but as composers developed greater ambitions for instrumental music – for it to be listened to without dancing – they needed alternative ways of determining structure, pace, duration or changes of mood. Instrumental pieces lacking the purpose of dance to guide them were potentially formless and anarchic without some kind of map, and in an age of order and decorum, where the hierarchies of society were rigidly observed – at least until various revolutions sparked off – formless music was anathema. So it became imperative to establish design templates for instrumental music, even if the template was hidden beneath the surface of the music.

The building of these musical maps had its most sophisticated manifestation in the growth and popularity of the symphony, but the form that underpins every symphony composed between around 1750 and 1900 actually has a name inherited from a smaller-scale instrumental work: 'Sonata Form'. I must confess I find Sonata Form a numbingly tedious subject and am not going to dwell on it. Suffice to say that its rules – state your theme, elaborate on it, state your second theme, elaborate on it, change key, elaborate more, return to where you started but in a new key-family (mostly, *quelle surprise*, IV or V) – were taught to every budding composer of the late-eighteenth and the nineteenth and twentieth centuries as if set in stone, so it is hardly a shock to discover it was where they all tended to start their careers. It is still a significant component in the teaching of undergraduate composition.

For most modern-day music lovers, music is something mysterious, unpredictable, sensual and, above all, emotional. Some people even put music on a par with a religious experience, tapping into some other-worldly part of their conscious or unconscious existence. This is utterly different from the way craftsmen like Haydn saw their art. Haydn's aim was the manufacturing of beauty and elegance in the material world; he was conscious that what he was doing was artifice, not a divine intervention. In order to create pleasing after-dinner entertainment for the guests of his royal employer, Prince Nikolaus Esterházy, he was going to have to find a way of making melody and harmony appear flawlessly proportioned, to harness nature's wild features and tame it into man-made perfection. These delightfully proportioned amusements would therefore need all the help they could get from formal blueprints like Sonata Form, and from musical versions of the balanced layouts of Capability Brown's gardens, or Robert Adam's buildings.

Haydn didn't invent the symphony. He didn't even conceive its classic shape of four movements – quite fast, slow, gentle dance in triple time, faster than before – a shape that composers were still loosely following even at the beginning of the twentieth century. But what he did do was perfect the obsession of the next two centuries: taking a small tune and manipulating it in lots of ways in order to make a unified, more substantial framework out of it.

Haydn had learnt about the symphony from pioneers like Wenzel Birck, Georg Wagenseil and Johann Stamitz, all now virtually unknown. Stamitz, who was born 120 kilometres from Prague and baptised Jan Stamic, has probably the greatest claim to being the inventor of the symphony as we know it, though posterity has largely forgotten him nonetheless. Stamic worked at the Court of the Elector Palatine in Mannheim, Germany, where he changed his name to Stamitz, and where he had access to an orchestra that was famous throughout Europe for both the unusual skill of its players and its incredible size, by the standards of the 1750s. Stamitz's Mannheim orchestra had twenty violins, four violas, four cellos, two bass violones (the predecessor of the double-bass), two flutes, two oboes, two bassoons and four horns, as well as two clarinets (much to Mozart's envy, when he visited in 1777, the latter being a relatively new instrument at this time). This tally of instruments, occasionally beefed up by timpani and trumpets, was the template for the classical orchestra as used by Haydn, Mozart, Beethoven, Schubert and their contemporaries.

Stamitz's music is at best agreeable, but he does demonstrate an important first step in the process of creating proportion from basic melodies. His mini-tunes, once stated, are immediately repeated. Whatever the peculiarities of the first mini-tune, an audible sense of 'rightness' emerges through the repetition. It is the musical equivalent of dropping a random blob of ink on a piece of paper: by folding the paper and creating a symmetrical double, a pleasing shape is suddenly formed. Almost everything Stamitz does is provided with a response of the same length and shape. Though it is repetitious and – I am afraid to say – increasingly annoying to listen to, this technique soon accustoms our ears to expect equal weight in a tune's two halves. This melodic symmetry had not been a noticeable feature of the more onward-flowing, unpredictable tunes of Bach and Handel, whose phrases were so often guided by the metre of the words they set. From Stamitz and Bach's sons onwards, though, symmetry became paramount – much as it was for late-eighteenth-century buildings.

Haydn took the Mannheim-style orchestra and the idea of proportion and balance, and went one crucial step further. *His* balancing phrase was not typically identical but slightly different in character, creating a symmetry without simply repeating itself. While a Stamitz mini-tune might be made up of a handful of notes, Haydn extended the phrase, testing the short-term memory of his listener, then coaxed a slightly altered or ornamented second phrase from it. The second halves of his melodic ideas may have been the same length as the first but then they might, for instance, mirror or invert the direction of travel, or continue the journey to a different resting place. A tune that gradually snaked upwards in its first half might gradually snake downwards in its second. A tune that moved from chord-base I to chord-base V in its first half would travel back from V to I in its second. Thus, out of his small but well-proportioned phrases, he cleverly constructed larger units that smoothly transformed into longer and longer chains, every part of the chain fitting neatly into the overall shape as if mathematically calculated (which they were not). Haydn taught the world, apparently effortlessly, how to organise and develop melody in such a way that a piece of fifteen or twenty minutes would sound unified.

Haydn was so adept at sculpting a tune from small beginnings that the younger Mozart and Beethoven simply copied the technique in their own way. Indeed, 'developing' tunes like this soon became essential for composers of orchestral music. Deconstructing and manipulating tunes, passing them between the instruments, wandering off into new key-families in search of fresh colours, and so on was what nearly all composers between 1770 and 1900 did when they wrote symphonies, with a few notable exceptions.

This was the point of a symphony; it was like an essay, or a detailed, blow-by-blow experiment. A song could simply be a nice meandering tune, plain and simple. An opera was a series of songs, linked by a plot. But symphonies were supposed to be explorations, journeys to find out what would happen if you took a clutch of short melodic ideas and elaborated on them.

The odd thing about the symphony as it blossomed in Haydn's, Mozart's and Beethoven's time is that it doesn't have any direct parallels in any other artistic field. Poems of the period were either descriptions of objects, plants, weather conditions, geographical features or emotional states, or they followed a narrative. William Wordsworth's and Samuel Taylor Coleridge's *Lyrical Ballads*, for instance, published in 1798, included Coleridge's 'Rime of the Ancient Mariner' and Wordsworth's 'Strange fits of passion have I known', both of which attached reflections on emotional states to journeys. The eighteenth century had seen the development of the novel, extended prose fiction, in which unfolding stories acted as structures to allow the exploration of a range of themes and philosophies, from Daniel Defoe's *Robinson Crusoe* (1719) and Samuel

Richardson's *Pamela* (1740) to Frances Burney's *Camilla* (1796) and Jane Austen's *Sense and Sensibility* (1811). Meandering, non-narrative prose or poetry, like musical symphonies, would not find their literary equivalents until James Joyce's *Ulysses* or T. S. Eliot's *The Waste Land*, both published in 1922. Likewise, extended dance forms such as ballet didn't become separated from storylines until the mid-twentieth century. Paintings of the late eighteenth and early nineteenth centuries are still entirely figurative; Kandinsky's first abstract painting did not emerge until 1910.

But the symphony is a peculiar thing: sixty musicians simultaneously interpreting instructions given them by one person with no narrative, no plot and no literal meaning, nor, until Beethoven's *Pastoral* symphony of 1808, a *description* of anything. Even after the *Pastoral* symphony, in the mid-nineteenth-century 'symphonic poems' of Liszt, for example, a listener who had not been forewarned by the concert programme *what* was being portrayed in the music could never have guessed simply by listening to it. The symphony form's four loosely related seven- or eight-minute sections of instrumental music at slightly different speeds, created solely for the cerebral fun of it, is a strange and unique cultural activity in the late-eighteenth and nineteenth centuries.

Being at odds with the other arts was not the only aspect of the symphony that dislocated music from its time. Haydn's and Mozart's obedient following of their favourite symphonic formula – Sonata Form – could not have come at a more *dis*obedient junction in social and political history.

Haydn, Beethoven and Mozart all lived through the American and French Revolutions, and Mozart diced briefly with political jeopardy when he composed an operatic setting of a banned play, Beaumarchais's *The Marriage of Figaro*, in 1786. The widespread alarm, though, that gripped the European aristocracy – the paymasters and patrons of musicians, remember – is hard to detect in the bulk of Haydn's and Mozart's symphonies, sonatas and concertos, and in the early work of Beethoven. The overwhelming impression is of an ordered, untroubled world. It is as if composers felt their job was not to join the revolutionaries, but to keep the aristocracy calm. 'All will be well,' they seem to be saying. 'We will create a *virtual* world of order and harmony.'

Listening to the playfully vivacious music Haydn was writing in 1793, his ninety-ninth symphony, while the Terror raged in Paris and agents of the mob were cutting off Marie-Antoinette's head, makes one wonder if he even knew what was going on in the outside world. (Which of course he did: the execution of France's Austrian queen deprived Haydn of his most famous and outspoken admirer.) Even allowing for the traditional plea of composers to be immune from political events irrelevant to their art, Haydn's symphonies sound as if they were written in a vacuum. The charismatic composer-conductor who championed and oversaw the premières of Haydn's six 'Paris' symphonies (nos. 82–7) between 1785 and 1786, Joseph Bologne, Chevalier de Saint-George, was denounced and imprisoned by revolutionary tribunal in 1793. Bologne, the first mixed-race colonel in the French Army, was thereupon abandoned by all his previous patrons and friends, and died in impoverished obscurity. Meanwhile, Haydn was setting Beethoven counterpoint exercises while on summer retreat at the palace of Eisenstadt.

The happiest months of Haydn's life, according to the composer himself, were those spent being treated like a celebrity in England, in 1791–2 and again in 1794–5. The clamour surrounding his appearances there, much written-up at the time and oft-quoted since, should not blind us to the reality that, when we talk of fame in this context, it means 'among the rich and privileged'. Haydn was fêted by the likes of Messrs Darcy and Bingley rather than by the Bennets and Lucases. The Bennets, had they lived in London and as a special treat visited an opera house or theatre, would more likely have queued to see Colman and Arnold's immensely successful comic opera *Inkle and Yarico*, which also delighted audiences in New York, Dublin, Jamaica, Philadelphia, Boston and Calcutta in the last decade of the eighteenth century. *Inkle and Yarico*, an interracial love story set in Barbados, in which the heroine is saved from slavery, not only reminds us that attitudes among the middle classes were not as instinctively racist as we might suppose, but also falls into a long tradition of popular entertainment reflecting or influencing public opinion – in this case on the subject of slavery – with greater efficacy than its more sophisticated equivalent. John Gay's *Beggar's Opera* was an early example of this, and later the music hall songs of Arthur Lloyd, and Sam Cooke's 'A Change is Gonna Come'. (Before we leave Samuel Arnold, composer of *Inkle and Yarico*, organist of Westminster Abbey and yet another musical Freemason, I feel compelled to report that he holds the British record for the musical publication with the longest single word in its title: his 1781 comic opera *The Baron Kinkvervankotsdorsprakingatchdern*.)

Other than during his sojourns in England, Haydn's long career was mostly unaffected by what the public thought of his music. The reason for this was that he worked for an aristocrat, Prince Esterházy, at his private houses. Haydn would be the last major composer for a hundred and fifty years to whom this artistic luxury was granted without question, but the price he paid for this security was being treated as a glorified footman by the prince. In the 'Upstairs, Downstairs' world of eighteenth-century European nobility, the in-house composer was definitely Downstairs, even one with an international reputation as prestigious as Haydn's. In any case, this sort of arrangement was on its way out: between Haydn and his young friend Mozart lies the fault line that divides the old world of musical patronage and the modern concept of the freelance composer offering his or her wares to an open, public market.

Unlike Haydn, Mozart needed the public to enjoy his music in order not to starve, carving out for himself in Vienna what we would call a portfolio career, involving public performing, teaching, writing on commission, composing for the theatre and producing a considerable body of dance music. This may explain why Mozart's music is so full of catchy melodies. Melody was a way to win an audience's heart, whether that audience was in the public gallery at Vienna's unstuffy Freihaus-Theater auf der Wieden, singing along to *The Magic Flute* in 1791, or the cream of the Habsburg ruling class at the Imperial Court Theatre (Burgtheater) chatting their way through *Die Entführung aus dem Serail* (*The Abduction from the Harem*).

Mozart was by far more daring than Haydn, but then he was also younger. The main difference between Haydn's style and Mozart's is really quite simple: if you can instantly remember the tune, it's by Mozart. A brutal assessment, but a true one. Technically, Mozart's approach was similar to Haydn's – the same orchestra, the same chords, the same architecture – but he had the melodic gift of a god. If he composed it, a tune sings like no other. Try, if you will, this little test: listen to the first thirty or so seconds of the aria for the Chinese princess Angelica, 'Palpita adogni istante', from Haydn's opera *Orlando Paladino*, first performed at the Eszterháza Palace in December 1782. The conductor and expert on eighteenth-century music Nikolaus Harnoncourt describes the opera as 'one of the best works in eighteenth-century music theatre' – praise indeed from an impeccably knowledgeable source. The opera was the best-liked of all Haydn's fifteen operas during his own lifetime. But play the opening statement just once and then try to sing it back to yourself. Then listen to the first fifteen seconds of Mozart's aria 'Welche Wonne, Welche Lust' from his opera *Die Entführung aus dem Serail* of the same year. Unless something has distracted you in the meantime, I bet you can sing back that opening Mozart phrase immediately. It isn't *better* than the Haydn; it is just catchier.

Something else emerges in Mozart, though, beyond the sublime melodies, that Haydn's music does not anticipate. Mozart, as well as being intrigued by the hidden curiosities and mystical secrets of Freemasonry, unashamedly celebrated in *The Magic Flute*, was fascinated by the supernatural, and by what we would call psychological motive.

In the decorously polite world that Mozart inhabited but never wholeheartedly embraced – aristocratic Vienna of the late-eighteenth century – his operatic visions of heaven and hell, of the spiritual and the carnal, allow us to catch a glimpse of something very different and surprising. To be sure, people sensed he was an oddball at the time, disconcertingly gifted, outspoken, irreverent – in short, a strange mix of child and sage. Indeed, rather like Michael Jackson in our own time, Mozart's childhood had been forfeited to make way for a career as a freakishly talented boy prodigy to be touted around an adult world. Both artists retained in their grown-up writing a sense of the fragility and potential pitfalls of close relationships. One of Mozart's earliest friendships was with the young English prodigy Thomas Linley, whom he met and befriended in Italy. There is a famous painting of the two boys together in Florence in 1770, Mozart at the piano, Linley with the violin. Mozart was devastated when his childhood friend was killed in a boating accident just eight years later, the same year as the death of Mozart's mother.

Thus, when we glimpse life's darker side in Mozart's music, or sense loneliness or insecurity – as in the desperately sad middle (slow) movement of his twenty-third piano concerto of 1786 – it is as if a veil has momentarily slipped. Other composers, especially Beethoven and Berlioz who followed in Mozart's wake, do little else than expose their internal turmoil all over the music, as though they are in a modern-day self-help group of composers with personality disorders. Mozart's emotional subtext, on the other hand, is disguised beneath the sheen of decorum and poise required of an eighteenth-century artisan. His dignified compassion in the face of life's challenges makes his music irresistible, even when it is tranquil. We have responded to this distant Austrian's voice across the years and the continents so spontaneously because his music seems simply to flow out of him, intuitively, without cynicism or intellectual pretension. Like the Gainsborough and Reynolds portraits painted during his lifetime, Mozart's music says, 'I will do my best to make this beautiful because that's what life, at its best, can be.' The 1770s and '80s may have been dirty, unhealthy and dangerous for anyone but the most privileged, and life was grim and unfair, but it wouldn't have occurred to Mozart, nor Gainsborough or Reynolds for that matter, to reproduce that misery. They wanted to ennoble humanity. They succeeded.

Much myth now surrounds Mozart, who was venerated in the nineteenth century as a kind of St John the Baptist to Beethoven's Christ, and in the later twentieth century as an innocent vessel transmitting God's message through music, sacrificing his health and ultimately his life in order to complete his final, incomprehensibly beautiful masterworks. Even in death he holds a quasi-religious significance for his devotees. If you visit Vienna's Saint Marx cemetery, on the city's outskirts in an undistinguished part of town, you can – if you have nothing better to do in that culturally plentiful capital – wander solemnly up its leaf-strewn gravel paths until you find the non-grave of Amadeus Mozart. I say non-grave, because his remains are not under the headstone that marks the spot. Indeed, the memorial plinth itself was constructed in more recent times to satisfy Mozart's Grave tourists and is placed in what amounts to a random spot in the garden. Not only are the whereabouts of his bones not known but, along with many others, his remains were dug up after his death, possibly crushed to reduce their bulk, and reinterred somewhere else, location also unknown. There is a theory that his skull was implausibly identified by a local gravedigger in 1801, ten years after Mozart's death, and that it eventually found its way to the vaults of the Mozart Foundation in Salzburg, but DNA tests have produced more or less the same divided outcome as with carbon-dating of the Turin Shroud: science says it's impossible, 'believers' continue to hope.

But worrying about this great composer's remains is surely missing the point, as is the now two-hundred-year-old 'mystery' concerning Haydn's skull, long since separated from his body and the object of scrutiny and ghoulish bounty-hunting worthy of Indiana Jones. Mozart left us far more poignant and permanent keepsakes of his existence than his bones: he left us his extraordinary music. What's more, unlike the paintings bequeathed to posterity by Constable or Rembrandt, his music has not ossified, frozen for ever in time. Every time his music is performed it lives again, fresh, newly awoken, sometimes interpreted surprisingly or unexpectedly but always experienced in the here and now. This is music's most spectacular conjuring trick. Far from dying, it is in a perpetual state of rebirth.

What mattered to Mozart was that his music should be enjoyed, not that he should be worshipped or revered, and it is this quality of treasured delight that captures his age. His music, whether in the unutterably lovely slow movement of his clarinet concerto, or the majestic optimism of his *Jupiter* symphony, or the coming to life of a dead man's statue in the concluding moments of *Don Giovanni*, or the heart-stopping delicacy of his later piano concertos, wants you – whoever and wherever you are – to feel good. That Beethoven changed the way society viewed composers should not cloud our judgement of his brilliant predecessor who sought and gave one thing: pleasure.

It is not known definitively whether Mozart and Beethoven ever met, despite their lives overlapping by twenty-one years, but two more different artists, creatively or temperamentally, it is hard to imagine. While Mozart's aim was to charm, seduce and occasionally tease his audiences, Beethoven's mission was to confront them. With him, the composer as agent provocateur had arrived.

Traditional histories like to equate Beethoven, the colossus of music in the early 1800s, with his contemporary Napoleon Bonaparte, revolutionary-turned-Emperor and serial military adventurer. This convenient comparison is given extra poignancy by Beethoven's reference to the French despot in his momentous third symphony, these days known as the *Eroica* but originally dubbed the *Bonaparte*. In fact, neither the well-worn anecdote about a disenchanted Beethoven 'scratching out' the title page of his symphony bearing a dedication to Napoleon, nor the composer's musical radicalism are quite what they seem.

Beethoven wasn't one composer but three. He started off as a

Mozart clone with a flair for playing the piano, became a tormented version of Haydn, and ended up isolated from the world by deafness, composing music that was to baffle, bewitch and amaze every European musician of the next hundred years. Whatever you think of him, you cannot escape the fact that virtually everything that happened in nineteenth-century music in some way began with Beethoven. All roads lead from him.

He comes to us saddled with a fair amount of baggage. He was a moody, complicated man, possibly suffering from some degree of clinical depression, who found himself in possession of musical talents even he couldn't quite come to terms with. But 'revolutionary', the adjective often used of him, feels like the wrong word for a man who was fundamentally conservative, who rubbed shoulders with the political and aristocratic elite of his day and whose music, until quite near the end of his life, was well within the cultural mainstream of the early nineteenth century. As we see time and again, cutting-edge innovators like those of Beethoven's youth were composers whose names are now mostly forgotten: Johann Dussek, Louis Spohr, Muzio Clementi, Étienne Méhul, François-Joseph Gossec . . . Beethoven's genius was to convert their modernity into something that would, in due course, become the mainstream.

Beethoven's eighth piano sonata, known as the *Pathétique*, was written when he was twenty-eight and making a name for himself in Vienna. Compared to the music of his teacher Haydn or to Mozart, it seems much more dramatic and pianistic, almost to the point of theatricality, than anything they had written for the same instrument. In the context of 1790s Vienna, it sounds daring, emotionally charged and original. Beethoven, though, knew his contemporary music, and particularly the groundbreaking piano music of two London-based composers, Italian Muzio Clementi and Bohemian Johann Dussek. This pair were boldly pushing the virtuoso and expressive boundaries of the instrument, in consultation with the leading piano builder of the time: John Broadwood, another Londoner. Clementi's and Dussek's music was virtually unknown outside Britain, though, but

Beethoven had found out about it and learnt from their innovations in style and playing technique.

Seven years after composing his *Pathétique* sonata, Beethoven stopped sounding like Mozart or Dussek or Haydn and started creating music *beyond* what they had imagined. The first major sign that he was breaking away from established formulas was his *Eroica* symphony of 1804, which was a considerable challenge for audiences of the time, exciting and alarming his fellow Viennese in more or less equal measure. The *Eroica* deliberately sought to disrupt what an audience expected to hear in a symphony. Its first movement alone was roughly the length of a whole early Haydn symphony. For audiences reared on the regular, predictable patterns of Haydn and Mozart, the *Eroica*'s many noisy surprises would have been both titillating and bewildering. Even its opening two chords seem to be bellowing, 'WAKE UP!'

The story goes that Beethoven first composed the *Eroica* in honour of Napoleon, hero of the French revolutionary struggle, but that he scrubbed out Bonaparte's name in a rage and replaced it with the inscription 'Heroic Symphony . . . composed to celebrate the memory of a great man', on hearing that Napoleon had contradicted his earlier appeals to liberty, equality and fraternity by proclaiming himself Emperor. His student and later biographer Ferdinand Ries claims to have heard Beethoven fume when hearing the news: 'Is he too, then, nothing more than an ordinary human being? Now he, too, will trample on the rights of man, and indulge only his ambition!' It may be that this oft-told anecdote underwent some layers of exaggeration as Beethoven's fame spread – not least because Beethoven dedicated a mass to Napoleon six years later, even after the Emperor's troops had besieged and bombarded Vienna, with Beethoven (and a dying Haydn) in it.

Musicologists love to wax on about the ambitious first movement of the *Eroica* symphony, mainly because it is unusually long and complex, and provides fuel for seemingly endless analysis and scholarly scrutiny. Beethoven takes a relatively simple tune and builds from it a giant tapestry of ideas and musical meanderings.

For me, though, it is not the clever-clogs first movement that carries the killer punch but the funeral march that follows it.

What is different, and new, about this movement is not its structure, orchestration or technical bravado, but its attitude. Whereas both Haydn and Mozart aimed to reveal human emotions through the filter of a gentlemanly, well-bred composure, the funeral march in *Eroica* is remarkable for the unflinching grip of its mood. It is not at all fanciful to link the mournful quality of the 'Marcia funebre' – Beethoven had borrowed the idea of a funeral march from French revolutionary music, the first of its kind in a symphony – with Beethoven's discovery during the months of composition that his deafness was becoming worse and would not be curable. There are many aspects of the movement that must have seemed strange to contemporary audiences. It seems to be restless, for one thing, as if looking for a resolution it never finds, moving briefly into a sunnier major key, then returning to its darker starting point, only to be churned around, experimented with and fragmented. It plunges into a period of Bachian counterpoint (fashionable, by that time, only in sacred choral settings, where its old-fashioned earnestness seemed appropriate), followed by an impassioned, busy episode, with flurrying strings and slower-moving woodwind. Finally, the processional march is recalled, this time disjointed, exhausted and spent: the tune announced so confidently at the beginning now unexpectedly disintegrates. So for the perplexed audiences who first heard it in 1804 and 1805, even the funeral march is denied its thundering climax, collapsing rather than concluding. Grief is grief, pain is pain, and music, Beethoven seems to be proclaiming, is the art best placed to confront such darkness. Within the next two decades or so, most of his educated contemporaries gradually came to the same conclusion. For the first time since the death of Bach, the music of the moment seemed to be attempting to portray more accurately the sadness and anxiety that people were actually experiencing.

From the *Eroica* symphony onwards, Beethoven self-consciously became a composer with a mission: he would change the world through his art. His music became serious-minded and earnest, but it is debatable whether he changed the world. Not at any rate in the way his contemporaries William Wilberforce fought to end slavery, or Mary Wollstonecraft articulated the rights of women, or Edward Jenner developed the smallpox vaccine – but Beethoven certainly changed his art.

This was Beethoven's great significance, not through form or musical language, but in recalibrating what music was *for*. Single-handedly he turned it from genteel, ignorable after-dinner entertainment into an all-encompassing emotional experience, a way of perceiving life as a mighty struggle, the cry of the soul, the voice of conscience. He did not curry favour; rather, he was seeking a relationship with destiny: his music yearned to be the expression of humanity's deepest desires and anxieties. Bach, Handel, Haydn and Mozart made music in the moment, for the moment. Beethoven challenged his listeners to return time and again to the unresolved conflicts that characterised his art. There would be no instant gratification, no easy triumph. Instead there would be ambiguity, dynamic conflict and doubt. All the composers of the next hundred years were affected by this profound change of purpose. It is no exaggeration to say that after and because of Beethoven music approached the status of a religion, complete with gods and goddesses for worshipping, a state of affairs that persists to this day.

Had he been a level-headed craftsman, like his friend Johann Hummel, composer and pianist, this transformation would not plausibly have caught the imagination of onlookers, but Beethoven's own personality oscillated between poignant vulnerability and raging anger. He gradually subsumed his own personality – his frustrations, burdens and (mostly unfulfilled) desires – into his music and the result was highly combustible. Beethoven could not hide his unstable emotions from the music, nor did he use the job of music-making as a distraction from the difficulties of life. Whatever else Beethoven's music may have been, it was certainly not intended to be escapist.

★

The cult of the isolated, divine or demonic genius, of which Beethoven was the first outstanding musical example, did not happen in a vacuum but rather as part of a general literary and artistic movement in the first three decades of the nineteenth century. It is a movement often labelled Romanticism, although, like the terms 'Renaissance', 'Baroque' and 'Classical', it presents considerable difficulties when applied to music.

In a nutshell, the problem with labelling anything 'Romantic' is that it has subsequently come to mean virtually anything, from the poetry of Lord Byron to the songs of Taylor Swift. Don't get me wrong, Swift's contemporary High School take on Romeo and Juliet, 'Love Story', is a crackingly well-crafted pop song that I wish I'd written, but it has little in common with Pushkin's poem 'The Captain of the Caucasus' or Schumann's piano concerto, both of which also carry the descriptor 'Romantic'. If 'Romantic' still means anything specific in the history of music, it best refers to a period when the composer's or performer's personal emotions, or sentiment, became paramount in the dialogue between music and audience. And Beethoven was the composer who began this transformation. Feeling is everything to Beethoven, as is the importance of his individual, original voice, and a generation of composers reverentially followed in his wake, equally obsessed with the passionate confession, through music, of tender feelings – or, as Jane Austen reminds us, 'Sense and Sensibility'.

Beethoven and his contemporaries even made the natural world an extension of their feelings. A century earlier, God was the king of Creation and all nature reflected his power. Now, with the Romantic attitude, nature was all about humankind. Musicians and poets saw the countryside as a roughly hewn wilderness, supplying countless images to convey the swirling emotional torrents of the yearning lover. Of course, none of them actually had to *work* the land. You observed peasants from the comfortable distance of your artistic nook but you wouldn't want to be one. They were more like present-day privileged Western students trawling the developing world and writing blogs about how the world's poorest people enabled them to broaden their horizons.

When Beethoven wrote his sixth, or *Pastoral*, symphony, in 1808, celebrating the delights of rural nature, his home town of Vienna would still have been virtually unscathed by the industrial boom that was scarring the landscape and rupturing the communities of northern England. This was the same year in which William Blake evoked England's 'dark, Satanic mills' in his poem 'Jerusalem', but Beethoven's easy-listening *Pastoral* is not about the industrial rape of the countryside. It is not really about the countryside at all; nature is there purely as a metaphor for feelings, as it was for Wordsworth and his daffodils, Shelley with his skylark and Keats with his nightingale. As Beethoven's contemporary Wordsworth put it, 'And led by nature into a wild scene / Of lofty hopes'.

No one followed Beethoven's lead in reflecting emotion through nature more passionately than his near contemporary Franz Schubert, also based in Vienna. For Schubert, the birds, the bees, the woods and the trees came into their own above all in song-writing, at which he was simply unmatched before the twentieth century. As well as nine symphonies and much chamber music, he wrote over six hundred songs before his death in 1828. Among them are three outstanding song cycles, *Die schöne Müllerin* (The Pretty Mill Girl) of 1824, *Winterreise* (Winter Journey) of 1827 and *Schwanengesang* (Swan Song), collated and published posthumously. All three dwell on the pain of love, embodied poetically in the natural world. In 'Auf dem Flusse' (On the stream), from *Winterreise*, for example, a frozen brook represents the state of the distraught wanderer's heart, beating powerlessly beneath a hard, icy surface. He will carve the name of his now hopelessly lost beloved into the ice with a stone.

It is hardly surprising that a composer like Schubert should be attracted to poetic texts that placed emotions in the relative safety of natural metaphor. Relationships between young men and women of his unpropertied class were fraught with restriction and inhibition. The tragedy is we have no way of judging a mature

Schubert's thoughts on love because he didn't live long enough
to have them: he died aged thirty-one. Wilhelm Müller, the writer
of many of his song lyrics, died aged thirty-three. The study of
the first half of the nineteenth century in art song is the study of
young men with very little true understanding of women – who
are typically portrayed as unattainable, goddess-like, simple, uneducated creatures or just plain 'cruel' (that is, not interested in the
men). Indeed, it is hard to find a composer of the nineteenth
century who didn't develop an infatuation or series of infatuations
with his piano pupils, mostly single young women whose higher
social status placed them – officially – out of bounds. A song like
'Abendstern', (Evening Star), composed at the time Schubert was
enduring a burning but impossible love for his eighteen-year-old
piano pupil Countess Karoline Esterházy, whom he called 'a certain
magnetic star', treats with great sensitivity the pain and loneliness
of unfulfilled love. Not many songwriters in history can match
the touching pathos of the song's plaint – 'I am the faithful star
of love . . . I sow no seed, I see no shoot, And remain here, silent
and mournful' – with such simple resources.

In a sense, Schubert is the inventor of the three-minute song
with universal appeal, a form that is still thoroughly alive today,
and one reason for this is his deliberate avoidance of the complex
musical language he might have used in a symphony or string
quartet. His songs were meant to sound like up-market folk songs:
immediately memorable, lyrically easily understandable and relatively predictable in shape. The distance in form, intention, mood
and expression between Schubert's songs for voice and piano and
those of, say, Adele is remarkably short, considering they are
separated by two hundred years. The only thing that would shock
Schubert about 'Someone like you' is the fact that a young woman
is the song's creator, not its object.

The Romantic spirit's darker manifestation, much in evidence in
Beethoven's personality and creative output, was the idea that
artists were in some way possessed of unnatural powers that it

was their duty to give to the world, whatever the cost to their soul. For this aspect of their troubled genius Beethoven and his contemporaries had two irresistible fictional role models: Faust and Prometheus. Though myths centred on both characters had existed for centuries, they were revived with enormous impact in two epic works by a writer whose imagination gripped composers for the whole of the nineteenth century: Johann Wolfgang von Goethe. His *Prometheus* was published in 1789 and *The Tragedy of Faust: Part One* in 1808, the year of Beethoven's *Pastoral* symphony.

Faust, as portrayed by Goethe, was an intellectual who sold his soul to the devil for worldly knowledge, power and pleasure. Both Goethe's play and Christopher Marlowe's *Doctor Faustus* of 1604 seem to have drawn inspiration from an actual alchemist, Johann Georg Faust, who lived in early-sixteenth-century Germany. Prometheus was a Greek god who championed mankind, stealing fire for them from Zeus, being tortured for eternity as his punishment. Romantic-era poets, painters and novelists were haunted by but irresistibly drawn to Prometheus, who was sometimes compared with Napoleon in poems and cartoons of the day, with spin-offs ranging from Blake's 'Prometheus Bound' and Jean-Louis-César Lair's 'The Torture of Prometheus', to Percy Shelley's play *Prometheus Unbound* and Mary Shelley's hugely influential novel, *Frankenstein, or the Modern Prometheus*. Beethoven tackled both figures, composing 'Mephisto's Flea-song' in tribute to Goethe's *Faust*, and a ballet score, *The Creatures of Prometheus*, in 1801. His was the first of a flood of musical responses to the two legends in ensuing decades.

Why were the figures of Faust and Prometheus so important to artists of the nineteenth century? Because they were both handy metaphors for the idea of the troubled, isolated genius whose gifts separated him from ordinary mortals, who represented the power that could be granted by divine (or Satanic) intervention. Beethoven was music's first Faustian figure: a difficult, edgy, unpredictable maestro, a musical version of Lord Byron – mad, bad and dangerous to know (or so his mesmerised audiences doubtless

imagined) – but many others were to follow. These included Hector
Berlioz (*Symphonie fantastique*, 1829 and *The Damnation of Faust*,
1846), Felix Mendelssohn (*Die erste Walpurgisnacht*, 1832), Clara
Wieck Schumann ('Le Sabbat' from *Quatre pieces caractéristiques*,
1835), Fanny Mendelssohn (*Szene aus Faust, der Tragödie*, 1843),
Robert Schumann (*Scenes from Goethe's Faust*, 1853), Franz Liszt
(*Faust* symphony, 1857), Charles Gounod (*Faust*, 1859) and Gustav
Mahler (eighth symphony, 1906).

Perhaps the most extreme example of the new wave of star
performers who followed in Beethoven's wake was Italian violin
virtuoso Niccolò Paganini. Paganini was rumoured to have struck
a deal with the devil himself, Faust-style, in order to acquire super-
human powers on his instrument and to put off the inevitability
of death – a piece of fantastic spin fuelled by the fact that he
refused the Last Rites on his deathbed and that his body was
consequently not buried for another thirty-six years.

In Aeschylus's fifth century BC telling of the Prometheus legend,
Prometheus Bound, the rebellious Titan's gifts to man, as well as
fire, include the tools for civilisation: writing, mathematics, agri-
culture, medicine and science. In the first decades of the nineteenth
century, surrounded by the march of the Industrial Revolution,
writers and artists grappled with a new scale of civilisation: bigger
cities, methods of communication and, inevitably, more powerful
armies and weapons. Beethoven clearly found the warlike times
in which he lived strangely inspiring, given the number of his
pieces that refer to victorious struggles of one kind or another
(*Coriolan*, 1807; *Egmont*, 1810; *King Stephen*, 1811; *Wellington's Victory*,
1813) or whose music has a martial theme, such as extended
passages of several of his symphonies (especially the *Eroica* and
the fifth).

As with industrial and scientific progress, so the symphony
orchestra, which in the hands of Beethoven and Schubert increased
in size and volume with every première. By the time he was
halfway through his nine symphonies, Beethoven had at his
disposal double-basses, which had supplanted the gentler bass

violones, to fortify the bottom end of his sound. And as well as a full complement of strings – anything from twelve to thirty violins, four to twelve violas and the same number of cellos – his fifth symphony of 1808 added a very high-pitched piccolo, very low-pitched contra-bassoon and three trombones to the line-up for its noisy final movement. He surpassed himself at the première of his stirring seventh symphony in December 1813, with a violin section featuring four other distinguished Vienna-based composers of the time: Louis Spohr, Johann Hummel, Giacomo Meyerbeer and Antonio Salieri (the man quite wrongly accused in popular fiction of having conspired to murder, or at least silence, his 'rival', Mozart). The big hit of the evening was the second movement, the *Allegretto*, which has remained a public favourite ever since, notably providing the moving musical climax of the 2010 film *The King's Speech*. The symphony was being composed as Napoleon's Grande Armée was retreating from Moscow and though Beethoven did not mean it as such, the *Allegretto*'s steady, funereal character has been associated ever since with that chilling cortège of half a million doomed Frenchmen.

The scale of Beethoven's seventh symphony was to be overtaken in a dramatic way, however, by the ambition of his ninth and final symphony. Indeed, the shadow of this mighty *Choral* symphony was to loom majestically over the entire nineteenth century.

Much has been made of the fact that the fourth and final movement adds a large chorus and four solo singers to the already sizeable orchestral forces, the first time such a multitude had been glued on to the symphony. But large choruses, soloists and orchestra were bread and butter to Bach in his Passions, Handel in his oratorios, Mozart in his *Requiem* and Haydn in his grand choral works. Beethoven, inspired by study of and admiration for Handel and Bach, merely had the idea of appending to a symphony something you might expect in an oratorio. The reason for the additional singers was not just to fill the hall with a magnificent noise but to proclaim Beethoven's hopes for the future.

In the face of political and social uncertainty, his answer to the anxieties of the hour was an appeal, originally written by German Enlightenment poet Friedrich Schiller in 1785, that all people should unite in brotherly joy and revere the Creator – a brotherhood, incidentally, in which beggars and princes would be equals. He had first expressed an interest in setting the poem to music when he was in his early twenties, before the full weight of the Napoleonic Wars began to envelop Europe. It may therefore be an unusual mixture of youthful dreams and mature exhortation, yet the 'Ode to Joy's' arrival in the final movement of the *Choral* symphony, revealed to the world in two subscription concerts in May 1824 – one packed with friends and admirers, the other virtually empty as the public struggled with Beethoven's modernity – is surely one of the most riveting and uplifting eighteen minutes in all nineteenth-century music.

The most significant thing about Beethoven's ninth, though, is not his introduction of a choral element into the symphony per se; it was his demonstration that the symphony as a form could and would thereafter mean anything it wanted, the bigger the better. This monumental new piece announced to the next generation of composers that the symphony was now to have an epic dimension. Never has an invitation to young composers been more enthusiastically embraced. For better or worse, the coming decades were to be about music taking on the task of reforming humanity, dreaming up a new Utopia and leading the arts to unite mankind. I am not exaggerating: composers of the second half of the nineteenth century really did believe that this was their role. And the Messiah who had rallied them to the cause was Beethoven.

Even the modern world has found it hard to shake off this legacy. When the Berlin Wall was breached in 1989, a special performance there of the ninth symphony was broadcast around the world, with the word 'joy', (*Freude!*) replaced with the word 'freedom', (*Freiheit!*), lending those extraordinary events (its organisers doubtless believed) profundity, universality, meaning.

The irony of what happened after Beethoven's ninth, with composers from Berlioz to Wagner indulging in preposterously overblown claims for the importance of their work for the future of humankind, is that what Beethoven himself did next was the exact opposite.

In the last two years of his life, now profoundly deaf and mostly bedridden by severe illness, Beethoven withdrew into a private sound world, composing six string quartets of astonishing, unapproachable intensity. They were modern not by the standards of 1826 but by the standards of a century later. These late quartets are almost embarrassingly private. It is as if he was working out some tortured mind game on the page, or distracting himself from an unbearable sadness. Most of his contemporaries didn't know what to make of these late quartets. It was as if someone had time-travelled from 1930 and played twentieth-century music to the mystified people of 1826. Could Beethoven hear the music of the distant future? If this was it, his vision was a bleak, uneasy one. The late quartets have a musical detachment about them, an intensity without warmth, and it seems as if the Pleasure Principle of the previous decades has been replaced with an urge to experiment with harmony at all costs: they are beautiful in an unsettling way.

After Beethoven's death in 1827, a kind of parting of the waves took place between two versions of what a composer might do: whether to seek popularity with an audience or to become a martyr to your cause, suffering for your terribly important art. It is a tussle that continues to smoulder.

The most popular composer in Beethoven's final years, even in Vienna where he lived, was not Beethoven himself but the Italian Gioachino Rossini, whose light-as-a-feather smash-hit comic operas, such as *The Barber of Seville* (1816) – all laughs, saucy farce and hummable tunes – were arguably closer to the general public's idea of an 'Ode to Joy'. The two composers did meet once, an encounter brokered by the kindly Antonio Salieri, and we have it word for word since Beethoven, being deaf, had to have the conversation written down. The rules of engagement between the two

types of composer were even evident in their short back-and-forth
in 1822, with Beethoven congratulating Rossini on his success but
warning him not to write anything other than comic opera as 'his
character wouldn't suit it'. It is a conversation that continues to
be played out between self-styled 'serious' composers and 'crossover' composers to this day.

Robert Schumann and his friend Felix Mendelssohn were
German successors to Beethoven of a gentler mould. Like
Schubert, they appealed to their audience not through comic
opera, Rossini-style, but by providing bitter-sweet, mostly tender
reflections on love, art and life that were instantly enjoyable.
Neither Mendelssohn nor Schumann planned to take over the
world with his art, though both suffered for it nonetheless.

Mendelssohn was the most conspicuously gifted young musician
of the nineteenth century, producing a fabulous octet for strings
aged sixteen and an orchestral tribute to Shakespeare's *A Midsummer
Night's Dream* aged seventeen that dazzled all who heard it at the
time. In fact, both pieces are still among the most performed of
all nineteenth-century favourites, in a dauntingly strong field. In
later years Mendelssohn composed incidental music for a production of the play itself, with additional scenes and characters,
including a wedding march – *the* wedding march – that has since
been used at what must now be millions of weddings.

But Mendelssohn had to struggle against both snobbery and
bigotry. The very fact that his music was so instantly popular with
audiences – particularly among prosperous middle-class Britons
and indeed Queen Victoria, with whom he became friends – was
enough for there to be a backlash against him. His critics, often
motivated by anti-Semitism, branded him old-fashioned or lacking
in originality – originality being the most overhyped quality in the
history of music. Wagner's comments in his toxic *The Jews in Music*
(1850) were fairly typical, if more long-winded than most:

Whereas Beethoven, the last in the chain of our true music-heroes,
strove with highest longing, and wonder-working faculty, for the

clearest, certainest Expression of an unsayable Content through a
sharp-cut, plastic shaping of his tone-pictures: Mendelssohn, on the
contrary, reduces these achievements to vague, fantastic shadow-
forms, midst whose indefinite shimmer our freakish fancy is indeed
aroused, but our inner, purely-human yearning for distinct artistic
sight is hardly touched with even the merest hope of a fulfilment
. . . . The washiness and whimsicality of our present musical style
has been, if not exactly brought about, yet pushed to its utmost
pitch by Mendelssohn's endeavour to speak out a vague, an almost
nugatory Content as interestingly and spiritedly as possible.

In 1889, the enormous popularity in Britain of Mendelssohn's
oratorio *Elijah* caused George Bernard Shaw to lampoon its
'Sunday-school sentimentalities and its Music-school ornamen-
talities'.

The composer who stands at the antithesis of Mendelssohn,
who took Beethoven's call to arms most to heart, adopting early
on the 'possessed maestro' option, all cutting edge and misunder-
stood angst, was the French firebrand Hector Berlioz.

Despite being French, Berlioz may as well have been German,
so keen was he to assume the Beethovean throne. He too was
drawn to the same literary icons like a moth to a flame: Sir Walter
Scott, Lord Byron, Goethe and Shakespeare. His personal identi-
fication with romantic heroes such as Romeo in *Romeo and Juliet*
seemed to have fuelled not just musical inspiration but his crazed,
desperate infatuation with a Shakespearean actress, Harriet
Smithson. Mind you, without his twelve-year obsession with her,
the world wouldn't have had Berlioz's hugely influential *Symphonie
fantastique: Épisode de la vie d'un Artiste* in 1830, the oratorio *Roméo
et Juliette*, the operas *Les Troyens* and *Béatrice et Bénédict* and his
musical treatments of *King Lear* and *Hamlet*. In December 1832, he
premièred in Paris a sequel to the *Symphonie fantastique* called *Lélio,
Le retour à la vie* (Return to Life), part of which was a fantasia on
The Tempest. At this performance he finally met Harriet, who was
somewhat taken aback at how much she seemed to feature in

Berlioz's works, and their tempestuous, unrealistic and ultimately destructive relationship erupted into life, despite the fact that neither spoke the other's language.

A comparison of Berlioz's *Grande Messe des morts* (Requiem) of 1837 with Beethoven's *Choral* symphony of just thirteen years earlier provides a stark illustration of how far the ambition of large-scale music had already ballooned. It calls for a minimum of two hundred singers, a string section alone of one hundred and eight players, twenty woodwind players (including two cors anglais and eight bassoons), twelve French horns, eight cornets, twelve trumpets, sixteen trombones, six tubas, four ophicleides (a cross between a bass tuba and a prototype saxophone that had only been patented sixteen years earlier), ten timpani players (on sixteen drums), four gongs, two bass drums and ten pairs of cymbals. Even the most generously funded rendition of Beethoven's ninth would require a meagre third of those forces. While at the heart of Beethoven's symphony lies a vision of a better civilisation led by a benign deity, Berlioz, a life-long atheist, attempts to evoke the Apocalypse and Final Judgement in sound. In the intervening years, music has grown from joyful servant of humankind and the Almighty to a bigger experience than both of them. Liszt and Wagner idolised Berlioz, which would explain much that happened in the second half of the nineteenth century, a torrid drama that will unfold in the next chapter.

Berlioz never flinched from reminding whoever would listen of his great troubles and adversities, nor from absorbing those torments in his music, much of which is richly rewarding to listen to. His relationships were stormy and plagued with bad luck. The death of his son in 1867 more or less killed him. Yet he survived to the relatively impressive age (for the time) of sixty-six and made a good living as a conductor, music critic and chief librarian of the Paris Conservatoire. Compared to the nightmare existence that Robert Schumann endured, it was a walk in the park, though surprisingly Schumann's is the music of greater tranquillity and warmth.

Schumann was, however, one of a group of composers who between them made the piano the essential nineteenth-century instrument. The tender serenity found in much of his piano music he and his clique had learnt not so much from Beethoven and his theatricality but from the example of a lesser-known Irish composer, John Field, who made his name first in London, then in Catherine the Great's Imperial capital of St Petersburg. Field is one of those composers who has been dealt an inexplicably poor hand by posterity but who had a huge influence on other composers in their own time. It is to Field we owe the piano nocturne, a form taken up enthusiastically by Chopin and later many others, and his flowing, rapturous piano style became a rough template for what a composer in the nineteenth century was expected to do at the instrument. Describing Field's piano music fifty years later, the Hungarian composer-virtuoso Franz Liszt poetically summed up how the Irishman captured the spirit of the early-century Romantic movement in music: 'these half-formed sighs floating through the air, softly lamenting and dissolved in delicious melancholy'. Quite apart from all that delicious melancholy, there was something else going on, or not going on, in Field's nocturnes that was to reverberate through the coming century and that was a major break with the Haydn-Mozart era.

Field's nocturnes are not journeys, they're mood pictures. He abandoned the structural architecture of the previous half-century, Sonata Form, and let his passion at the keyboard have a rhapsodic, free rein. This possibility – simply evoking an unidentified atmosphere in sound – was to lodge in the minds of many composers in the coming decades and bear rich fruit.

Field's first set of nocturnes were published in his adopted home of Russia in 1812, while Napoleon's colonial ambitions there were being buried under a mountain of snow, fire, starvation and disease. Two years earlier, he had married his former piano pupil Adelaide Percheron and together they shared the stage as touring pianists. While it may sound a vaguely familiar story – one we will encounter shortly with the similarly passionate and professional partnership of pianist-composers Robert and Clara Wieck Schumann – it is important to note how exceptional the concept was, before the twentieth century, of a woman being able to pursue any professional career in music. These significant exceptions were possible thanks to the piano.

The early nineteenth century was the beginning of a new era of amateur musicianship, a mass movement of skilled and semi-skilled musical participation that was unprecedented in history and which centred on the piano. Before gramophones and radios, the piano was the only source of music in many a middle-class home and the sharing of home-made music was a habit that lasted for many families until the Second World War. The middle classes proudly installed factory-made pianos in their drawing rooms and needed music to play on them. Composers from Field and Beethoven onwards were happy to oblige, in vast quantities; what's more, here was a chance for women to become involved in composing and performing – pursuits from which they had largely been excluded up until now. The fact that piano music could be written in the privacy of the home and sent off to a sheet music publisher allowed women, who were routinely taught piano skills from an early age, to compose and – in due course – to perform in public, despite virulent parental disapproval in all but a handful of cases.

Felix Mendelssohn's older sister Fanny grew up as musical as her brother, their music tutor Carl Zeller writing to Goethe in 1816 about their father Abraham Mendelssohn, 'He has adorable children and his oldest daughter could give you something of Sebastian Bach. This child is really something special.' As her talents developed, so did family resistance to her taking up music as a career. Felix published some of her songs under his name and her husband, artist Wilhelm Hensel, was broadly supportive of her composing and of her occasional performances at the piano. Her compositions are delightful – they include exquisite songs in the Schubert tradition, like 'Die Ersehnte' (The Yearned-for One), and a characterful portrait of the months of the year for solo piano, *Das Jahr*, which compares well with her brother's enormously popular collection of *Songs Without Words* – and her death aged just forty-two deprived music of a talent formidable enough to have challenged many myths surrounding musical women in the Victorian era.

The reality was, though, that while it might be possible, with good reading and writing, to become the author of a novel, as Jane Austen, the Brönte Sisters or George Eliot proved, it was practically impossible to write large-scale forms such as a symphony or an opera without years of instruction and specialist knowledge. This was the barrier – training – that most prevented women composers coming to the fore in the nineteenth century.

In 1838, twenty-eight-year-old Robert Schumann composed an eight-part homage to Johannes Kreisler, the fictional musician who featured in the comic novels of E. T. A. Hoffmann, Beethoven enthusiast and author of *The Nutcracker*, *Coppelia* and *The Tales of Hoffmann*. Although Schumann dedicated the *Kreisleriana* to his friend Frédéric Chopin, what it was really was a musical love letter to Clara Wieck, the young woman Schumann would soon marry despite legal proceedings instigated by her father. As well as nurturing and inspiring her husband, even as mental illness drove him to attempted suicide and an early death, Clara Wieck was a composer of distinction, from her astonishingly adept and undeservedly neglected piano concerto, written when she was just seventeen, to her passionate set of six songs for Denmark's Queen Caroline Amalie, culminating in the enchanting 'Die stille Lotusblume', with its unexpectedly bluesy opening chords. She became one of the most famous concert pianists of the century. In a sixty-year career on the concert stage she tirelessly championed the music of her husband, of Brahms and of Chopin. One day, I hope, her immense contribution to Western music and the courage of her determination to pursue music at the highest level against all odds will be properly recognised. The composer who probably owes her the greatest debt of gratitude, Frédéric Chopin, she first met in Paris, when, aged twelve, she played to him one of his own exquisite nocturnes (opus 9, no. 2).

Of the generation that followed Beethoven, Chopin was the composer whose influence was slowest to make its impact. The reason for this is that, like Beethoven's late quartets, Chopin's music is unusually intimate. He preferred not to perform in large concert halls, as was increasingly the vogue, but rather in small salons and private homes. Consequently his fame spread person by person, fan by fan. He was arguably more like a novelist than a composer in this respect, people falling for his music as they would a newly discovered secret passion.

Listening to Chopin after the helter-skelter psychological drama of Beethoven or the theatrical bravado of Berlioz, it is as if someone has opened a window and let in some fresh, balmy evening air. Though he settled in France, the quality that most pervades Chopin's style is homesickness for his native Poland. Unlike expat composers Rossini, Cherubini, Meyerbeer and others drawn to Paris in the nineteenth century, seeking career upgrades and access to a lucrative Parisian penchant for opera, Chopin arrived there as a refugee from political repression at home. Sometimes he expressed his longing for Poland, at that time swallowed up in the Russian Empire, through his highly stylised adaptation of Polish folk dances – mazurkas and polonaises. Though they were intended to evoke such rustic dances, they were meant to be played and listened to, not as accompaniment for actual dancing.

Chopin stands at the critical pivot in nineteenth-century music. In his over sixty heartfelt mazurkas, love letters to a homeland he would never see again, he anticipated composers in every European country in the second half of the century, especially those in nations struggling to shrug off an imperial yoke, finding inspiration in the folk music of their own communities.

In his twenty-one nocturnes and twenty-seven études Chopin managed to set a staggering standard of technical virtuosity for players at the same time as creating something beautiful for listeners to enjoy, and he initiated a golden age of the piano; his example was still proving influential for the likes of Debussy, Ravel and the jazz legend Bill Evans in the twentieth century. Chopin's rich and ambiguous harmonies, interwoven intricately between the hands, looked to the future, leaving behind the primary-colour certainties of Gluck, Mozart, Haydn and early Beethoven once and for all. After a period of simplicity, Chopin was nudging music's pendulum back towards complexity once more.

There is a delicacy and gentleness to Chopin's music, though, that represents the final curtain call of the age of elegance and gracefulness, of sense and sensibility. His heroes, notwithstanding the underrated John Field, were Mozart and Bach, composers in whose music dignity was everything. Ill health plagued Chopin throughout his life, and in his final three years he became so weak he needed round-the-clock care; TB finally killed him in 1849. His last public concert was given at London's Guildhall in November 1848, a fund-raising event for Polish refugees. He may have been unable to return home to Poland to die, but his heart had never left it.

The year of Chopin's final concert, 1848, was one of huge political upheaval across Europe; it was a year of revolutions. One of the rebels clamouring for social change in an uprising in Dresden was a young Richard Wagner. Trouble was brewing, and a period that began with fear of Apocalypse was replaced with one in which the Apocalypse might be played out within music itself – by that same firebrand on a Dresden street.

5

The Age of Tragedy
1850–1890

'Whether I shall turn out to be the hero of my own life, or whether that station will be held by anybody else, these pages must show,' says David Copperfield in the opening line of the eponymous novel by Charles Dickens, published in 1850. It is a book about the twists and turns of destiny and, it being an English novel rather than a German, Italian, French or Russian one, despite tragedy along the way, all ends satisfactorily, with a fresh start in the New World the reward for stalwart and honest perseverance.

The second half of the nineteenth century was, for music, all about destiny too, though since music was dominated by Germans, Italians, Frenchmen and Russians, tragedy triumphed, and it all ended in death. Indeed, Continental European composers of the second half of the nineteenth century were completely obsessed with death and destiny; it is hard to find a piece of music written between 1850 and 1900 that *isn't* about one or the other. Composers were never happier than when they were able to combine them both, preferably bolted on to a doomed love affair. In an opera.

But what these Victorian Age composers didn't realise was that destiny was about to give them a tremendous jolt. As the six million visitors to London's Great Exhibition of 1851 were prophetically promised, the future was about two things: technology and the world *beyond* Europe.

If you were looking for a starting point for the death and destiny craze in music you could do a lot worse than Berlioz's *Symphonie*

fantastique: Épisode de la vie d'un Artiste . . . en cinq parties, first
performed in Paris in 1830. Although it is called a symphony,
Berlioz's intention with the five-episode orchestral fantasy was to
tell a story, without words, a story that begins with a dream (which,
unsurprisingly, turns into a nightmare, this being the nineteenth
century). His written introduction to it explains:

> The author imagines that a young musician, afflicted by the moral
> sickness which a well-known writer [François René de
> Chateaubriand] has called 'the wave of passions' [*la vague des*
> *passions*], sees his perfect, idealised woman, and falls desperately
> in love with her. Curiously, the image of his beloved only ever
> comes into his mind associated with a musical theme, which –
> passionately – reminds him of her nobility and shyness. Both the
> melodic image and its model pursue him incessantly like a double
> *idée fixe*. That is the reason for the constant appearance, in every
> movement of the symphony, of the melody that begins the first.
> The transitions from this state of dreamy melancholy, interrupted
> by fits of inexplicable joy, to delirious passion, with its outbursts
> of fury and jealousy, its returns of tenderness, its tears, its religious
> consolations – all this forms the subject of the first movement.

I feel emotionally wrung out already. It is worth pointing out,
since we have met her already, that the woman Berlioz himself
was dreaming about when he wrote this was the object of his
obsession, the Irish actress Harriet Smithson, but also that the big
tune, his so-called *idée fixe*, he had already composed a year previously as part of a cantata he had entered into a competition. In
the cantata the tune represented a tragic Muslim Princess, Erminia,
during the Crusades. Not for the first or last time, a composer
recycled a good tune that had not yet found its audience. The
Symphonie fantastique's musical narrative moves on to a Ball (or,
as Berlioz describes it, 'a festive orgy'), a gentler scene in the
countryside involving shepherds that is reminiscent of Beethoven's
Pastoral symphony, then two movements that descend into

Hammer-Horror-style darkness. The first is a 'March to the Scaffold', in which our hero poisons himself with opium, falls into a fevered, comatose state, sees himself murder the object of his infatuation, is duly apprehended and becomes onlooker to his own execution by guillotine – with a semi-comic musical effect depicting his head being chopped off. The innocent, late beloved has further torment in store in the afterlife, since the finale is a nightmare 'Witches' Sabbath', ostensibly convened to mark the (presumably) headless artist's funeral ceremony, though really its purpose is to escort the hapless girl to hell in a Breughelesque frenzy, a grotesque, diabolical grind show.

It would appear that this latter vision of semi-erotic infernal punishment was Berlioz's revenge on Harriet Smithson, who would not answer his letters of lovesick longing, nor agree to meet him, and was rumoured to be having an affair with her manager, though it could easily have been one of her other celebrity admirers, an impressive list that included Victor Hugo, Eugène Delacroix, Théophile Gautier and Alexandre Dumas. Heaven knows what the poor woman thought when she eventually heard the Berlioz piece at a Paris concert and read the programme notes, although it didn't prevent her from marrying him three years later.

The fusion of doomed love, nightmarish pandemonium and illustrative orchestral narrative that characterises the *Symphonie fantastique* lit a fuse in the imaginations of many other composers of the period, as we shall see, but it was inevitable that Berlioz, now smitten beyond sanity with Ms Smithson, would turn to arguably the greatest of all doomed-love romantic tragedies, that of Romeo and Juliet. Indeed it was seeing her in Shakespeare's play at the Paris Odéon that detonated the infatuation in the first place. Berlioz's *Roméo et Juliette* (1839) was a large-scale dramatic choral symphony – Beethoven's ninth with a story and cast of characters.

Berlioz was not alone in his obsession with this tragic love story. Romeo and Juliet's agonising predicament acts like wallpaper to nineteenth-century music: almost wherever you look it is lurking in the background, provoking decade-by-decade settings of many shapes, sizes and formats. The powerful chemistry of teenage innocence and sexual awakening, desperate longing against the odds, warring families, inevitable calamity, suicide and, finally, union in death more or less summed up the ingredients of the perfect nineteenth-century plot. Berlioz himself was encouraged in his endeavours after reviewing a performance in Florence of Vincenzo Bellini's opera *I Capuleti e I Montecchi* in 1834, one of several operatic treatments of the story that century, the most conspicuously successful being Charles François Gounod's *Roméo et Juliette* of 1867, which had three momentous openings that year, in Paris, New York and London. The latter production, at the Royal Opera House in Covent Garden, caused a sensation that rocked Victorian London when its two leads, Adelina Patti and Ernesto Nicolini, both married to other people, did in fact fall in love, kissing on the lips twenty-nine times during the balcony scene. They later settled down together at her splendid neo-Gothic castle in Wales, Craig-y-Nos, where she built her own opera house, and which is rumoured to be haunted by the spirits of Patti, Nicolini, composer Gioachino Rossini (next to whose grave in Paris Patti requested to be buried) and the children who died of TB there when the castle was used as a hospital between 1922 and 1986. The person most haunted by Berlioz's symphonic setting of *Romeo and Juliet*, on the other hand, was Richard Wagner, who used it as a stylistic template for his opera *Tristan und Isolde* in 1865.

Berlioz's temperament was, to be sure, suited to the fascinations of nineteenth-century opera – doomed love, death and destiny – even if it was not so well suited to the patient, collaborative process of putting on operas. His operatic Everest was the epic 'lyric tragedy' *Les Troyens* (The Trojans), a sumptuously passionate retelling of the fall of Troy and the suicidal liaison between Trojan hero Aeneas and the Queen of Carthage, Dido. The actual affair may not have lasted as long as the opera itself, its incredible five-and-a-half-hour length being one of the many obstacles to its being mounted in its entirety during Berlioz's lifetime. It was eventually performed whole for the first time in 1921, fifty-two years after his death.

In between revolutions, communes, epidemics and wars, Paris was the Vegas of the nineteenth century, and the grandeur of its opera productions stood at the pinnacle of a glittering high-society scene. Opera composers from all over Europe were drawn to its glitz and glamour, and the prospect of getting rich from musical tragedy. Luigi Cherubini was one such composer, born in Florence but able to flourish in Paris by tiptoeing deftly between opposing camps as political power changed hands before, during and after the Revolution. In all, he produced eighteen operas there, including some that, daringly, had a topically political flavour, such as *Les Deux journées, ou Le porteur d'eau*, which was a thinly veiled re-imagining of a contemporary political controversy. He was followed to Paris by Gaspare Spontini, favourite of the Empress Joséphine, whose *La Vestale* (The Vestal Virgin) of 1807 was the best-received of his eight Parisian premières. Italian-born Gioachino Rossini, already famous, moved to Paris in 1824 and presented five operas there, including *William Tell*. Giacomo Meyerbeer and Jacques Offenbach – the noms de plume, in fact, of two German Jews originally named Jacob – took the Paris opera world by storm in the 1830s and '40s. Meyerbeer's grand spectacles, particularly *Robert le diable* (1831), *Les Huguenots* (1836) and *Le Prophète* (1849), turned him into a wealthy and much-decorated celebrity – they were the most regularly performed new operas in the world during the nineteenth century. Offenbach, meanwhile, composed no fewer than ninety-eight operettas in Paris before his death in 1880, some of which, like *Orpheus in the Underworld*, *La Belle Hélène* and *La Vie Parisienne*, were outrageously popular, even among the not so well off.

Notwithstanding the universal admiration for Offenbach's comic operettas, the opulence of the Parisian experience of opera and its position in society still meant it was a luxury. But the relationship between opera and the populace could not have been more different in Italy, where opera was a popular art form. By 'popular' I don't mean some people quite liked it; I mean almost *all* city dwellers would have known the songs from the latest operas. If you lived in Turin or Milan or Naples in 1850, opera was your iTunes or your TV. This seems strange to us, aware as we are that even subsidised seats in modern-day opera houses cost upwards of £100, but in nineteenth-century Italy, opera *was* entertainment.

In his immaculately researched study of music and its audiences, *The Triumph of Music*, Tim Blanning sums up the scale of Italian operaphilia and the pivotal role of it in every community thus:

> the opera house . . . often included not just a stage and auditorium but also cafés, restaurants, gambling casinos and public spaces where people could just meet and socialise. Many people went four or five times a week. Nowhere else in Europe and at no other time in European history has so much opera been performed as in Italy between 1815 and 1860. In Milan there were six theatres in which opera was performed regularly; in Naples there were five plus one more occasional venue.

Opera was the soul of the Italian people as well as its chief off-duty pastime. The hummable operas of three composers, Rossini, Donizetti and Bellini, dominated the first half of the nineteenth century but no one captured the hearts of all Italians more completely than Giuseppe Verdi, whose first hit was *Nabucco* in 1842. He reigned supreme for half a century and his early offerings, *Nabucco* included, had plots carefully chosen to whip up the Italian people's desire for self-government, the movement known as the Risorgimento. Thanks to this, Verdi became a political as well as a cultural icon.

Like his crowd-pleasing predecessor Donizetti, Verdi's first dozen or so operas were concerned mostly with giving the audience a series of show-stopping solos and choruses hung on a stirring plot from history or legend, generally involving heroism, self-sacrifice, defiance of neighbouring powers, bandits, brigands, highwaymen and dastardly villains. They were not so very different from Hollywood movies of the 1930s to '60s. Battles were big, especially if they involved bullies being trounced by minnows, so Peruvian tribespeople standing up to the Spanish Conquistadors (*Alzira*, 1845), lowly Joan of Arc against the brutish English (*Giovanna d'Arco*, 1845) or plucky Lombards taking on all comers (*I Lombardi alla prima crociata*, 1843, *La battaglia di Legnano*, 1849) were typical. But then, in around 1850, Verdi's approach changed gear.

Whether he sensed his audiences were hungry for something different or the impulse came from his own shifting priorities, the result was a direction of attention to more contemporary issues and plot lines, even those that were ostensibly set in the past. This new attitude, at least initially, scandalised as much as it excited: *Stiffelio*, first performed in Trieste in November 1850, provoked official condemnation and substantial censoring, telling as it does the tale of a married Protestant minister learning to forgive his adulterous wife. It was based on a play that had been published only the previous year and was set in recent times rather than in the safely distant past. His next project, *Rigoletto*, was also based on a recent (banned) play by Victor Hugo, *Le Roi s'amuse*, which lampooned an immoral, corrupt king – Hugo had had Louis Philippe I, last king of France, in mind – and accordingly encountered further difficulties with the authorities, in this case Venetian, who insisted scenes be removed and the period and setting be changed. A tragic melodrama of fate and revenge, *Il Trovatore*, followed in January 1853, immediately becoming one of the most popular operas in history, but even this did not prepare Verdi's now thronging admirers for the shock of *La Traviata*, which was put in front of an astonished public just three months later, in Venice.

La Traviata is about a doomed love affair and parental interference in a young couple's unlikely liaison – once again echoing *Romeo and Juliet* – climaxing in the agonising and symbolic death, from TB, of the once-promiscuous female protagonist, Violetta. The opera's title translates approximately as 'the woman who went astray', though a modern colloquial translation might be 'The Slut'. Based on a recently published bestseller, *The Lady of the Camellias* by Alexandre Dumas, *La Traviata* was met at first with moral outrage. To death and destiny Verdi had now added sex. The Venetian authorities demanded that the opera's present-day setting be put back a hundred and fifty years, to reduce its potential to shock, while Queen Victoria was advised not to attend the London première three years later for fear of being seen to endorse its 'immorality'. But though its birth was controversial, *La Traviata* eventually swept (nearly) all before it. To date there have been over twenty film adaptations and it is the second-most-performed opera of all time, after Mozart's *The Magic Flute*.

Of course, stories like *The Lady of the Camellias* allowed nine-teenth-century audiences to have their cake and eat it – to enjoy being spectators of what they thought of as lewd behaviour, and then to have their hypocritical morals endorsed by seeing the naughty woman who indulged in it die a horrible death. Violetta does not expire, mind, before she has broken the audience's defenceless hearts with an adieu of choking beauty, the aria 'Addio, del passato bei sogni ridenti' (Farewell, lovely, happy dreams of the past).

It is no coincidence that the figure of the Fallen Woman stalks through so many operas, novels and paintings of the second half of the nineteenth century. With increased male middle-class spending power came astonishing levels of prostitution. Social historian Judith Walkowitz calculated in her authoritative *Prostitution and Victorian Society* (1980) that nineteenth-century industrialised cities had on average a staggering ratio of one pros-titute per twelve adult males. *La Traviata* confronts this sexual hypocrisy: that every woman had her price, and yet should be condemned for it. The death of Violetta was meant to strike shame into Verdi's audiences' hearts, as it did the meddling father of her lover in the final scene. It was a bold attempt to change prevailing social attitudes by a man who was second only to Garibaldi, hero of the struggle for Italian independence, in fame. And Verdi understood that opera was at its most powerful when attempting to impart universal truths through emotionally engaging morality fables. By making his fellow countrymen and -women confront their double standards, their prejudices and insecurities through his accessible, sweeping melodramas, he arguably *did* do as much to better the lives and self-esteem of Italians in the nineteenth century as Garibaldi.

Throughout his gloriously successful career of twenty-eight operas, Verdi managed to convey emotions, stories and often layered concepts of deeply felt intensity without disappearing into a private world of musical complexity that only other musicians could appreciate – an alarmingly common tendency that crept into opera as the decades rolled on. His tunes were firmly rooted in an easy-to-grasp, enchanting-to-sing Italian vocal style, so that ordinary folk really *could* leave the theatre humming. Those who couldn't afford a ticket need not have missed out, either. Barrel organists and other itinerant musicians would hang around the theatres, learn the tunes and make a living busking them in the street the next day.

So solid was the foundation Verdi created for populist Italian opera that even when, in the early twentieth century, classical music became convulsed in turmoil and discord, he was able to hand over seamlessly to composers like Leoncavallo and Mascagni. But without doubt Verdi's greatest successor was Puccini, whose death-and-destiny-heavy masterpieces belong to the mindset of the nineteenth century even though they were written at the turn of the twentieth, their generously melodic melodramas bucking the trend of modernism. In all art, there are few more poignant critiques of the abuse of power than Puccini's *Tosca* of 1900, or of rapacious imperialism than *Madama Butterfly* of 1904, both of which were presented, then as now, as mass-market commodities without pretension or snobbery.

★

If it had been left to the Italians, classical music would have made it to the modern age without so much as a scratch, still completely mainstream, still loved by everyone. As late as 1936 La Scala in Milan could still première such enthusiastically received comedies as Ermanno Wolf-Ferrari's delightfully tuneful and quaint *Il Campiello*, based on a play written for the Venetian Carnival of 1756, and which would not have been stylistically out of place had it opened a whole century earlier – rather than in the same year as the BBC began television transmissions. North of the Alps, though, things had been developing very differently indeed.

If instrumental and symphonic music of the first half of the nineteenth century was totally dominated by Beethoven, music in the second half belonged to a French-speaking Hungarian born in what is now Austria: Franz Liszt. What is odd about this statement is that virtually everyone has heard of Beethoven and can probably recall some piece of music by him, but very few can name a piece by Liszt, even if they have heard of him. He was a genius other composers slavishly followed for well over half a century, yet to most modern listeners he is just a name, alongside his colleague Brahms. But Liszt was a trailblazer, an experimenter, a pacesetter. To do justice to the increased obsession with death and destiny, someone needed to turbocharge music's engine. Liszt was that man.

Disturbing emotions were conjured up in Liszt's harmonies; flashy set pieces thrilled and terrified a sensation-seeking public. Liszt, Mr Trick or Treat, was the composer who, more than anyone else in the mid-nineteenth century, recalibrated music's forces, so it is worth looking in detail at some of the many innovations he brought to fruition.

First, he kick-started a craze for extravagant, Hallowe'en-style music, full of dark, deep, crashingly loud chords and abrasive strings. It is a craze that has yet to abate. His theatre of the macabre, as seen in his scary *Totentanz* (Death-dance) of 1849, for solo piano and orchestra, didn't inspire just composers of his own period, like Saint-Saëns's *Danse macabre* (1874), or Grieg's 'March of the Trolls' (1891), or Liyadov's *Baba Yaga* (1904), but also film composers of our own time, including the chillingly ingenious Danny Elfman. Elfman's Lisztian score for Tim Burton's 1989 *Batman*, for example, gives edge-of-the-seat action sequences an undercurrent of avenging menace.

Second, Liszt was a spectacular pianist who more or less single-handedly – or indeed two-handedly – forced piano builders to adopt iron frames to replace wood ones, because they simply broke under the hammering he gave them on stage. His use of the piano as fairground of effects bedazzled audiences at his live concerts. One of his party-piece show-stoppers was a Grand Chromatic Galop, composed in 1838, which can be seen as the template for Offenbach's hallmark cancans of twenty years later (for example, the 'Galop infernal' from *Orpheus in the Underworld*). Showy, circus-like turns, though, were only a tiny part of what he could do at the piano in his 'recitals' – a term he coined for a solo piano concert. In his thirties, Liszt became music's first inter-national star, embarking on a merry-go-round of European tours, where he was known, and treated, as 'The King of the Piano'. According to contemporary reports, some female fans became 'hysterical' at the mere sight of him on stage. (This aspect of his celebrity was, I fear, rather overhyped in the late-twentieth century in an attempt by classical record companies to make him more relevant to a younger generation in the pop era. Although the term 'Lisztomania' was first used in 1844 by the German writer Heinrich Heine in his review of a series of recitals in Berlin, the 1975 film by Ken Russell, *Lisztomania*, unsubtly likened the adora-tion of Liszt's female fans to the phenomenon of Beatlemania and subsequent similar manias. Ever since the film, a lazy identi-fication of Liszt as 'the first rock star' has developed. Granted, he inspired unprecedented levels of dedicated fandom for his day, but a few anecdotes about female concert-goers swooning or hoping to take away some memento from a live Liszt appearance – a handkerchief or, in one report, a discarded cigar – hardly measures up to the Fab Four arriving in a helicopter to perform at the open-air Shea Stadium in August 1965 in front of 55,600 screaming, weeping, fainting fans whose noise deafened the hundreds of NYPD officers deployed to protect the artists and totally over-whelmed the stadium's PA system.)

Liszt's third innovation was his perfection of a keyboard style that shimmered and gleamed, an aural equivalent of the blurred vibrancy of an oil painting by Monet, where sounds melted and smudged into one another like colours. This technique in music has since been described as 'impressionistic' and specifically attached to the works of the French composer Claude Debussy, whose pieces had visually evocative titles such as 'Reflections in the water', 'Footprints in the snow', 'The Hills of Anacapri' and 'Gardens in the rain'. Debussy's 'Gardens in the rain', though, was composed in 1903, a good thirty years after the Impressionist painters had first begun exhibiting their works to a disconcerted Parisian public. If the term 'impressionistic' belongs to anyone, it is not Debussy – who disliked the comparison between the move-ment in art and his music – but Liszt, whose *Fountains of the Villa d'Este*, for example, dates from 1877, just three years after the First Impressionist Exhibition. This was a piece that was well known to the young Debussy, who revered Liszt as a disciple, and who was honoured to be able to play for him in person in 1888.

Liszt's fourth innovation was in the field of orchestral music. He invented what he called the 'symphonic poem' and wrote thirteen of them, templates of a form that was to be taken up enthusiastically by composers as varied as the Czechs Bedrich Smetana, Antonin Dvořák and Leoš Janáček, Russians Mily Balakirev, Modest Mussorgsky, Alexander Borodin, Nikolai Rimsky-Korsakov, Alexander Glazunov and Anatoly Lyadov, Germany's Richard Strauss and Finland's Jean Sibelius.

The idea behind Liszt's symphonic poems was to reduce the traditional four-movement symphony as exemplified by Beethoven into one concentrated, shorter piece that would be a musical response to a *non*-musical artwork. His subjects ranged from Prometheus, mythical hero of Ancient Greece and muse of

Beethoven et al, to Shakespeare's Hamlet, from Orpheus in the Underworld to a contemporary painting of a battle in AD 451 between Attila the Hun, the Visigoths and the Roman Empire. While Beethoven had framed his Sonata Form *Pastoral* symphony around visual images – a walk in the country, a thunderstorm, peasants' merry-making – he was more interested in his own feelings than in the pictorial effect of his scenes. Liszt's symphonic poems, on the other hand, were a departure from this trend in that they *intended* to conjure up in music the pictures or the stories themselves. Liszt was moving away from the idea of music as an abstract entity, something to be listened to attentively for forty or so minutes, towards orchestral music as a representation of something extra-musical. In its purest form, the symphonic poem style is what orchestral film music grew out of in the 1920s and '30s, its job to support and describe something outside music.

Though old-style, four-movement symphonies continued to be written, even until the mid-twentieth century, lots of composers leapt enthusiastically on Liszt's symphonic poem alternative. Beethoven's third symphony, *Eroica*, had had at its core an idea – heroism (and its betrayal) – but it nonetheless retained the musical form of a symphony. Much the same can be said about Mendelssohn's *Hebrides* overture (1830): it may have had a guiding thought – a holiday visit to those islands, in particular Fingal's Cave – but its form was still determined by a musical template. Liszt's *Tasso, Lamento e Trionfo*, however, followed the path of an actual period in the life of the sixteenth-century Italian poet Torquato Tasso, to the extent of weaving in a traditional gondoliers' folk song to evoke Tasso's relationship with Venice, and creating an anguished first section in the mental asylum where Tasso, possibly suffering from schizophrenia, was for a while imprisoned. The form of the piece, crucially, was dictated by the story.

This was a new emphasis for purely orchestral music. (Opera, of course, had been shaped by story and characterisation for many years.) Liszt's own comments about *Tasso*, which was completed

in 1849 and revised in 1851 and 1854, reveal how specific his approach
to telling the tale was intended to be:

> Tasso loved and suffered at Ferrara, he was avenged at Rome, and
> even today lives in the popular songs of Venice. These three
> moments are inseparable from his immortal fame. To reproduce
> them in music, we first conjured up the great shade as he wanders
> through the lagoons of Venice even today; then his countenance
> appeared to us, lofty and melancholy, as he gazes at the festivities
> at Ferrara, where he created his masterworks; and finally we
> followed him to Rome, the Eternal City, which crowned him with
> fame and thus pays him tribute both as martyr and as poet.[1]

This shift in emphasis spearheaded by Liszt, from purely orchestral to more illustrative music, is particularly notable in his
symphonic poem *Hunnenschlacht*, the one devoted to the 1850
painting of Attila the Hun's battle by Wilhelm von Kaulbach.
Fought in AD 415, against the now Christian Roman Empire and
their allies, the encounter was a rare occasion on which Attila and
his heathen Huns were beaten. At the beginning of the piece,
Liszt's music is meant to depict the ghostly armies of the battle
mustering for the fight; it is marked to be played 'tempestuously',
and to recreate the effect of the painting's spirit soldiers in the
sky, the strings are instructed to play with their mutes on, thus
dampening and thinning the sound. Interspersed among the lively,
whispery strings are little military outbursts from the horns. In
the painting there are relatively few actual soldiers depicted, the
emphasis being more on the ordinary men and women engulfed
unwittingly in the conflict, so Liszt is careful not to make his
orchestra too percussive and martial, at least near the opening.

Eventually the battle proper kicks off and, in the midst of the
tumult and chaos, Liszt introduces on trombones an old plainsong

---

1 Translation from Humphrey Searle's book *The Music of Liszt* (London: Williams
& Norgate, 1954).

chant, 'Crux fidelis' (Cross of faith), to represent the caped figure in one corner of the painting who carries a gleaming, golden cross. This is followed by a triumphant fanfare and then the introduction of a gentle, holy organ. The plainsong theme is carefully interwoven into increasingly agitated string activity in the final three minutes or so, giving a general sense of the great victory about to be celebrated, which, when it is, leaves you in no doubt whatever of the scale and meaning of the Roman-Christian forces of civilisation coming out on top. The muscular victory music is topped off with extra off-stage brass reinforcements and an instruction regarding the organ, *'Dans le cas où l'harmonium ne serait pas assez puissant pour couvrir l'orchestra à la fin, n'en faire aucun usage'* which translates roughly as 'if it can't be louder than the whole orchestra, don't bother'. The final climax is the kind of heavyweight flourish you have heard in countless Hollywood adventure film scores, from Elmer Bernstein's parting of the Red Sea in *The Ten Commandments* (1956) to Hans Zimmer's body-shaking battle music for *Gladiator* (2000).

Liszt's fifth innovation was a product of the particular political geography into which he was born. The small town of his birth, Doborján, then in the Kingdom of Hungary, now Raiding in Austria, was populated by a mixture of Magyar Hungarians and German-speaking Austrians, all of whom were absorbed into the Austrian, later Austro-Hungarian, Empire under the Habsburg monarchy. By the nineteenth century many of the majority ethnic Magyars in Hungary were dejected by their lack of self-government – though Liszt himself was far from the turmoil for most of his life. As a child his musical ability had quickly been spotted and he was soon in Vienna receiving training from, among others, Salieri, and encountering both Beethoven and Schubert. As an adolescent, after his father's death, Liszt and his mother moved to Paris, where he adopted French as his 'first' language. For the rest of his life he was thoroughly cosmopolitan, travelling widely, living for twenty years in Weimar, and for six years near Rome, where he took holy orders. A recent centenary conference and festival devoted to him in modern Hungary simply described him, correctly, as 'European'. But even though he wasn't brought up in Hungary, Liszt held on to some vestiges of Hungarian patriotism beneath his pan-European façade. In 1839 he returned to his homeland for the first time since his childhood and was greeted rapturously by crowds chanting 'Hail! Franz Liszt!'. He ostentatiously wore national costume as a gesture of solidarity with the Magyar cause and defiantly performed in public his piano arrangement of the popular but banned 'Rákóczy March', honouring Prince Francis Rákóczy, who had led a revolt against Austrian domination in 1703–11. In an emotional speech at Hungary's National Theatre in January 1840, Liszt declared his support for his countrymen's aspirations for independence.

It is this same sympathy with the country of his birth that is reflected in Liszt's set of eleven piano arrangements of folk songs, the *Magyar dalok* (which includes the 'Rákóczy March'), compiled in 1839–40, and his nineteen *Hungarian Rhapsodies* for solo piano, composed on and off between 1846 and 1885. That they were intended to have a patriotic, as well as a nostalgic, purpose is clear from his dedication of the most famous of the set, no. 2, composed in 1847, to the Hungarian nationalist, revolutionary and statesman Count László Teleki. Teleki's association with the Hungarian uprising against Austrian rule in March 1848, a revolt that was crushed by Imperial armies and followed by a punitive policy of Germanisation, led to him being sentenced to death.

Liszt's musical identification with the folk song and dances of his native Hungary was, alongside Chopin's polonaises and mazurkas, the first wave of a movement that was to sweep through music over the ensuing half-century, given powerful momentum by the fact that so many of Liszt's contemporaries – Brahms, Grieg, Joachim Raff, Smetana, Tchaikovsky, César Cui and Rimsky-Korsakov, to name just a handful – were in thrall to him and his every move.

The formula that Liszt put to use in his *Hungarian Rhapsodies*, and which was much imitated thereafter, was simple enough. It started with a stately, meandering, slightly exotic first section, known as a *lassan* or *lassu*, which was paired with a frantic second section called the *friska*, from the German word *frisch*, meaning brisk. The third important component of the collection and all subsequent spin-offs was the ultra-vigorous *csárdás* dance, which had much impressed Liszt when he was treated to a private recital in May 1846 by the Jewish 'father of the csárdás', Márk Rózsavölgyi. Rózsavölgyi's background was poor and he was most likely introduced as a child to the Eastern European Jewish folk music known as *klezmer*, and as a young man he travelled through Hungary, Slovakia and Romania picking up the local folk dances on his violin. Later he became a well-known musical figure in Budapest; some of his melodies (either newly composed or collected by him, that is) were integrated into Liszt's *Hungarian Rhapsodies*. (Liszt did not claim the melodies were his, merely that he was arranging them for piano in his own style.)

But Liszt, like the other composers of his time, was more than a little confused about what indigenous Hungarian music actually was, believing it to be the same as 'gypsy' music, which in turn was often muddled up with 'Turkish' music. In reality, gypsy (Romani) music was in fact quite distinct from Turkish folk music and also quite distinct, as it happened, from Hungarian (Magyar) folk music. For the well-to-do Viennese of the late-eighteenth century onwards, however, including composers like Haydn and Mozart, using the terms 'gypsy', 'Hungarian' or 'Turkish' was like saying 'random foreign music by poor people'. Indeed, we now know that Liszt and his contemporaries were quite wrong about the provenance of what they called 'gypsy' music. The music they all *thought* was 'gypsy' was in fact either Hungarian folk music played by Lautari (professional Romani musicians) in Budapest and Vienna for the benefit of restaurant or café patrons, or it was 'gypsy-style' pastiche based not on old, anonymous folk songs and dances but on tunes from popular stage shows or drawing-room ballads, their original composers' names wittingly or unwittingly lost over time. (They have since mostly been identified.)

The real Romani of nineteenth-century central Europe, whose fundamental ethnic origins were Indian, kept their own music to themselves.

Liszt thought, though, that Hungarian folk music *was* gypsy music and the publication of his first book of *Hungarian Rhapsodies* in 1853, in a generic folkloric style dressed up for the sophisticated Western European salon, prompted a craze that virtually all composers in Europe emulated. Some plundered their own country's rustic folk dances, some opportunistically arranged the folk music of other countries, while others dipped into the non-specific well of travelling gypsy band music. This boom has subsequently been labelled 'musical nationalism', but I find this terminology problematic. The flaw in describing it as 'nationalist' is that, while it was sometimes identified with political movements seeking self-determination, as in the case of Liszt's *Hungarian Rhapsodies* or Sibelius's *Finlandia*, in other cases it was merely an excuse for inserting ethnic idioms and sounds into salon or concert-hall music with no national or political motivation whatever. Or at best a confused motivation, as with Liszt's well-intentioned misunderstanding of Romani music. Likewise, the magpie-like composers of the nineteenth century sometimes even made use of such material from regions that were not their own, or, as members of the imperial ruling class, found inspiration in the music of subjugated tribes and communities within their empire's domain – in which cases the term 'nationalist' is, surely, highly inappropriate. We will encounter examples of all these variants.

To be clear, the phenomenon of repackaging ethnic music may in many cases have been motivated by a deep and sincere love of country, and of the traditions and roots of peoples who felt oppressed by other more powerful nations, no doubt about it, but what it was not was a bottom-up, grass-roots movement whereby peasant troubadours presented the treasures of their communities to the world. In all cases, the movement that used to be called 'nationalism' in music was concocted by highly trained, sophisticated, well-travelled, middle-class composers, mostly trained in

Leipzig, Vienna or Paris, who took bits and pieces of folk song and dance that they had heard, probably in city taverns, not even in the rural heartland, and whipped them up into what were essentially mainstream Austro-German musical caricatures for the amusement of an audience who had no interest in the genuine struggles of peasant culture at all.

Among the most popular collections of the type that Liszt's example engendered were Johannes Brahms's *Hungarian Dances* of 1869 and 1880, which exploit all the usual folksy dance forms of *lassan, friska* and *csárdás*. Brahms, who was more than a little in awe of Liszt's talent and status (but found his music too progressive to enjoy), was a self-confessed musical conservative, following in the more formal tradition of Beethoven, Schubert and (his friend) Schumann, and though his unsheltered boyhood was partly scarred by piano playing in seedy bars and brothels near the Hamburg docks, his familiarity with genuine Hungarian folk music would have been wholly second- if not third-hand. His *Hungarian Dances* are great fun and highly polished but – make no mistake – if you had played one of them to a passing Magyar milkmaid on the banks of Lake Balaton in 1870 and asked her what it was she would have likely answered, 'Nice. Some kind of fancy German music.'

The integration of pseudo-peasant style into the piano and orchestral mainstream was an unstoppable flood, yielding many of the best-loved gems of nineteenth-century music, from the Bohemian (Czech) composer Dvořák's *Slavonic Dances* of 1878 and 1886 to Finnish composer Sibelius's *Karelia* suite of 1893, from Bohemian (Czech) Smetana's *Má vlast* (My country) of 1879 to Hugo Alfvén's Swedish rhapsody, *Midsommarvaka* (Midsummer vigil) of 1903. Popular *csárdás* dances were pastiched by Frenchman Delibes (in his ballet *Coppelia* of 1870), Russian Tchaikovsky (in his ballet *Swan Lake* of 1877) and, perhaps best known of them all, Italian Vittorio Monti, whose 'Csárdás' of 1904 was later adopted by genuine Romani Lautari bands and orchestras across Europe to play to their foot-tapping clientèle. What goes around comes around. Liszt himself wrote three piano csárdás, between 1881 and 1884, including, naturally, a 'Csárdás macabre'.

Nowhere were the moral questions surrounding the borrowing of elements from ethnic music and putting them into mainstream music more sharply highlighted than in the United States, where one composer in particular found himself at the centre of a highly divisive debate.

Middle-class Americans of the late nineteenth century were keen not to be outdone by their European counterparts, so they built concert halls, established orchestras and invited star names across the Atlantic to perform. Antonin Dvořák, by the late 1880s already well known outside his homeland, especially in Britain, was invited to New York by a wealthy philanthropist in 1892, to become director of the new National Conservatory of Music, at twenty-five times the salary he had been paid to do the same in Prague. He lived in New York for three years, producing, among other things, his now extremely familiar ninth symphony, *From the New World*, in 1894.

Dvořák's clear and oft-stated aim at the college, published in newspaper articles shortly after his arrival, was to encourage young American composers to adopt and develop the melodies of Native American and African-American communities in their orchestral music, as he and his Bohemian students had done with Czech and Slavic folk music back in Prague. He wrote,

> I am now satisfied that the future music of this country must be founded upon what are called the Negro melodies. This must be the real foundation of any serious and original school of composition to be developed in the United States. . . . These beautiful and varied themes are the product of the soil. . . . These are the folk songs of America, and your composers must turn to them. . . . In the Negro melodies of America I discover all that is needed for a great and noble school of music. They are pathetic, tender, passionate, melancholy, solemn, religious, bold, merry, gay, or what you will. It is music that suits itself to any mood or purpose. There

is nothing in the whole range of composition that cannot be supplied with themes from this source.

Dvořák's optimism was as much scoffed at as admired, and his comments about 'Negro music' made front-page news on both sides of the Atlantic. Italian composer Puccini remarked a few years later, 'There is no such thing as American music. What they have is Negro music, which is almost the savagery of sound.' Added to European snobbery was white American scepticism about Dvořák's public statements. Bostonian composer Edward MacDowell, who himself had trained in Paris and Frankfurt rather than America, and who mostly wrote German-style music, responded, 'We have here in America been offered a pattern for an American national music costume by the Bohemian Dvořák . . . though what Negro melodies have to do with Americanism in art still remains a mystery.' Nonetheless, MacDowell's own mother, Frances, did provide a scholarship for a young African-American musician, Harry Thacker Burleigh, to join Dvořák's classes at the National Conservatory of Music, where he introduced the Bohemian composer to spirituals and assisted him with orchestral part-copying. Burleigh arranged some of these spirituals, published in 1901 as *Six Plantation Melodies for Violin and Piano*, and later had considerable success with song arrangements of spirituals and the composition of sentimental ballads, including 'Little Mother of Mine' (1917), 'Dear Old Pal of Mine' and 'Under a Blazing Star' (1918). Of Dvořák's other students, Rubin Goldmark responded to his call to arms with a setting of Longfellow's *Hiawatha* and, in 1923, one year before the première of his own pupil George Gershwin's *Rhapsody in Blue*, a *Negro Rhapsody*. Dvořák's other notable student, organist and composer Harry Rowe Shelley, may not have heeded the call as conscientiously, certainly not if his orchestral works *Souvenir de Baden-Baden* and *The Crusaders* are anything to go by.

But if Dvořák's teaching methods raised eyebrows among his adopted countrymen, his own American compositions were to prove even more controversial. His *New World* symphony of 1894 in particular was scrutinised for the extent to which it was actually 'American', the original source of its melodies, and whether it was even Dvořák's right to appropriate folk music styles (if not actual melodies) of another community for his composition.

One very vocal opponent of the tide of ethnic imitation was the writer, civil rights activist and co-founder of the National Association for the Advancement of Colored People, W. E. B. Du Bois. He was at pains to point out in *The Conservation of Races* (1897) and in his seminal essay collection *The Souls of Black Folk* (1903) that the slave ('Sorrow') songs of the plantations were not, as Dvořák would have it, a national resource open to all Americans. Rather they were quite specifically the voice of the oppressed African-American – 'these songs are the articulate message of the slave to the world' – and should remain so. He described having heard the 'Sorrow' songs as a child, including 'Swing Low, Sweet Chariot', which he called 'the cradle-song of Death', recalling that they 'came out of the South unknown to me, one by one, and yet at once I knew them as of me and of mine . . . This was primitive African music . . . the voice of exile.' For Du Bois, the Negro people of America had to resist absorption into white America: 'their destiny is not a servile imitation of Anglo-Saxon culture, but a stalwart originality which shall unswervingly follow Negro ideals. . . . We are the first fruits of this new nation, the harbinger of that black to-morrow which is yet destined to soften the whiteness of the Teutonic to-day. We are that people whose subtle sense of song has given America its only American music, its only American fairy tales, its only touch of pathos and humor amid its mad money-getting plutocracy.'

One of the *New World* symphony's greatest controversies concerns its slow movement, still instantly recognisable thanks to its innocently memorable tune, rather like a hymn, and also because it was subsequently co-opted for a bread commercial in which it evoked rural Edwardian England (which fact in itself should alert us to the dangers of music's ability to reinforce 'national' characteristics). Its similarity to a hymn tune was spotted not long after its première at Carnegie Hall in December 1893, since it was given holy words and turned into a sacred song, 'Goin' home', by another of Dvořák's pupils, William Arms Fisher. Persistent claims have been made that Dvořák heard the tune from Harry Burleigh, a theory proposed, for example, in a 1922 letter written by the composer Victor Herbert: 'Dr Dvorak was most kind and unaffected and took great interest in his pupils, one of which, Harry Burleigh, had the privilege of giving the Dr some of the thematic material for his Symphony. . . . I have seen this denied – but it is true.'[2] Burleigh himself later wrote, 'I gave him what I knew of Negro songs – no one called them spirituals then – and he wrote some of my tunes (my people's music) into the New World Symphony.' Another claim was made for African-American guitarist W. Philips Dabney, who suggested it was based on his own plantation melody 'Uncle Remus', which he had played to Dvořák in his Conservatory office and, he reported, copied down on to manuscript. The tune has often been compared to the spiritual 'Deep River', while another of the symphony's melodies has been likened to 'Swing Low, Sweet Chariot'.

Dvořák certainly intended his symphony's skipping rhythms and melodic shapes derived from the five pentatonic notes we have encountered before (the 'black' notes on a keyboard), those common to all the world's music cultures, to sound like those of Native American peoples. Even before his arrival in America, he had read a musicological essay published in Germany in 1882 called 'On the Music of the North American Indians'. He stressed, though, with regard to the symphony, 'I have not actually used any of the Native American melodies. I have simply written original themes embodying the peculiarities of the Indian music, and, using these as subjects, have developed them with all the resources of modern rhythms, counterpoint and orchestral colour.'

2 See also: Simpson, Anne Key, *Hard Trials: The Life and Music of Harry T. Burleigh* (The Scarecrow Press, 1990).

Further stimulus for enquiry regarding Dvořák's sources for the tunes in the *New World* symphony were prompted by his admission that he had previously been developing ideas for a musical setting of Henry Wadsworth Longfellow's epic poem, loosely based on Indian tribal legends, *The Song of Hiawatha*. Dvořák abandoned the Hiawatha project but claimed to have absorbed research he had conducted for it into his musical thinking for the symphony. Without definitive documentary evidence of particular sources we may never know if this research included tribal melodies he later passed off as his own. (By far and away the period's most successful setting of Longfellow's poem was *The Song of Hiawatha*, an oratorio trilogy completed in 1900 by English mixed-race composer Samuel Coleridge-Taylor. The hugely oversubscribed première of its first instalment, *Hiawatha's Wedding Feast*, in November 1898 at the Royal College of Music, was described by the composer Sir Hubert Parry as 'one of the most remarkable events in modern English musical history'.)

Just as Longfellow's intention in writing the poem was not colonial exploitation but rather an attempt to portray the Native American tribespeople as 'noble savages' with much in their folklore to value and enjoy, so Dvořák's aim in composing his symphony was to raise the aspirations of American music-makers and music lovers. He wanted them to have pride in their own heritage, not to see it as a second-rate imitation of European culture. The irony of course was, as Leonard Bernstein pointed out in a blow-by-blow analysis of the symphony in 1956, that in his well-meaning but superficial imitation of 'primitive' Native American and African-American melody types, Dvořák's style also sounded like that of other non-mainstream cultures. These included Chinese and Scottish, as well as some Eastern European ethnic folk music. Dvořák himself acknowledged that irony, saying in a newspaper interview, 'I found that the music of the Negroes and of the Indians was practically identical,' going on to affirm that 'the music of the two races bore a remarkable similarity to the music of Scotland'. James Huneker, reviewing the first performance of the symphony, identified the

'Swing Low, Sweet Chariot' theme in the first movement, describing it as 'negro or oriental, just as you choose'.

All of which brings us to the question of whether it is legitimate to plunder the musical content of another community's cultural inheritance, placing it in an alien and artificial milieu for the benefit of a very different audience. Why did it matter whether Dvořák's source melodies for the symphony were borrowed from Native American and African-American folk songs, or whether they were newly composed? It mattered because Dvořák's *New World* symphony has to be seen in the context of the period. American territorial expansion in the nineteenth century had repeatedly been justified by a firm belief in 'Manifest Destiny' – the notion that white Americans had a God-given right, or even duty, to colonise the whole continent. Time and again, though, Manifest Destiny was revealed as little more than a euphemism for the violent appropriation of Native American land for the benefit of white settlers. Would survivors and relatives of the Lakota Sioux Indians butchered at the Wounded Knee Massacre, which took place just three years before the symphony's first performance, have recognised its melodies as theirs? If they had, would they not have seen it as yet another form of theft?

Even Dvořák, champion of African-American musical advancement (one hundred and fifty of his six hundred students at the National Conservatory were black, a startling statistic of integration in a deeply segregated age), was able to dismiss some Native American culture as all but worthless: 'I have heard black singers in Haiti for hours and, as a rule, their songs are not unlike the monotonous and crude chantings of the Sioux tribes.' The moral debate as to whether it is ethical for a richer people to adapt the music of a poorer people for their musical entertainment – often uncredited and unpaid – has never gone away and is just as hotly debated in our own time, not least in the fields of Blues, jazz and world music. We will meet it again in the next chapter.

But for the time being, at the end of the nineteenth century, there was another great controversy on the horizon. Indeed, any unease generated by Dvořák's relationship with the culture of oppressed peoples was a walk in the park compared to the hornet's nest provoked by Liszt's most needy and argumentative disciple of them all: Richard Wagner.

The colossus of Wagner is an inescapable reality of late-nineteenth-century music, indeed of recent Western civilisation. He is both brilliant and problematical, and it is fair to say that his towering legacy has had more impact on the worlds of literature, philosophy and politics than, strictly speaking, on musical development. This is because his style was so particular, his agenda so ambitious and his stature as a German national figure so all-embracing that other composers found it impossible (or unpalatable) to follow his example.

Of Liszt's many gifts to the musical world, arguably his most significant is what he mostly unintentionally taught this man who would eventually become his son-in-law. Wagner's debt to Liszt is so great, in fact, that it is fair to say there is no innovation, no technique, no supposed great leap forward in expression or style anywhere in Wagner's monumental output that is not found somewhere, first, in Liszt. Sometimes, as in the final movement of Liszt's *Dante* symphony, 'Purgatorio', composed in 1856, it is as if whole passages have found their way – doubtless subliminally – into Wagner's texture (in that case, *Tristan und Isolde*). Elsewhere, the gifts are technical. Take Wagner's dismantling of harmony.

One of Wagner's favourite tricks was to take the building block of all Western harmony – the common triad – and either squash it slightly, to make a *diminished* chord, or enlarge it slightly to make an *augmented* chord. Diminishing or augmenting chords does strange things to the way they behave. They become unstable and have a tendency to unsettle the mood because they deviate from comfortable convention, seeking relationships with unfamiliar chords. They are music's drifters and grifters. They create a sense of nervousness, of anxiety and uncertainty. Wagner uses them prolifically throughout his ten most famous operas to evoke pain or anguish, or to tell you something grim might be about to happen. In the first part of his epic *Ring* cycle, *The Rhinegold*, for example, angry diminished chords are often used to signify the dangerous power of the Ring itself.

Diminishing and augmenting chords Wagner may have made his own, but they are all over Liszt's daring, dark harmony. His *Faust* symphony of 1855 begins with an anguished opening theme entirely made up of augmented chords, followed not long after by an outbreak of demonic pain, punched out in a series of very loud diminished chords. (Liszt's *Faust* is not just noteworthy for presaging Wagner. Its opening theme, albeit not instantly hummable, consists of twelve notes: it uses all twelve notes of the Western scale without repeating any of them. So what, you may ask? Well, when the Austrian composer Arnold Schoenberg proposed a new form of musical organisation, whereby a melody was obliged to use each of the twelve notes of the Western scale in a sequence before being allowed to repeat any of them, a method known as twelve-tone serialism, it threatened to bring about the collapse of musical civilisation as we know it. We shall encounter it later. The remarkable thing is that Liszt's experiment with the same idea pre-dated Schoenberg by sixty-eight years.)

Wagner's debt to Liszt is evident even in Wagner's most famous chord – so famous, in fact, that it has its own name. Whole books have been written about it and academics have built careers on it. It is called the 'Tristan' chord. The Tristan chord comes from Wagner's opera *Tristan und Isolde*, and while it has been accorded the kind of mystique and reverence usually reserved for Newton's First Law or Einstein's Special Theory of Relativity, it is, when all is said and done – wait for it – a diminished chord.

It has been credited, the humble Tristan chord, with signalling the end of four hundred years of order in Western harmony and the beginning of modernity – a bold claim, to say the least, and even bolder considering Liszt had been using this chord, and many others of its ilk, for years before Wagner wrote it into the opening phrase of *Tristan und Isolde* some time between 1857 and 1859.

Notwithstanding Wagner's debt to Liszt, it would be churlish not to stress that the greatest composers have always tended to synthesise the styles and currents of their time, that they were not necessarily innovators, and Wagner's music in any case has far better tunes than Liszt's. *Tristan und Isolde* is an out-and-out masterpiece, with sweeping, yearning themes, deserving of its place in music's pantheon, whatever it may or may not have innovated. As a musical experience it is luxuriant and overwhelming, and has the two greatest build-ups to a climax in all music (only one of which is consummated, as it were; the first veers off at the last moment). What it is not, though, is the one thing that Wagner most wanted to bring to the world: musical drama. Clara Wieck Schumann saw the opera in Munich in 1875 and her summary says it all: 'During the entire Second Act the two of them sleep and sing; through the entire last act – for fully forty minutes – Tristan dies. They call that dramatic!!!' (Like Verdi's *La Traviata*, twelve years earlier, *Tristan* is about a doomed love affair, death and destiny. Of course.)

The relative inertia of *Tristan*'s plot, with so little action taking place over nearly six hours in the theatre, makes it closer in form to an extended symphonic poem with singing than even Wagner's other operas. It is the most extreme example in his catalogue of another striking hallmark of his style. It is *not* Italian.

For a good part of the eighteenth and all of the nineteenth century, the populist, light, tuneful Italian style of opera was what most people went to an opera house for. Italian style in opera was completely dominant. So much so that even an Austrian composer like Mozart should really be seen, stylistically, as a German-speaking Italian. All but one of his famous operas is literally Italian, from *The Marriage of Figaro* and *Così fan tutte* to *La Clemenza di*

Tito and *Don Giovanni*. (The exception is his German 'singing play', *The Magic Flute*.) The other centre of operatic style in the nineteenth century was Paris, though French opera at that time was essentially a grander version of Italian opera. Wagner did not fit either of these moulds. Indeed, one of the reasons musicians from all over Europe flocked to hear Wagner's music dramas at Bayreuth in the 1870s was because they were so radically out of step with the mainstream. Notwithstanding his debt to Liszt, Wagner's sound was, to them, incredibly daring and original. The essence of that originality was to take what composers normally did in symphonies – long, abstract, streams of 'pure' instrumental music – and turn it into a sung drama on stage. Even the *idea* of attempting this was bracingly novel.

Despite the fact that Wagner had learnt his trade writing pseudo-Italian operas, by the time he reached his maturity, he had moved decisively and deliberately away from an Italian style. Instead of a series of clearly defined solos, called *arias*, narrative prose-like singing that carried the plot, called *arioso*, duets, and sweeping choruses, with a bit of ballet thrown in, as was the Italian way, Wagner preferred a continuous musical flow, with all those elements mixed in together. Thus an Italian opera, typically, was a series of well-defined 'numbers', a glorified variety show, with something for everyone and plenty of opportunity for lead singers to have their turn at impressing the audience. A showy solo in an Italian opera might elicit spontaneous applause and even encores. Such a reaction at a Wagner performance would have been considered blasphemous – to dare to interrupt the master's unstoppable narrative flow. For Wagner, nothing was allowed to distract from the unfolding musical story and he would happily intertwine chorus, solo, duets, instrumental interludes so that you could hardly tell when one ended and another began.

The other bonus of this approach, as far as he was concerned, was that it treated the symphony, not other operas, as a structural starting point. Whereas opera in his lifetime was dominated by Italians and Frenchmen, the symphony was still considered the quintessential *German* form (the Austrians being honorary Germans, in his and many others' minds). In his many hundreds of pamphlets, articles, books and letters, Wagner's contempt for the French was second only to his hatred of the Jews, seeing both as a threat to Germany's destiny, which was to lead Europe and impose an ethnically cleansed culture upon it. Inventing a uniquely German form of opera, therefore, for Wagner, was a political choice.

A nationalistic approach also began informing his choice of subject matter, especially after the Germans defeated the French in the Franco-Prussian War of 1870–71. Wagner aimed to honour a resurgent German Reich and he seized the moment to sell the idea, in his next batch of operas, of an invincible race of Aryan superheroes put to the test against various human or supernatural foes. Some of his operas even reinvented Germany's medieval past. In *Tannhäuser*, *Lohengrin* and *The Mastersingers of Nuremberg* he reworked ancient legend-fables so that his contemporaries would be uplifted by the chivalric pride inherent in the tales. The cod-historic world of these operas is one in which Teutonic moral strength is associated with poetry and lusty singing, of which there is an enormous amount, Wagner being a stranger to the notion of musical restraint.

This wasn't a unique experiment, though, and nor was patriotic heroism confined to music. Over the North Sea in Britain's Victorian empire, artists, writers and composers were dredging Albion's Arthurian roots, too. The Pre-Raphaelite group of painters were particularly fond of their St Georges, Sir Galahads and Ladies of the Lake in spotless glistening armour or see-through negligées, as captured, for example, in Edward Burne-Jones's *Sir Galahad* (1858), *Saint George and the Dragon* (1868) and *The Last Sleep of Arthur* (1881–8), Emma Sandys's *Elaine* (1865), John Everett Millais's *The Knight Errant* (1870), John William Waterhouse's *The Lady of Shalott* (1888), Dante Gabriel Rossetti's *Sir Launcelot in the Queen's Chamber* (1857) and *Before the Battle* (1858), and the model in that picture, artist Elizabeth Siddal's *The Lady of Shalott* (1853) and *The Quest of the Holy Grail, or Sir Galahad at the Shrine of the Holy Grail* (1857).

The unprecedented international popularity of historical fiction such as Sir Walter Scott's *Lady of the Lake* (1810), *Waverley* (1814), *Rob Roy* (1817) and *Ivanhoe* (1820), and the comparing of Britannia's invincibility with the legends and deeds of dragon-busting knights, inspired many an overture, play, pageant or opera. Sir Arthur Sullivan, whose comic operettas written with W. S. Gilbert success-fully lampooned Victorian pomposity, wrote one serious opera, *Ivanhoe* (1891). As suitable subject matter for Wagner, never mind Sullivan, Scott's legend of Ivanhoe ticked nearly all the boxes, telling as it does the struggle, in 1194, in the aftermath of the Third Crusade, of a noble Saxon against nasty Norman Frenchmen. But that it also concerns itself with unfair treatment of England's medieval Jewish population would have ruled it out for the arch anti-Semite Wagner.

When they are not concerned with mythical Teutonic heroism, Wagner's music dramas focus on sacrifice and self-denial, like *Tristan und Isolde* and *Parsifal*, or they tackle the inevitability of the corruption of power – or all of the above at once, as is the case in his monumental four-opera cycle, *The Ring of the Nibelung*.

It took Wagner twenty-six years to create his *Ring* cycle, completed in 1874. It is far and away the most ambitious undertaking in the history of European music. What's more, he wrote the libretto as well as the music, and drew up the specifications of the purpose-built theatre at Bayreuth in which it was to be performed. His aim was to produce nothing less than a modern equivalent of the drama of the Ancient Greeks. Works like Aeschylus's *Oresteia* trilogy had hoped to distil and dramatise the experiences of a whole society and this is what Wagner meant to do for his: a recently unified Germany still finding its feet as a modern nation. He sifted through many sources for his material but in the main he concentrated on a set of ancient Icelandic documents known as the *Eddas*. He mixed in various plot lines from Austrian, Norwegian and German sagas, and set about moulding them into a coherent dramatic whole.

The plot initially hinges on the idea that the love of gold leads to corruption and disaster, but it soon becomes embroiled in the legend of Siegfried, an innocent, brave nature man who sacrifices his life for the common good and has an incestuous relationship with his aunt. The story, spread over the four separate operas, begins with the theft of a precious Golden Ring from the depths of the River Rhine, which represents indomitable, deathless Germany. Along the way, there is internecine strife between the gods and some flying Hell's Angels, the magnificently apocalyptic Valkyries. The Valkyries, with their leader Brünnhilde, are the warrior daughters of Wotan, a Zeus-like overlord, and have the second opera of the sequence named after them. Their job is to fly around the world picking up dead warriors to act – when resurrected – as bodyguards for the gods' home of Valhalla. So they are airborne undertakers, in a way.

In the final opera of the four, *The Twilight of the Gods*, Wagner made mayhem with the Icelandic concept of *Ragnarok* – the destruction of the gods as preordained by fate. Valhalla is razed to the ground in a staggering climax, which includes Brünnhilde riding her flying horse into the flames and the Rhinemaiden mermaids leaping out of the overflowing river and reclaiming their stolen Golden Ring.

Wagner's vision was the product of a restless, angry age. All Europe was reeling from the implications of Charles Darwin's two shattering books, *On the Origin of Species* (1859) and *The Descent of Man* (1871). Darwin himself had come hard on the heels of Charles Lyell's *Principles of Geology* (1830–33), in which he showed that the world had not begun with a single act of creation, and Ernest Renan's *Life of Jesus* (1863), which questioned the Bible as historical truth. God himself, it was now being suggested, had been made in man's image, and not the other way round. This idea is now a commonplace, but in the middle of the nineteenth century its effect was devastating, not dissimilar to the revelation five centuries earlier that the earth travelled round the sun and not vice versa. So, in a monumental piece of symbolism that defined his age, at the end of the *Ring* Wagner annihilated the gods altogether in his musical Armageddon. That said, it is only fair to point out that Wagner's keenest interest was not the fate of the gods but rather what happened to humanity.

Without God, without judgement, without fear of retribution, mankind's biggest bullies could now, in theory, rule supreme. The formidable advance of science and technology in Wagner's time, instead of making people confident and liberated, made them fearful and vulnerable, ripe for exploitation. Throughout Europe, industrial capitalism, coupled with military force on a frightening scale, loomed ominously. It seemed to many, including Karl Marx who published the first part of *Das Kapital* in 1867, to promote nothing but widespread poverty, inequality and hopelessness.

The power of much of the *Ring*'s music reflects this dark, foreboding image of industrial might: during the first opera, *The Rhinegold*, we are taken down into the depths of a menacing and fiery mine, with dehumanised workers slaving to extract gold. Other artists shared this sense of despondency. The French writer Emile Zola, for example, thought that the Industrial Age had brought to working people untold misery and cruelty. The vast, devouring machine of technology in Zola's *Germinal*, set in a grim coal-mining landscape with money-crazed bosses brutally abusing their workers and treating their women as little more than sex slaves, finds considerable resonance in the *Ring*. Zola himself also embarked upon a project as vast and all-encompassing as Wagner's *Ring*, a twenty-book epic called *Les Rougon-Macquart*, which follows the fortunes of a family living in mid-nineteenth-century France.

But the greatest single influence on the *Ring* cycle – and indeed on two of Wagner's other operas, *Tristan und Isolde* and *Parsifal* – was not Karl Marx or Charles Darwin but rather the German philosopher Arthur Schopenhauer. Schopenhauer's theories, like Wagner's operas, could not be described as succinct, and they are consequently hard to summarise briefly, but the idea that caught Wagner's imagination was that we humans are essentially irrational, emotional animals. As Zola also sought to demonstrate in

Les Rougon-Macquart, the trajectory of our lives is predetermined by our genetic inheritance. All efforts to reform or control our desires are therefore pointless. Our sexuality, our cravings and our longings totally dominate our minds, and since our appetites can never be satisfied we are always projecting our happiness into the future: we are always *preparing* to live.

In Schopenhauer's world view there is no God, no afterlife, no heaven, no redemption – just oblivion. The only way to kill off our insatiable desire is through death. One can interpret the end of the world in the *Ring*'s finale, *The Twilight of the Gods* (*Götterdämmerung*), as the destruction of greed and overbearing authority, or as a sort of Buddhist oblivion. Either way, the outcome is nothingness. According to this philosophy, Tristan's and Isolde's forbidden love (she is married to his friend Mark) can only be properly consummated in death. (Schopenhauer's deeply pessimistic outlook can also be detected in the novels of Thomas Hardy, for example *Far from the Madding Crowd*, which was completed in 1874, the same year as Wagner's *Ring*. Hardy's characters are buffeted around by their fates, over which they have absolutely no control. In the end, the good and the bad get roughly the same deal from life.)

Above all, Wagner's focus was on the *psychology* of his characters. Their actions were merely the symbolic manifestation of their deeper desires. In this respect he was pre-empting Sigmund Freud's revolutionary way of looking at the motives and behaviour of men and women. Wagner's characters were archetypes: models for Everyman. In the *Ring*, he was much more interested in what his heroes and heroines *felt* than what they *did*. As Freud was to do some years later, Wagner tackled taboo and controversy head-on. His operas are unabashed in their treatment of sexuality and eroticism, race, death and incest. All this in the 1860s and '70s.

In order to help us perceive a character's feelings or motivations, Wagner needed tools at his fingertips to be able to enrich and layer the music. One such technique is his use of fragments of melody, or rhythm, or harmony, as calling cards of a character, a place, an idea, an object or a memory. These musical cells, from which he created the whole web of the music, he called *leitmotif*. He did not invent the leitmotif, the credit for which lies squarely with the opera composer and distinguished writer E. T. A. Hoffmann, sixty-odd years earlier, and it owes a fair amount to the *idée fixe* in Berlioz's *Symphonie fantastique* too, but he did ultimately make it his own, such was the power, breadth and ingenuity with which he deployed it.

At its simplest, leitmotif is a straightforward association of a nugget of tune with a character. Every time the character appears, or is mentioned or thought of by someone else, we hear that nugget. In the *Ring*, every character has his or her own leitmotif, or signature tune. Other motifs in the story are attached to concepts, for example 'transformation' or 'love' or 'servitude', or to things, such as a 'spear', the 'gold' or the 'River Rhine'. There are in fact hundreds of leitmotifs in the *Ring*, which can be layered simultaneously on top of each other or introduced in quick succession. By the end of each opera they are cropping up at an astonishing rate, sometimes several in every bar. They become a vast tapestry on which the music and the story hang.

Thus the orchestra, instead of merely providing the musical backing for the characters to sing to, was able to express or hint at the meaning of the stage action, even in passages without singing. While in Verdi's dramas the orchestra reflected and underpinned the human drama acted out by the singers, in the *Ring* it was the opposite: what was seen on the stage was a visual representation of the music. Not content with the orchestra as inherited from the concert hall, the demands of the *Ring*'s score included instruments that needed to be especially adapted for the purpose, or even prompted the development of new instruments altogether. For example, though Verdi had used anvils as part of a gypsy chorus in his opera *Il Trovatore* in 1853, Wagner outdid him in *The Rhinegold* and *Siegfried* by employing eighteen bespoke tuned anvils – that is to say, they were calibrated to sound particular notes as determined by the score. The *Ring* also called for the invention of subsequently dubbed 'Wagner' tubas, a hybrid that combined elements of the French horn, trombone and euphonium.

To stage the *Ring*, Wagner had his own theatre erected at Bayreuth. Much about its design was revolutionary. Instead of having a distracting orchestra pit in front of the stage, he instructed his designers to hide the musicians underneath it and had their sound waft up into the auditorium. He ordered the modernisation of the stage and lighting effects, had scenery moving silently on and off sideways, had a steam curtain invented and played optical illusions with perspective to make his giants giant and his dwarfs dwarfed. Wagner's theatre was an early attempt at what we would associate with the cinema, rather than the theatre, experience. It was a darkened magic lantern show, fantastical and all-embracing. For the *Ring*'s first complete performance, Wagner decreed that the house lights should be dimmed. This was such a novelty at the time it drew gasps from the audience.

Wagner's ambition was nothing less than the creation of the art form of the future, in which all the arts would combine and fuse, led by the unequally greater power of music. The *Ring* may have aspired, through ancient myth, to explain and explore basic human instincts, yet it was still, by and large, a series of oversized operas. But having destroyed the old gods in its finale, *The Twilight of the Gods*, Wagner's next move was to found a new religion.

In his final piece, *Parsifal*, of 1882, Wagner turned the theatre into a temple, the plot into a sacramental ritual and the leitmotifs he bestowed with sacred power. Instead of calling it an opera, or even a 'music drama', Wagner omnipotently referred to *Parsifal* as 'a festival play for the consecration of the stage', insisting that the exclusive rights to perform it should remain in perpetuity at Bayreuth, other theatres and opera houses being thought unworthy of doing justice to such a precious creation. In fact, the exclusion lasted only until 1903, not the end of the world, as he had hoped.

Though this proviso may sound far-fetched, Wagner's admirers had indeed begun to see Bayreuth as a very special place, the holiest of holies, well before he embarked on *Parsifal*. Audience members saw themselves as communicants, humble supplicants at the high altar, even while Wagner was still very much flesh and blood. It is ironic that, as a young man, Wagner had raged against the arts world as a nauseating, bourgeois, elitist clique that was closed to the masses, the *Volk*, who needed its balm and illumination most. He frequently extolled the all-encompassing virtues of Ancient Greek theatre, which drew its audience 'from the government and judicial buildings, from the country, from ships, from military barracks and from the furthest regions'. *His* operas would be for the common people, at sensible, knock-down prices. *His* operas would rip to shreds the comfortable and suffocating morality of the middle classes.

The reality was that Wagner could only have a theatre built for him and his own pieces put on there thanks to the generosity of the very people he had previously so detested. And there is no opera house in the world more exclusive than Bayreuth. A few years after Wagner's death, Mark Twain gave a striking impression of what the unsuspecting visitor might expect from a visit there:

> I have seen all sorts of audiences – at theatres, operas, concerts, lectures, sermons, funerals – but none which was twin to the Wagner audience of Bayreuth for fixed and reverential attention, absolute attention and petrified retention to the end of an act of the attitude assumed at the beginning of it. This opera of 'Tristan und Isolde' last night broke the hearts of all witnesses who were of the faith, and I know of some who have heard of many who could not sleep after it, but cried the night away. I feel strongly out of place here. Sometimes I feel like the sane person in a community of the mad; sometimes I feel like the one blind man where all others see; the one groping savage in the college of the learned, and always, during service, I feel like a heretic in heaven.

George Bernard Shaw, on the other hand, was one of the adoring congregation, reporting, 'most of us at present are so helplessly under the spell of the *Ring*'s greatness that we can do nothing but go raving about the theatre between the Acts in ecstasies of deluded admiration.'

For musicians, the Wagner shrine at Bayreuth became a place of pilgrimage, sure enough, and because of the cutting-edge style of the vast, demanding music dramas mounted there, it also became a rallying point for all that was modern and progressive in music. Wagner followers gloried in the alarm his work often provoked among outsiders. The more difficult the mountain was to climb, the more avant-garde, the better, they believed. Indeed, it is possible to date the chasm that was to develop between the populist mainstream and the classical avant-garde in music to this place and time. The schism was to last over eighty years. Wagner's acolytes were happy to have retreated into their private Valhalla, where only the initiated, the learned and the bold would venture to tread. The composer Arnold Schoenberg, an admirer of the way in which Wagner seemed to mould audiences to his will, declared in 1946: 'Those who compose because they want to please others, and have audiences in mind, are not real artists.'

All religions, even musical ones, need their Eucharist, their *Pooja*, their *Shahada*, their *Pirit* – moments of high observance and ritual. Wagner provided his cult with the solemn act of devotion, purification and veneration that is *Parsifal*.

Set in medieval Spain, *Parsifal* is ostensibly a parable about the Holy Grail, the cup from which Christ drank at the Last Supper. It doesn't so much have a plot as a series of ritualistic scenes, and its imagery and context wouldn't be out of place if one stumbled across them at the secret tombs of the Knights Templar in Rennes-le-Château, on Glastonbury Tor, or in the pages of a Dan Brown novel. It is easy to pooh-pooh its symbols and magic, its Doctor-Who-like time travel and, since *Monty Python* covered the source material, it is always a struggle to see the Knights of the Holy Grail on stage without sniggering. But there is a deadly serious intent in *Parsifal*.

At its heart lies a theory Wagner drew from Schopenhauer, from Buddhism and from Christianity, that self-enlightenment, or personal redemption, is achieved by denying oneself gratification, resisting temptation and seeking an understanding of fellow-suffering. Compassion, the piece teaches, has a healing and liberating power. There is nothing mad or fanciful about this idea, and the first and third acts of *Parsifal*, the acts that take place in the Grail's mountain refuge of Montsalvat, contain music of breathtaking grandeur and beauty to match the deeply felt beliefs underpinning it. The so-called 'Transformation' music, during which the young Parsifal is taken into the castle to witness the Holy Communion of the Knights Templar, has to be one of the most awe-inspiring, heart-stopping moments in all European orchestral music. Though it is powerful, it is not triumphant; it is agonising – at its climax is a leitmotif associated with suffering. Fellow composer Gustav Mahler described hearing this as the 'greatest and most soul-wrenching experience of my life'.

Musically, *Parsifal* derives much of its seductive power from Wagner's frequent disruption of the listener's expectations. He had played with expectation and fulfilment liberally in *Tristan und Isolde*, but in that case the purpose of his harmonic delaying tactics was to portray sexual desire, arousal and consummation (or lack of it). In *Parsifal*, his agenda was spiritual rather than physical, and the technique he relied on to intoxicate the listener is called *chromaticism*.

The term 'chromaticism' comes from the Greek word for colour. It is the musical equivalent of filling a painted canvas with thousands of colours instead of just a few. This is how it works.

As we have already seen, all the world's musical systems recognise the natural and perfect relationship between a note made by plucking a string and its little brother made by plucking a string half the length: the helpfully named 'octave'. We have also seen that the number of times you subdivide the distance within this octave is up for grabs: in some cultures there can be as many as sixty subdivisions between the two, or even – theoretically at least

– three hundred and sixty, in an ancient Chinese system, but in Western and Indian classical music the distance has in recent centuries been divided into twelve steps. Western music, being more orientated towards harmony than its non-Western counterparts, gradually formed hierarchies among the twelve notes, so that the listener's ears latched on to a 'home' in the sound. It was a little bit like shaping a wild, natural landscape into identifiable patterns for the benefit of the human onlooker.

As soon as there was a centre of gravity, or a 'home' in the sound, the relationship between chords also started to coalesce into hierarchies. For Mozart or Haydn, the hierarchy of chords was so strict that the listener is never far from the 'home' key centre. As the nineteenth century progressed, though, the lure of the three governing triads, I, IV and V, began to pall and the strength of the previously well-defined chords began to blur. The more weight composers gave to the junior notes and lesser chords, the more they allowed the harmony to lose its sense of familiarity, reassurance and comfort. It was a deliberate attempt to make harmony sound unstable and more exotic in flavour. By the time of Liszt and Wagner, the hierarchies were all but gone.

In the opening prelude of *Parsifal*'s third act, the music shifts and slides around, avoiding settling on one key or chord for more than one beat. This is extreme chromaticism at work. You are *meant* to feel disorientated and in the grip of mysterious powers. The harmony is in meltdown because Wagner has used chromaticism, the promiscuous use of all the subdivisions in the scale, to put you in an unsettling place. As it happens, that place is the Temple of the Holy Grail, Montsalvat, and the atmosphere is tense and unresolved.

As an intriguing footnote to the rich world of chromaticism, the Russian composer Alexander Scriabin, who was ten years old when *Parsifal* opened, took the 'colour of notes' idea to a whole new level in theories he developed from around 1907 onwards. He assigned each of the twelve notes in the scale a different colour, based on *Opticks*, Sir Isaac Newton's 1704 study of light, colour and diffraction. He also helped his friend, chemist and electrical engineer Aleksandr Mozer, invent a light-projecting colour organ, the 'Chromola' (also known as the *clavier à lumières* or *tastiera di luce*), which could 'play' the coloured lights corresponding to the twelve notes of a keyboard, as directed by Scriabin's score. Part of this contraption, looking dare I say it like something that has fallen off a stall at a fair, is preserved in the Scriabin Museum in Moscow.

Scriabin's music, as heard in his complex *Prometheus: Poem of Fire* (1910), is highly idiosyncratic, not to say hallucinogenic, like an intermingled Chopin and Debussy, with *Parsifal* and Stravinsky's *The Firebird* being played simultaneously in the background. Scriabin was born on Christmas Day and died at Easter, and rather aptly toyed with the idea that he might be the reincarnation of Christ, once writing, 'I am God. I am nothing, I am play, I am freedom, I am life. I am the boundary, I am the peak.' Wagner wasn't the only one who believed music and mysticism could fuse to become the religion of the future.

As for Wagner, he was at pains to point out in his autobiography the symbolism of his having had the idea for an opera of the Parsifal legend on Good Friday: 'I suddenly remembered that the day was Good Friday, and I called to mind the significance this omen had already once assumed for me when I was reading Wolfram's *Parsifal* . . . its noble possibilities struck me with over-whelming force, and out of my thoughts about Good Friday I rapidly conceived a whole drama, of which I made a rough sketch with a few dashes of the pen, dividing the whole into three acts.' With its heady concoction of chromaticism, rich, sweeping orchestral landscapes, ethereal musical representations of heavenly bliss, its highly developed leitmotifs and its fervent invocation of compassion and enlightenment, *Parsifal* is undoubtedly the work of a mountainous talent sincerely seeking to give meaning to life and the world around him. A fairly typical summary of the thousands of pages of reverential prose that it prompted when first performed is that of Charles Albert Lidgey, whose 1899 book on Wagner concluded, 'As the "Ring" is the embodiment of human Love, so is "Parsifal" the expression of the Love Divine. "Parsifal", in truth, is not a drama – it is a religious ceremony. It is one of those works from which the cold lance of criticism glances without piercing . . . It is more seemly to regard it as the last message to his fellow-creatures of a man who laboured with all his strength to propagate the noble truth – Love is of God. As such let us honour both it and its author.'

There is, however, another side to the philosophy driving *Parsifal*, and it is a side that for some Wagner worshippers flipped a switch.

It is not possible to sidestep the fact that the climax of this Crusader story homes in on the magical properties of the spear that allegedly pierced the side of the crucified Jesus of Nazareth (only ever referred to as the 'Redeemer' in the text). The 'pure' blood of Christ, the Holy Grail containing it, and the sacrificial significance of Good Friday are all presented as both real and miraculous. The holy blood itself is seen as purifying: purging the evil, the weak and the sinful. Plotting against the innocent Christian Parsifal is the Darth Vader of the tale, a malicious sorcerer called Klingsor whose magic garden lies in the Arabic south of Spain and who – until the 1950s – was typically portrayed in *Parsifal* productions as of Arabic or Jewish origin.

Klingsor, who has castrated himself, is accompanied by a possessed shape-shifter, Kundry, a reincarnation of the cursed Jewish princess Herodias. Klingsor forces Kundry to seduce Parsifal in the hope of contaminating his purity. She enlists the help of her teenage 'daughters', the Flower Maidens, in her task of sexual entrapment. The much-abused Kundry, having converted to Christianity at the last moment and been duly released from the curse that has trapped her in time, is then killed off at the moment the 'pure' Parsifal becomes chief protector of the Grail, blessed by a dove from heaven. Her final humiliation and the triumph of the Aryan hero Parsifal were not very subtly concealed metaphors for what Wagner wanted to happen to German culture. Two years earlier he had baldly compared 'the superiority of the revelation through Jesus Christ to that through Abraham and Moses'. He may have died seven months after the opening of *Parsifal*, but tragically the toxic legacy of his views on Aryan supremacy did not.

Although Wagner regarded all foreign influences as potentially threatening to German purity, he singled out the Jews for particular venom. Unfortunately, in nineteenth-century Europe, anti-Semitism was rampant, but Wagner's views were excessive even by the standards of the time. His fanaticism partly stemmed from his own experiences of being a struggling opera composer in his earlier career, in Paris, where he developed a personal loathing for the most successful of the grand opera composers of the moment, Giacomo Meyerbeer. It was also stoked by his reading *The Inequality of Human Races* by Frenchman J. Arthur Gobineau, in the 1850s, in which Gobineau declared the superiority of the white European and coined the idea of 'degenerate' or inferior, impure races. Gradually Wagner adopted a virulently anti-Semitic attitude that polluted his views on almost everything. His avowed agenda was to give the Germans a sense of their historical destiny through the arts. To fulfil this destiny, as he conceived it, he believed that it would be necessary to remove all Jews – and all trace of Jewish culture – from the German Reich.

He was not alone in wishing this outcome. Three years after *Parsifal* opened, in 1885, German Chancellor Bismarck legislated to expel all Jews and Poles from the Prussian Reich; within forty years this ultra-German nationalism evolved into the cancerous ideology of Nazism. It's no good pretending Wagner wasn't accessory to this slide into xenophobic vitriol. In one of his many inflammatory publications, *Erkenne dich selbst* (Know Thyself) of 1881, he urged the German *Volk* to awaken and bring about a 'great solution' to the Jews' 'now so dreaded power among and over us': their eradication. On another occasion he 'joked' that all Jews should be herded into a theatre, for a performance of Gotthold Ephraim Lessing's 1779 play *Nathan the Wise*, set during the Third Crusade and calling for religious tolerance, and immolated.

Wagner could not, of course, have predicted that the Nazis would take him at his word, nor that Hitler would one day proclaim, 'Whoever wants to understand National Socialist Germany must know Wagner', or, 'I intend to base my religion on the Parsifal legend.' But there is no doubt that the Nazi top brass treated Bayreuth as a shrine. They were welcomed with open arms by Wagner's surviving family members; there was even a suggestion that Hitler, known as 'Uncle Wolf' by the Wagner children, might have proposed marriage to Winifred Wagner, the composer's English daughter-in-law. Bayreuth, in fact, had become Montsalvat itself, the mountain-top resting place of the Holy Grail, the high temple of Aryan culture. Joseph Goebbels, head of the Nazi propaganda ministry, idolised *Parsifal*, which was put on twenty-three times at Berlin's Deutsche Oper alone during the period of the Third Reich. (The 1938 production witnessed the début of young soprano Elisabeth Schwarzkopf as a Flower Maiden. Schwarzkopf, darling of the Reich's culture department, later allegedly took the SS General and Nazi Governor of Lower Austria, Dr Hugo Jury, as her lover. He committed suicide on the day of the German surrender; her career never looked back.) New productions of *Parsifal* were mounted at Bayreuth in 1934 and 1937, though revivals of it were suspended during the war so as to spare the war-wounded the insensitivity of scenes involving the wounded knight Amfortas. Propaganda images in Nazi Germany variously depicted the Führer as a Montsalvat knight, or indeed as Parsifal himself, with the dove of benediction hovering above him.

Fully understanding the racial implications of *Parsifal*'s message and its pre-eminence in Nazi ideology, it is uncomfortable for us to hear Wagner's sublime music without wincing. In one way, this became the most dangerous music ever written, because, despite being motivated by a devotion to self-denial and compassion, it undoubtedly inspired hatred.

Wagner's influence on the other, non-musical, arts was considerable. During his lifetime alone over ten thousand books and articles were written about him. The painter Renoir asked if he could paint a portrait of him and crossed Europe to do so. Picasso made a drawing in response to *Parsifal* in 1934, a precursor to his world-famous *Guernica*. D. H. Lawrence wrote a novel, *The Trespasser*, which was inspired by Wagner's version of Siegfried. Poets, philosophers and playwrights gushed and paid homage to him, including T. S. Eliot, James Joyce and Oscar Wilde, whose sinister Dorian Gray was an early Wagnerite.

Despite all this, his immediate effect on other *composers* was patchy. Though they were blown away by what he was attempting, very few followed his example into through-composed music drama, except the one-hit-wonder German composer of the opera *Hansel and Gretel*, Engelbert Humperdinck. French composer Jules Massenet wrote a *Parsifal*-inspired medieval epic for the opening of the Great Paris Exposition of 1889 called *Esclarmonde*, complete with sorceress, magic sword, masked knight, dastardly Saracens, tele-transportation and a bishop and attendant group of monks performing an exorcism. But despite its scale and mystic pretensions, *Esclarmonde* is musically only fleetingly Wagnerian in its biggest orchestral moments, following instead in the French grand opera tradition of Massenet's twenty-five other operas, with gigantic triumphant choruses, pipe organ, and a lead soprano required to sing an almost impossible series of high, 'coloratura' virtuoso solos. The latter, never mind everything else about Massenet, would have been anathema to drama-obsessed Wagner. Meanwhile, Czech composer Zdeněk Fibich trotted out three pseudo-Wagnerian operas in the 1890s, *Hedy*, *Šárka* and *Pád Arkuna*, much to the irritation of his anti-German Czech compatriots, and an Englishman, Rutland Boughton, set up what he hoped would be a British Bayreuth at Glastonbury, complete with grand (though low-budget) Arthurian music dramas, a festival that ran from 1914 to 1926.

Even Boughton, though, whose fairy opera *The Immortal Hour* opened at Glastonbury twenty-two days after the British Empire declared war on Germany in August 1914, didn't emulate Wagner's musical style. He found stimulus in Anglo-Celtic folk music instead.

The Glastonbury Festival's future wasn't exactly Bavarian chic and hushed reverence either.

It is not so far-fetched to suggest that, without his link to the Nazis, most people who were not hardcore opera lovers would by now have lost interest in Wagner. That may sound harsh, but the evidence of Wagner's musical impact is nothing like as convincing as his disciples would have us believe. Everywhere you look in the 1880s, outside Bayreuth, you see composers carrying on as if nothing had happened.

Even relatively nearby, in Vienna, Brahms ploughed his symphonic furrow, stylistically unaffected by the Bayreuth hurricanes. Brahms, admittedly a complex personality himself whose music resolutely resisted the modernising currents that hovered around him in his later years, never quite came to terms with the open hostility Wagner always showed him and his music. The problem was that Wagner felt that writing symphonies was no longer a worthwhile pursuit. In his mind, all art had been subsumed into his 'new' form of music drama. He once wrote scornfully in an article, 'On Poetry & Composition', of Brahms's attempts to add to Beethoven's hallowed nine symphonies, 'I know of some famous composers who in their concert masquerades don the disguise of a street singer one day, the hallelujah periwig of Handel the next, the dress of a Jewish Csardas-fiddler another time, and then again the guise of a highly respectable symphony dressed up as Number Ten.'

Brahms completed his majestic, abundantly tuneful, highly respectable third symphony a few months after Wagner's death; its first performance, by the Vienna Philharmonic Orchestra in December 1883, was disrupted by Wagnerite hecklers but it was nevertheless well received by everyone else. On Brahms's death, four years later, the English composer Charles Hubert Parry wrote an 'Elegy for Brahms', one of the loveliest tributes ever paid by one composer to another and a stylistic homage that acknowledges the deep and lasting impact the *Poco Allegretto* (third) movement of Brahms's third symphony had made. In Britain, Parry's Brahmsian lead was followed with conspicuous success by Edward

Elgar. Listening to his *Enigma Variations* of 1899 or his first symphony of 1908, which Elgar openly admitted was modelled on Brahms's third symphony, it is as if the whole Wagner experiment had happened in a vacuum.

While Brahms held his nerve against the Wagnerian tide, however, his fellow symphonist Anton Bruckner did not, his numbingly long nine symphonies reflecting in various degrees his adoration of the man he unselfconsciously called 'The Master'. Bruckner's third symphony of 1873 was dedicated to Wagner and in its first version contained melodic quotations from his idol's operas. His seventh symphony received its première at a Wagner memorial concert in December 1884, its second movement, *Adagio*, being in the form of a funeral lament for Wagner. (One has to wonder whether Bruckner's obsession with Wagner's music dramas was in part motivated by a voyeuristic attachment to the sexual content in them, particularly the *Ring* cycle and *Parsifal*. As a lifelong bachelor with an erotic appetite focused exclusively on young girls – whom he continued to stalk, observe and proposition even into his seventies – the mental image of the seductive Flower Maidens in *Parsifal* must have enhanced his guilty pleasure in the music no end.)

Bruckner aside, most of Wagner's contemporaries, while quick to assert his musical brilliance, were as at sea with the whole Wagner-and-the-future-of-all-art project as they were with the cultural agendas of his dramas. Tchaikovsky described *Parsifal* as 'inconceivable nonsense', Wagner's services to opera 'of a negative kind' and, commenting on the overall impact of his works, 'as regards the dramatic interest of his operas, I find them very poor, often childishly naive'. Debussy had this to say on his legacy: 'All that remains will be beautiful ruins in whose shadows our grandchildren will dream of the former greatness of this man who was under-endowed only in humanity to be truly great.'

After Wagner's death, Verdi, now in his seventies, produced two final operatic triumphs, both based on Shakespeare plays: *Otello* (1887) and his only comedy, *Falstaff* (1893). As with Elgar, it is as if Wagner had never existed. Perhaps it is even more remarkable in Verdi's case, since his was the field of musical theatre, so transformed, or so it was claimed, by the Bayreuth 'revolution'. The two composers, both born in 1813, had pursued parallel but quite separate careers in opera. Wagner's attitude to his Italian rival can be ascertained by his writing a four-hundred-page survey of the state of their chosen art, *Opera and Drama*, in 1851, without once mentioning the most famous living composer in the form at the time. For his part, Verdi spoke nothing but praise about his acid-tongued contemporary, writing that *Tristan und Isolde* was 'one of the finest creations that has ever issued from a human mind'.

Wagner apart, there was certainly no evidence that Verdi's style had become unfashionable or was deemed old-fashioned by opera lovers in the sixteen-year gap between *Aida* (1871) and *Otello*, nor in the six further years before the unveiling of *Falstaff*. *Falstaff*'s première at Milan's La Scala in February 1893 was particularly successful, and was followed within months by equally rapturous openings in Vienna (conducted by Gustav Mahler), Paris, Hamburg, London and New York. Its sparkling score has a light-hearted family resemblance to the Italian-style operas of Mozart, fond nods and winks to his own colourful back catalogue, and even – I venture – a trace of Gilbert and Sullivan's *The Yeomen of the Guard* of five years earlier, doubtless in tongue-in-cheek recognition of the opera's subject matter. But what there is *not* is an echo of anything remotely Wagnerian. Old Giuseppe was doubtless heeding the advice of his lead character Sir John Falstaff, '*Va, vecchio John, va, va per la tua via*' (Go, old Jack, go your own way).

It was understandable that Wagner might want to speculate about the art world of the future, one that would encompass within it all the arts, centred on human dramas of love, death and destiny. But it wasn't to be *his* vision that fulfilled the promise. Motion pictures were to be the artwork of the future, a technological breakthrough that stuttered into life just after his death, the first ever moving picture, Louis Le Prince's *Roundhay Garden Scene*, dating from 1888.

No. Wagner's main contribution to the music that followed him was that all the key composers of the next thirty years, particularly in France, Russia and the New World, were inspired not to emulate him, but to contradict, repudiate and sidestep him. These negative responses to his legacy were to blow music apart. An age of revolution, as radical and savage as anything he might have imagined, was just around the corner.

6

The Age of Rebellion
1890–1918

In the thirty-one years between the death of Richard Wagner in 1883 and the outbreak of the First World War, music was shaken by a series of gigantic convulsions, fundamentally reshaping its sound, its function and its attitude. Much of the impetus for these changes came from places and people whose voices had not yet been heard on the world stage. For all their pre-eminence in the eighteenth and nineteenth centuries, composers from Austria and Germany would soon be competing for attention with a kaleidoscope of musical stars from elsewhere, notably Russia, France and the USA.

Aside from developments in music, the spotlight of history would shift dramatically towards Russia as the new century dawned, and to the growing industrial might and territorial expansion of the USA, which in the same period added over a dozen new states to its size. Though the period saw the high-water mark of the oversized, increasingly ungovernable European colonial empires (British, Austro-Hungarian, Russian and, to a lesser extent, German, French, Portuguese, Spanish and Dutch), and for many (white) citizens of these empires life had never been more luxurious, pleasurable or decadent – fertile conditions for the blossoming of musical activity – cracks were beginning to show. The Pax Britannica, for example, was maintained by the fighting of multiple colonial campaigns in South Africa, Bechuanaland (Botswana), Nigeria, Sudan, Zanzibar, Ashanti (Ghana), Afghanistan, the Indian North-West Frontier,

Burma, Tibet, China and Venezuela, and all European cities were liable to terrorist outrages perpetrated by anarchists and separatists whose catalogue of assassinations would eventually trigger the First World War. The rebellions that were to shake music, however, were almost entirely divorced from political realities. Even the October Revolution in Russia in 1905, an event with thunderously far-reaching implications for society at large, had minimal impact on the contemporaneous upheavals in music.

Music's battles were about direction of travel. Where could Western music go once – as it seemed at the end of the nineteenth century – all possibilities of the existing system of twelve notes and key-families had reached saturation point? Though composers were divided on whether to follow the 'total art-form' experiment of Richard Wagner, or the extreme chromaticism of parts of *Parsifal*, or his building of large musical structures by the manipulation of small cell 'motifs', all were agreed that his Bayreuth revolution was a watershed that had to be responded to one way or another.

Russian composers like Tchaikovsky mostly treated the brouhaha surrounding Wagner's music dramas with disdain. César Cui wrote to fellow composer Nikolai Rimsky-Korsakov, 'Wagner is a man devoid of all talent. His melodies, where they are found at all, are in worse taste than Verdi . . . All this is covered up with a thick layer of rot. His orchestra is decorative, but coarse. The violins squeal throughout on the highest notes and throw the listener into a state of extreme nervousness. I left without waiting for the concert to end, and I assure you that had I stayed longer, both I and my wife would have had a fit of hysterics.'[3] Stravinsky's view, having seen *Parsifal*, was equally scathing: 'What I find revolting in the whole affair is the underlying conception which dictated it – the principle of putting a work of art on the same level as the sacred and symbolic ritual which institutes a religious service. And,

3 Letter from Cui dated 9 March 1863, quoted in Nicolas Slonimsky, *Lexicon of Musical Invective*, 2nd ed. (University of Washington Press, 1969), pp. 230–31.

indeed, is not all this comedy of Bayreuth, with its ridiculous formalities, simply an unconscious aping of a religious rite?'[4]

The most extreme response to Wagner's music, though, came from France, where it became for many musicians a matter of patriotic duty to spurn the musical fruits of the country that had humiliated them in the Franco-Prussian War of 1870–71, and where an entirely alternative musical approach was developing. The Société Nationale de Musique, a club with the motto '*Ars Gallica*', was symbolically launched during the German bombardment of Paris with the express aim of promoting a French style that would carve out a non-German identity. Even without the provocation of his German flag-waving, most French composers took a dim view of Wagner – and in any case they had their own pacesetters to follow: Camille Saint-Saëns and César Franck, two of the co-founders of the Société Nationale de Musique, and between them mentors to virtually all the post-Wagner generation of French composers. Despite attempting opera, not very successfully, and composing a symphony that reasserted the possibilities of the form in France (where it had become neglected in favour of grand opera), Belgian-born Franck's main contribution to French music was in the field of chamber music. Here, the delicacy and economy of his style, in sharp contrast to the grandiose scale of so much of the music of the second half of the nineteenth century, was to be an inspiration to his pupils and protégés.

If the French revered any German composer, it wasn't Wagner but Bach. When they began to tire of the excesses and sentimentality of their own nineteenth-century grand operas, never mind everyone else's, they went back to Bach for inspiration. They loved his clarity, his neatness and his formal discipline. When the crowd-pulling Charles-Marie Widor played his new organ Symphony no. 5 (from which the celebrated 'Toccata' comes) at the Palais du Trocadéro as part of the great Parisian World Fair of 1889, the only other composer on the programme was Bach. Like Widor,

4 Igor Stravinsky, *Igor Stravinsky: An Autobiography* (Norton, 1962), p. 39.

Franck and Saint-Saëns were both expert organists, and learning the organ, then as now, meant learning Bach inside out. Saint-Saëns's music is particularly Bachian, parts of his piano concerto no. 2 (1868) being at times close to pastiche.

Saint-Saëns's most distinguished student was Gabriel Fauré, who, as well as being exposed by his mentor to what was then considered the modern work of Schumann and Liszt, had a thorough grounding in plainchant and sacred choral music. The simple but meandering melodic lines of plainsong were to exert a considerable influence on his composing style as he matured. Above all, Fauré had the confidence to turn his antipathy towards the many-layered complexity of Wagner's music dramas into a much purer, emotionally restrained sound. Even his student compositions, such as the ravishing *Cantique de Jean Racine* (1865) for choir and organ, served notice of an unequivocal change of direction away from lush excess, paving the way for the effortlessly tranquil beauty of his *Requiem*, completed twenty-three years later. Listening to Fauré after Brahms, Liszt, Wagner or Tchaikovsky is comparable to someone spring-cleaning and redecorating a teenage boy's bedroom. Gone are the posters of death, psychological torment, superheroes and tragedy. The augmented piles of clothes have been put away, and the windows have been opened to dispel the diminished air. Fauré's exquisite, modest music, from his lilting *Pavane* for small orchestra (1887) to the song cycle *La Bonne chanson* (1894), composed to express his secret love for Emma Bardac (they were both married at the time), sounds as if it might have been written on a different planet from the one that housed Wagner's Bayreuth. Which was, of course, the idea.

An even more radical rejection of complexity can be heard in the piano miniatures of Erik Satie, Fauré's eccentric, half-English contemporary. His first *Gymnopédie* of 1888, as well as sounding like a long, hot afternoon in the Midi after a liquid lunch, can be seen as a deliberate attempt to debunk pomposity and de-clutter music. Described (rather unfairly) by his tutors at the Paris Conservatoire as the 'laziest student ever', Satie was a free-thinking intellectual whose obsessions ranged from Ancient Greece to the novels of Gustave Flaubert, and who preferred to spend his time with painters and poets in Montmartre than among other musicians. His intense fascination with the straight lines of Gothic architecture may also have contributed to the ultra-simple structures of his *Gymnopédies* and *Gnossiennes* of the following year.

No one tried harder than Satie to puncture the pretension of Bayreuth, even if his rejection of the Wagner legacy may have been at times rather puerile. In 1891 he announced the première of his new opera, *Tristan's Bastard*, poking fun at Wagner. It was a hoax. Two years later he founded his own church, *Eglise Métropolitaine d'Art de Jésus Conducteur* (The Metropolitan Church of Art of Christ the Leader), appointing himself as its only priest. (He was also its only member.) But Wagner wasn't the only composer who was guilty of creating unnecessary clutter in the eyes of an iconoclast like Satie. French composers of the melodramatic grand opera school – Jules Massenet and Charles Gounod, for example – were just as much a target for his often facetious pen. In 1916 Satie concocted a baldly insulting parody of themes from Gounod's opera *Mireille*, and several of his cabaret songs make fun of Massenet's supposed sentimentality.

All in all, French composers' attitudes to the vainglorious ritual of the Wagnerian spectacle, whether it was frivolous like Satie's, or philosophical like Fauré's, led to a new spirit in their music, soon to be dominated by the sensuous modernity of Claude Debussy and Maurice Ravel. Francis Poulenc neatly summed up the prevailing French ambivalence towards Wagner by saying that, after listening to him, it was necessary to cleanse one's spirit and ears by listening to Mozart.

Wagner might have expected the French, whose opera he despised, to rebel against his stylistic leadership; he would have been far more disturbed by the betrayal of German cultural supremacy embarked upon by the most distinguished Director of Music of the Vienna State Opera in its history, Gustav Mahler.

Mahler was born into a Bohemian corner of the Austrian Empire, into a German-speaking Jewish community of about a thousand souls whose existence was entirely wiped from the map during the Holocaust. It is a painful irony that, as Europe's leading opera conductor in the late-nineteenth century, this most Jewish of composers should have been such a fervent champion of the works of music's most notorious anti-Semite, Richard Wagner. Indeed, his own music, to some extent, takes over from where Wagner's *Parsifal* left off – although, like Liszt, Mahler had a thoroughly cosmopolitan, non-nationalistic outlook and career.

As a Bohemian subject of the Austrian Empire, as a poor boy in a profession full of the privileged, as a Jew working in an overwhelmingly Catholic culture, it's not surprising that Mahler should have sought comfort by identifying with the folklore and sounds of his childhood, flavours he liberally sprinkled throughout his ten completed symphonies. These include strolling klezmer (Jewish folk band) musicians, passing military bands and lusty children's choruses.

Though he was inevitably drawn to the musical metropolis of Vienna, and there is more than a little of the *gemütlich* charm of the Viennese in Mahler's music, occasional whiffs of marzipan cake and the swish of the waltz alongside rustic mountain dances, what Mahler did was absorb influences from just about the whole continent. He was a sort of musical embodiment of Ellis Island, with all Europe's exhausted, oppressed cultures finding refuge and a new start in his symphonic embrace. Mahler's symphonies were a new start all right: he is music's gateway to the twentieth century.

But it is not just his pan-European style that make Mahler such a paradigm for twentieth-century composers; he is also notable for the directness of his musical expression. This is encountered most conspicuously in a set of orchestral songs he composed between 1901 and 1904, the *Kindertotenlieder* (Songs on the death of children).

Even in the most heartfelt of previous composers' works – the Funeral March of Beethoven's *Eroica* symphony, for example, or the songs and piano pieces Robert Schumann wrote for love of his wife

Clara – euphemism and generic description allowed there to be a degree of detachment between the creator and listener. Thus Chopin would entitle a piano work 'Mazurka' or 'Nocturne', which might have some deep, personal emotional relevance to him as a composer – connected with a memory, a person, an atmosphere, a place in his life – but which can only be guessed at by the listener. Even the most intimate songs of Schubert, Schumann and Mendelssohn soften raw emotion with a poetic image – rejection being portrayed as an iced-up lake, or happiness as a bird singing. In the lovely, deservedly famous Schumann song 'Ich grolle nicht' (I bear no grudge) of 1840, for example, the details of the broken love affair it refers to are oblique: there is mention of diamonds unable to illuminate the lover's dark heart, and a poisonous snake with an addictive sting, and the protagonist says he will not complain even if the rupture is final. Added to the language of metaphor present in so many musical settings of art songs like 'Ich grolle nicht' was a tendency, often admittedly at the request of censors, to remove the issues and conflicts tackled in operas to a previous era or location, or to retreat into the shady world of myths and fables, gods and goddesses. In his *Ring* cycle, Wagner tackles the subjects of incest, or the abuse of power, or greed – all pertinent to nineteenth-century Europe – but transports the action to the distant mists of prehistory. It is as if his operas carry the familiar film disclaimer 'Any resemblance to real persons, living or dead, is purely coincidental'.

Mahler, on the other hand, abandoned the smokescreen of euphemism and tried to address difficult issues head-on. He did not flinch from addressing, musically, his darkest fears. The five poems by the German poet Friedrich Rückert that Mahler compiled into the *Kindertotenlieder* cycle confront any parent's most unspeakable nightmares. Rückert had written over four hundred poems in the wake of the death of his own children from scarlet fever. His appalling loss bleeds off every line of the poems and Mahler's music accordingly ranges from utterly bleak numbness, as in 'Nun will die Sonn' so hell aufgeh'n' (Now the sun wants to rise as brightly as if nothing terrible had happened during the night), to unbearable sadness, as in 'Nun seh' ich wohl, warum so dunkle Flammen', in which the dying child challenges the parent to look into her eyes, to frantic distress, as in the frighteningly turbulent 'In diesem Wetter' (In this weather, in this windy storm/I would never have sent the children out/They have been carried off,/I wasn't able to warn them).

In 1907, four years after his setting of the poems, Mahler's own five-year-old daughter Anna Maria died of scarlet fever, and he confessed to his friend Guido Adler that having lost his daughter he could not then have written *Kindertotenlieder*, the pain being too great to bear. Mahler himself was diagnosed with a terminal heart condition the year of Anna Maria's death. When he too died, in 1911, aged fifty, he was laid to rest in her grave. (His younger daughter, Anna Justine, survived the illness, became a sculptor and fled Nazi Austria for Hampstead, London, where she died in June 1988.)

The *Kindertotenlieder* cycle, and movements of Mahler's symphonies of similarly extreme vulnerability, were to inspire virtually all the giants of twentieth-century classical music, long before he was introduced to millions through recordings (in large part by Leonard Bernstein, his unstinting champion in the 1960s). One of so many examples is Shostakovich's thirteenth symphony, *Babi Yar* – the subject of which is the Nazi massacre in a Kiev ravine of 33,771 Jews over the course of forty-eight hours in September 1941 – which is stylistically unthinkable without the pervasive influence of Mahler. Other composers whose work is indebted to his include Igor Stravinsky, Arnold Schoenberg, Alban Berg, Sergei Prokofiev, Jean Sibelius, Leoš Janáček, Karol Szymanowski, Béla Bartók, Paul Hindemith, Kurt Weill, Aaron Copland, Benjamin Britten, Leonard Bernstein and, in film music, Franz Waxman, Erich Korngold, Alfred Newman, Bernard Herrmann, Miklós Rózsa, James Horner, Danny Elfman, James Newton Howard, Howard Shore, John Corigliano and John Williams.

There is no hidden agenda in Mahler's music: he felt isolated in a mean-spirited age, as many Jews did, victims in the last twenty years of the nineteenth century of widespread anti-Semitic persecution all over Europe. Mahler himself was forced out of his post at the Vienna State Opera, notwithstanding his world-class artistic success there, as a result of anti-Semitism. But despite the understandable sadness and alienation we hear in his music, there is, incredibly, hope of something better, usually associated with childhood and youth, as in his *Das Lied von der Erde* (The Song of the Earth), composed in 1908–9.

> The dear Earth everywhere blooms in spring
>   and grows green, as new,
> Everywhere and for ever
> A blue sky in the distance
> for ever . . . for ever . . . for ever.

The concluding three or so minutes of the final movement of the symphony, *Der Abschied* (The Farewell), is music of astonishing transcendence, as the cadence repeatedly attempts to come to rest under the reiterated word *ewig* (for ever), seemingly unable to accept its final conclusion. Indeed, Mahler's instruction at the end of the piece is for the sound to fade away, imperceptibly, to nothing, blurring the moment when the music dies and the silence begins – a respectful nod towards the not dissimilar ending of his friend Richard Strauss's symphonic tone poem, *Tod und Verklärung* (Death and Transfiguration) of 1889. The resulting, long final chord of *The Song of the Earth* – Western music's symbolic 'home' of C major, naturally – was described by the mid-twentieth-century English composer Benjamin Britten as being 'imprinted on the atmosphere'.

Mahler's symphonies and songs were unappreciated by critics, who either found them too abrasive, too loud, too neurotic and too structurally complicated, or, like the Austrian *Reichpost*, simply objected to Mahler himself, reporting on his appointment to the State Opera in October 1897, 'Only the fullness of time will reveal whether this Jew-boy will prove worthy of such acclaim or will find himself brushed aside when reality strikes.' His music was, however, mostly enjoyed by audiences in his own lifetime, and perhaps most significantly it exerted a huge influence on the debate over music's future direction. He had a direct, tutor-like impact on a wave of younger composers whose agenda was nothing less than the complete dismantling of the Western 'tonal' system – that is to say, the way notes are arranged into key-families with a sense of 'home'. Indeed, Mahler's own composing style had begun to destabilise this system, borrowing as it did from ethnic folk music of near and far – his *Song of the Earth* was a setting of ancient Chinese poetry in translation and its music was accordingly given a Chinese flavour – and seeking to convey dark and unsettling emotional states. Of all his impressionable Viennese pupils, none embraced this dismantling of tonality quite as enthusiastically as Arnold Schoenberg.

Schoenberg's idea – the adoption of a totally new 'tonal' system – was, like other authoritarian manifestos of the early twentieth century, strict on how everybody else should obey its rules but applied with remarkable laxity when it came to his own creative output. His goal was to sweep away the forms that had served music for a thousand years – the way melodies are constructed, the chords, the rhythms, everything – and replace them with a system based purely on a mathematical formula.

The 'twelve-tone' formula that Schoenberg began exploring in the early 1900s – the one arguably anticipated by Liszt's *Faust* of 1855 – treated each of the twelve notes in the Western scale as equals in order to do away with the sense of 'home' in any given piece of music. Not one of them was allowed to be repeated in a melodic phrase, which prevented the listener's ear from latching on to any note as the centre of gravity. It was as radical a formula for music as it would be for a language if you ruled that no letter of the alphabet could be used more than once in a sentence.

Fascinating and brain-teasing though this limitation might be, its main problem as applied to music was that the *only* people who understood or admired it were other musicians. The public, then as now, were simply baffled. Schoenberg's theoretical rebellion, which later acquired the labels 'serialism' or 'atonality', produced decades of scholarly hot air, books, debates and seminars, and – in its purest, strictest form – not one piece of music, in a hundred years'-worth of effort, that a normal person could understand or enjoy.

One positive function Schoenberg's twelve-tone formula fulfilled, though, other than provide for interesting analysis and debate, was to give composers in the twentieth century a challenging structure with which to grapple. Igor Stravinsky, for example, as he hit a mid-life lull in his composing energy in the 1950s, began experimenting with serial techniques as a way of hearing musical possibilities in a fresh way, saying about it, 'The rules and restrictions of serial writing differ little from the rigidity of the great contrapuntal schools of old. At the same time they widen and enrich harmonic scope; one starts to hear more things and differently than before. The serial technique I use impels me to greater discipline than ever before.' That said, Stravinsky composed relatively few works with the serial rules fully applied, the short third movement of his Venetian cantata *Canticum Sacrum* (1955) being one.

One thing is for sure: Schoenberg and his fellow-travellers in the redesigning of the Western note system were not courting a mainstream audience. When, during the next half-century, audiences reacted with hostility to serialist works, it seemed to confirm to the movement's adherents that it was a cause so noble that ordinary, lesser mortals without 'the knowledge' would inevitably reject it. 'Elitist' is an overused word, tinged with resentment, but in describing serialist self-justification of the twentieth century it is spot on. Schoenberg was so sure his new dodecaphonic system would take off that he declared triumphantly, 'I have made a discovery which will ensure the supremacy of German music for the next hundred years.' He was no prophet.

Had early serialism had any chance of appealing to a paying public, one composer who would surely have opted into it was Richard

Strauss, Germany's leading composer after Mahler's death and a man with a voracious appetite for musical adventure. Strauss, though, had other tricks up his sleeve.

He began his career, conventionally enough, in a musical style that owed much to Liszt and a little to Wagner, composing large-scale symphonic poems of which *Also sprach Zarathustra* (Thus spoke Zarathustra) is pretty typical. Based on the philosopher Nietzsche's treatise of the same name, its opening, 'Sunrise', is now legendary thanks to Stanley Kubrick's 1968 film *2001: A Space Odyssey*. The overall musical effect is cinematic: shock and awe for a *fin de siècle* generation seeking thrills and spills galore. At the same time, Strauss looked backwards at the dying century, in songs of heartbreaking, Mahlerish delicacy, like 'Morgen!' (Tomorrow!), composed as a wedding present for his wife Pauline in 1894.

And then, just a few years after writing *Also sprach Zarathustra* and 'Morgen!', Strauss catapulted himself into musical notoriety with an opera of such savage, erotic power that it shocked bourgeois society and created a sensation. In some cities, London and Vienna among them, the opera was immediately banned. In one fell swoop, Strauss had transformed himself from the genteel *Kappellmeister* of the Austrian Belle Epoque into the Che Guevara of the musical rebels. The year was 1905, the place Dresden, the opera *Salome*.

Strauss's decision to find a newly rebellious musical style for the opera had been brewing over the preceding few years, a period during which his career as an opera conductor, principally in Munich and Berlin, though briefly too at Bayreuth, had been blossoming. His first public opera, *Guntram*, had had a disastrous reception when it opened in Munich in 1894 – from musicians, theatre management, press and public alike – prompting him to scheme artistic revenge on a city he thought 'philistine'. The first stage of his retaliation was a satirical opera, *Feuersnot* (Fire-night), performed in Dresden in 1901, in which he lampooned the anti-artistic burghers of Munich, throwing into the caustic melting pot a crazed magician modelled on Wagner. The second stage was accompanied by an acknowledgement that any young composer hoping to make a splash on the opera world would need to be daring and – if possible – a little shocking. Strauss knew that concert hall audiences, for whom he had produced a series of highly successful orchestral tone poems, were easier to impress than those in opera houses, especially in Germany and Austria where the expense of mounting opera had caused it to become heavily politicised. Nonetheless, the stark modernity of his music for *Salome*, never mind its edgy subject matter, was undoubtedly intended to shock the conservative opera community of Munich, the town of his birth, who had haughtily dismissed his early operatic efforts.

Based not so much on the biblical original as the scandalous 1891 play by Oscar Wilde, in which the motivation for the beheading of John the Baptist became primarily sexual, Strauss's opera set a new standard for ear-splitting dissonance – and, as he had predicted, earned him immediate worldwide notoriety. Salome's exotic Seven Veils dance-striptease may have alarmed and excited its first-night audience, but her final solo of passion for the severed head of John the Baptist, which she then kisses, was the Tarantino moment. You can either read Salome as a strong, independent young woman who gets what she wants by exploiting her sexuality, cleverly outwitting her stepfather the king in the process, or as a kind of demented junkie who lowers humanity's moral standards to a new nadir.

Strauss apparently hedges his bets, giving the first necrophiliac kiss arguably the most dissonant chord that had ever been heard. To put this chord in context, summon to your mind the high, shrieking violin discords that accompany the murderous shower scene in Bernard Herrmann's score for Hitchcock's *Psycho* (1960). The two notes that create the ear-piercing clash are placed at a distance of eleven steps from one other: an E and the E♭ above it. This discord is a split-apart version of another discord, the 'minor second', which can also be made up of an E and an E♭ but the ones directly adjacent to one another rather than the ones just short of an octave apart. These two clashes are enough on their own, as in the Herrmann shower scene, to be unpleasant, scary and painful to listen to. Salome's death-kiss chord has a trilling minor second hovering above it, but the real meat of the dissonance lies in the lower bass cluster, made up of a clashing minor second sandwiched between two other clashes, a major second and a tritone (the 'devil in music' we encountered in an earlier chapter). Underneath this scrunch is an ugly, growling minor third – not particularly offensive in itself but very dark and foreboding at such a low pitch – while the high trilling 'A' creates a vicious clash with the A# that sits three octaves below it at the apex of the deeper cluster. It would be hard to find a more aggressively uncomfortable combination of notes.

After asking whether the taste of blood on his lips is actually the 'taste of love', Salome revisits the kiss, in supreme triumph. 'I have now kissed your mouth, Jochanaan!' she screams, and Strauss unleashes a musical earthquake that could be construed as representing sexual consummation. To further complicate the psychological torment of this terrifying end, Kind Herod, who had encouraged Salome to dance for him in the first place, orders his soldiers to kill his stepdaughter there and then. For the awful violence of this slaughter, Strauss reserves his angriest, most dissonant music yet.

Having led the rebellion against musical respectability with *Salome* and one other blood-and-guts opera, *Elektra*, Strauss then made his second unexpected switch of style: he spent the remainder of his career, thirty-five years of it, composing beautiful music of antique nostalgia, from his luxuriantly melodic, intoxicatingly enjoyable, bitter-sweet opera *Der Rosenkavalier* (first performed in January 1911) to his posthumously published 'Four Last Songs' (1948), which for many music lovers are worthy candidates for the title Most Beautiful Music Ever Written. The 'Four Last Songs' appeared at the end of the Second World War but could easily have been composed half a century earlier: they belong stylistically to the end of the nineteenth century, alongside Mahler's orchestral songs. Their unspeakable beauty may have as much to do with the sense of a lost world as it does with Strauss's final gesture of love and gratitude to his wife of over fifty years.

The instant and worldwide acclaim that greeted the birth of *Der Rosenkavalier* in 1911 seemed to underline the two-hundred-year Austro-German dominance of classical music that had begun with J. S. Bach. This hegemony looked likely to continue indefinitely. But even without the catastrophe of two world wars, the Austro-German dynasty was coming to an end. Instead, a new force had emerged, and was by the early twentieth century the most exhilarating sound in Europe. In the closing decades of the nineteenth century the sleeping giant of Russia had awoken. Music was never going to be the same again.

The signs had been there for a while. In 1890, for example, if you'd asked most educated people in the West to name a famous living composer, they would very likely have given you that of a Russian, Pyotr Tchaikovsky. Tchaikovsky wasn't the first heavyweight Russian composer who wrote in the mainstream international idiom, the same milieu as Beethoven, Berlioz, Verdi or Brahms. Instead, that position was filled by Mikhail Glinka, whose operas *A Life for the Tsar* and *Ruslan and Lyudmila* had firmly established Tsarist Russia as a musical force to be reckoned with in the 1830s. Tchaikovsky, though, was the first Russian composer to achieve meaningful fame outside Russia.

If, for Italians, the supreme expression of their love of music was the emotionally charged operatic aria, for Russians it was dance. Whereas Italian opera arias were suffused with the musical quality known as 'rubato' – meaning to be free and flexible with the rhythmic pulse – in Russia the invigorating, repetitious beat of dance was everywhere to be heard. At the ballet, in operas, on the concert stage, lilting, driving, whirling, tiptoeing, leaping, gliding, jumping, gyrating and twirling, Russian music can't get enough of it. Tchaikovsky's ballet scores are still among the most popular pieces in the classical repertoire. His enormous prestige and irrepressible gift for melody, harnessed to a penchant for orchestral excitement, was a stark reminder to the West that patronising the Russian Empire as an offshoot of the Austro-German 'mainstream' was dangerously wide of the mark. Between the 1870s and the 1950s, Russian music exploded into creative life in a manner that was unprecedented – and subsequently unmatched – in history.

The fuse lighter of this Russian firework display in classical music wasn't cosmopolitan, well-travelled, friend-of-the-Romanovs Tchaikovsky, though, but a former military cadet from Pskov who worked in the Civil Service and who had a fatal vodka habit: Modest Mussorgsky.

Mussorgsky, among the big-name composers, was the most original voice of the late-nineteenth century and probably the only one in any country whose ideas cannot be traced back to Liszt. There was a reason for this: he wasn't musically trained at a conservatoire and he wasn't a professional composer. He was self-taught and thus blissfully unaware of the rules he was breaking. It was as if he was inventing composition as he went along. His pieces lacked traditional form and structure; in *Pictures at an Exhibition* (1874), for example, he merely hung together a series of ten different piano reflections of the paintings of his late friend, the artist Viktor Hartmann. They were like written-down improvisations. There was without doubt a naivety in his style, which earned him more than a little ridicule at the time, Tchaikovsky's summary being fairly representative of a generally held view. 'Mussorgsky you very rightly call a hopeless case,' he opined. 'His nature is narrow-minded, devoid of any urge towards self-perfection, blindly believing . . . in his own genius. In addition, he has a certain base side to his nature which likes coarseness, uncouthness, roughness. . . . He flaunts . . . his illiteracy, takes pride in his ignorance, mucks along anyhow, blindly believing in the infallibility of his genius. Yet he has flashes of talent which are, moreover, not devoid of originality.'

Importantly, though, for all his rough edges, Mussorgsky showed that Russian music could obey its own rules, follow its own tastes and carve its own identity. It did not have to be Brahms-*ski*.

Comparing Mussorgsky's *Boris Godunov* with another, earlier, opera also evoking Russia's Tsarist past, *A Life for the Tsar* by Glinka, whose traditional classical training included spells in Italy, Austria and Germany, the difference in styles is a stark demonstration of the change of direction being undertaken as the nineteenth century drew on.

A Life for the Tsar (1836), known in Russia as *Ivan Susanin*, is set in the Kremlin and has as its triumphant final chorus a celebration of the victory of Tsar Mikhail, the first of the Romanovs, against the Poles in the early seventeenth century. The assembled throng sing, 'Glory, Glory to you, holy Rus'!' Their jubilant chorus is certainly exciting and suitably victorious; someone has clearly stirred the thronging mob into singing very high and repeating themselves a lot, in the manner of victory crowds. If you didn't *know*, though, that this was a Russian victory, as opposed to a French, Austrian or Italian one, would you be any the wiser? If you were an academic, a detailed examination of the chorus harmonies would reveal some Russian Orthodox flavours in there, for sure. The fact is, though, that there is a pan-European character to the music; it could just as plausibly have originated in Vienna, Berlin or Rome as in St Petersburg or Moscow. But when compared to the Coronation scene from *Boris Godunov*, also set in the Kremlin and composed just thirty-eight years later, it is hard to believe the two choruses come from the same country.

In the Mussorgsky chorus, the colours, voices and glittering effects, with its tolling bells and echoing orchestra chimes, make a joyous cacophony that couldn't possibly be a Parisian, Viennese or Roman celebration. There is such daring, such exuberance in this sound that only a truly original composer could have dreamt it up, and sure enough it would soon become a template for others to follow. At the time of Mussorgsky's death in 1881 his music was virtually unknown outside Russia. But that was about to change.

So many of the seeds of the rebellions of late-nineteenth-century music can be traced to one extraordinarily fertile event. It took place in Paris in 1889 – the centenary year of the French Revolution – but this event was all about peace and shared humanity. It was the Exposition Universelle, the World's Fair. Here music as an international pursuit, shared, developed and exchanged across frontiers – a defining feature of the coming twentieth century – really began to take shape.

In the Palais du Trocadéro, which overlooked the newly built Eiffel Tower, Widor first played his famous organ 'Toccata', and it was here also that the visiting composer Nikolai Rimsky-Korsakov conducted a series of concerts of Russian music that dazzled French and other Western musicians, among them the twenty-seven-year-old Claude Debussy. Debussy's regular visits to the World's Fair were to be for him a life- and music-changing experience. 'Never has a more refined sensibility expressed itself by simpler means,' he wrote on hearing Mussorgsky for the first time.

> It seems to be the doing of some curious savage led by nothing but his emotion to discover step by step what music is about. 'Form' is for him of no use whatever – or rather, the form he resorts to is ever-changing to the point of being quite unlike any of the established, so to speak administrative, forms. His music, drawn by light touches, holds together by some mysterious link between them – and by his gift of luminous clear-sightedness.

What Debussy learnt from Mussorgsky was that there was an alternative way of building up the architecture of a piece of music to the developmental method introduced by Haydn and Mozart, which was still in service as the nineteenth century drew to a close. The development approach involved taking small cells of melody or rhythm, or both, and making up a whole discourse from them over a twenty- or thirty-minute period of growth. Beethoven notably constructed a whole movement from his fifth symphony from this tiny idea:

Brahms, Liszt and Wagner greatly expanded the possibilities of developing big structures out of small or even minute ideas, but it was essentially the same concept. Mussorgsky, because he knew no better, and Debussy because it suited his taste for the manipulation of block chords merging into each other – of which more shortly – ditched a hundred years of studious development technique and started from scratch. Their approach was episodic. One musical idea would simply follow another. No transitional development was necessary to move from idea A to idea B, as had been the case in the symphony, the sonata and the concerto since Haydn; idea A could run its course then switch to idea B. Just like that.

The strange, passionate marriage of Russian and French modernism that was born at those Trocadéro concerts was to turn into something big, noisy and rebellious. The invigorating newness of Mussorgsky, whose art, thought Debussy, was 'free from artifice and arid formulae', was but one of the extraordinarily fruitful imports to the Exposition Universelle. What revolutionised Debussy's music more even than hearing Mussorgsky was a sound that came from much further afield, blown into Paris on an aromatic wind from Asia.

The World's Fair showcased exhibits and cultural tableaux from all over the planet. Thanks to increased communications, the 'global village' was starting to become a reality. Debussy, along with twenty-eight million other visitors, spent an engrossing time wandering around the exotic installations from distant continents. The most popular attraction after the Eiffel Tower, sad to say, was a human zoo of four hundred Africans. What particularly mesmerised Debussy, though – as well as painter John Singer Sargent and sculptor Auguste Rodin, both of whom made copious sketches, and Paul Gauguin, who struck up a relationship with a Javanese teenage girl who later became his maidservant and concubine – was a Javanese village, complete with dancers and musicians, sponsored by a Dutch tea company.

Debussy certainly wasn't the first European to be enchanted by the exoticism of Javanese music – Sir Francis Drake, mooring the

Golden Hind off the south Javan coast in 1580, was treated to a performance by an 'orchestra' laid on by the local ruler, Raia Donan, in response to his English musicians' serenading. He reported in the ship's log that the Javanese players made 'country musick . . . of a very strange kind, yet the sound was pleasant and delightfull'. In the early nineteenth century Sir Stamford Raffles, founder of Singapore, while supervising the British occupation of Java sent two gamelan sets back to Britain, housed today in the British Museum. His friend Raden Rana Dipura, a Javanese 'chief' and accomplished musician, travelled with Raffles to England in 1816 and performed in London on a number of occasions. Prior to the Paris Exposition, Javanese gamelan groups had performed at Dutch trade fairs in Arnhem (1879) and Amsterdam (1883), as exhibits of the Netherlands' colonial riches. A commercial presentation of a gamelan troupe with dancers from the Javanese region of Yogyakarta took place at London's Royal Aquarium in 1882, attended by the Prince and Princess of Wales, and caused something of a sensation in the popular press, whose columnists were as enraptured as they were amused by an orchestra made up of metallic objects.

The particular sonorities, harmonies and scales of the Javanese Gamelan Orchestra displayed and performed at the Paris fair, though, intrigued Debussy so much that he was inspired to attempt an evocation of its Eastern sounds on a Western piano. Although he couldn't replicate the unfamiliar tuning of the bells, gongs and other metal bars of the gamelan, or the exact division of the musical scale used in Asian cultures, he could approximate it in two ways.

One was to make copious use of the so-called *pentatonic* scale, the five notes that are common to all the world's musical systems and are especially prevalent in Eastern music – these are the notes that can most easily be found by playing just the black notes on a keyboard. His 'Pagodes' of 1903, from a collection of three piano pieces called *Estampes* (prints), makes subtle use of pentatonic scales in homage to east Asia, and by 1910, when he produced his first book of piano preludes, whole sections of *Voiles* (veils, or sails) had fallen under the pentatonic spell. The pentatonic aspect of Debussy's piano music provided much inspirational fuel for later generations of jazz pianists. Bill Evans's 'Peace Piece' of 1958 is typical of the pentatonica inspired by Debussy, whereby the simpler, limited menu of pentatonic notes forms the basis of the melody – or, in Bill Evans's case, improvised right-hand cascades – layered on to a more complete (i.e. Western) palette of notes for the left-hand harmonies.

The other trick Debussy employed in his evocation of the gamelan was to allow his chords to hang over each other, overlapping and ricocheting from one to the next, rather in the way the different tones of bell-ringing overlap one another; a bell, once struck, is not dampened to stop at any point, rather it carries on until it dies away naturally. This same effect is achievable on a piano by depressing the right-hand ('damper') pedal – often erroneously called the 'loud' pedal – which lifts the row of felt dampers that normally prevent the notes from reverberating into one another. (Some very grand pianos, including those used by Debussy himself, have a third pedal – 'sostenuto' – which allows the player to choose which notes hang and which are dampened, rather than all or nothing.) What this technique does is eke out as many as possible of the sympathetic resonances, or harmonics, latent in the reverberating strings, thus imitating the natural harmonics found in plucked strings and struck metal bars. Natural harmonics are 'hidden' notes, usually quite high in pitch, which are found within any given sound, like the additional colours of the spectrum that are contained within white light. So Debussy's hanging chords, with the dampers kept away from the strings, represented a kind of return to nature, a move away from the more artificial sound of block chords.

Putting all these ideas into the music he composed after the Exposition Universelle, Debussy created a new soundscape for the piano. The reformation of scales and harmonies that he introduced offered a daringly new palette of aural possibilities.

One way of looking at what Debussy did with his Asiatic sound colours is to brand it as colonial exploitation, a touristic theft no better than the Exposition's human zoo, or the appropriation of exotic artefacts by European archaeologists and plunderers that was rampant at the turn of the twentieth century. It recalls, to some extent, the furore surrounding Dvořák's interest in Native American tunes – although Dvořák at least was *in* America at the time. Certainly, Debussy's dalliance with non-European culture – like his contemporary Paul Gauguin's French Polynesia-inspired art – seems to be part of the 'asymmetrical' relationship between rich West and poor 'Other' that was famously and controversially identified by cultural historian Edward Said in *Orientalism* (1978), and which persisted until the late-twentieth century. Orientalism, in the form of a crude, one-sided peep show of the 'sensual' East, had been enjoying a boom in France for most of the nineteenth century, ever since Napoleon's inept military adventures in Egypt and Syria, in fact, and the resulting unstoppable flood of artefacts, including the Rosetta Stone, from the Nile delta to the banks of the Seine. Exotica, fictional or actual, became commonplace among the French educated classes, whether they were devouring Victor Hugo's poems, *Les Orientales* (1829), discreetly reading Gustave Flaubert's bestselling erotic novel *Salammbô* (1862), feasting their eyes on the harems and naked slaves in Jean-Léon Gérôme's paintings, or flocking to operas like Meyerbeer's *L'Africaine* (1865), Bizet's *The Pearl Fishers* (1863), Massenet's *Le Roi de Lahore* (1877), Gounod's *Le Tribut de Zamora* (1881) or Delibes's still-popular *Lakmé* (1883).

The French were not unique: the British had Kipling, the paintings of Frederick Goodall (no relation) and Gilbert and Sullivan's *The Mikado*, after all. But to the usual ingredients of the ludicrously contradictory Orientalist recipe – presumption of a childlike, uneducated civilisation, innate savagery, slaves to incomprehensible ritual, aptitude for servitude, propensity for laziness, dignified inscrutability, awe at European superiority – the French imagination added freely available, fetishistic sexuality.

Debussy's music, whether inspired by Javanese gamelan or his taste for *le japonisme* – an example of which is Hokusai's woodblock print *The Great Wave Off Kanagawa* (1829–33), which inspired the orchestral suite *La Mer* – is hardly exploitative in the way that Gauguin's nude of his adolescent Eurasian servant may be. Indeed, viewed another way, one might even say Debussy was part of a healing process that would gradually reunite all the world's musical cultures into one multitudinous (or dangerously homogenised, as some believe) mainstream, the reality of the twenty-first century. His harmonic experiments flowed freely into later incarnations of jazz, the origins of which were most certainly not European, and have become part of a common musical heritage. Edward Said himself believed music could be harnessed as a force for good in the resolving of cultural, political and social differences, even in the sublimating of national identity for a higher ideal, co-founding with Daniel Barenboim the West-Eastern Divan Orchestra in 1999. If the cooperative manner of music-making has any validity, it must surely allow not just for Palestinian and Israeli musicians to play Beethoven together, but also for the uninhibited interweaving of musical styles across geographical and racial boundaries.

The Exposition Universelle of 1889 was, in effect, the starting point of the twentieth century's preoccupation with what we now call 'world music'. With the benefit of hindsight it marks the beginning of the end of Western European musical aloofness and the emergence of Russia as a major cultural presence. Few if any of the audience for Rimsky-Korsakov's Russian concerts at the Trocadéro, though, could have guessed the scale, dynamism and turbulence that Russian music was to unleash on the world in the early twentieth century, through the shop window, once again, of Paris.

The Russian Imperial capital of St Petersburg had, by the end of the nineteenth century, become one of the greatest musical centres in the world. A dynasty of outstanding composers, each the mentor of the next, had developed along a timeline that began with Glinka in the 1830s and Mily Balakirev in the 1860s, running through Borodin, Mussorgsky and Tchaikovsky to Rimsky-Korsakov, the teacher of Stravinsky.

The years leading up to the October Revolution of 1905 had seen an awakening of interest in Russian ethnic art and architecture, a fashion to some extent promoted by the nationalist leanings of Tsars Alexander II and Nicholas II. The appointment of the patriotic Balakirev as director of music at the Russian Imperial Chapel in 1883 saw a deliberate abandonment of the Western-style choral chant in use at the time and the adoption of older, so-called *Znamenny* Russian Orthodox chants, with their deep basses and thick, eight- or sixteen-voice block chords. By 1900 this ancient sound had fed like a river into the choral texture of all Russian composers.

Sergei Diaghilev, art, dance and music lover, saw in this upsurge of Russian cultural pride an opportunity. He mounted an art exhibition in St Petersburg in 1905 that was intended to show the educated classes of the Imperial capital the great wealth of the country's artistic talents beyond the city's parochial horizon, a collection that he had spent a year researching throughout Russia. He and his colleague, artist Alexandre Benois, who had formed an organisation and magazine called *World of Art* (*Мир искýсства* – Mir iskusstva) then took a similar exhibition to Paris the following year, the success of which encouraged Diaghilev to present a season of Russian concerts there in 1907 and to mount Mussorgsky's 1874 opera *Boris Godunov* – in a revised version by Rimsky-Korsakov – in 1908.

Boris Godunov was just one of a series of operas that cashed in on the Russian aristocracy's growing obsession with the Empire's Asiatic and Slavic folklore; Rimsky-Korsakov mined the same richly colourful seam with such pageants as *Kaschei the Immortal*, *The Golden Cockerel*, *The Legend of the Invisible City of Kitezh*, *The Tsar's Bride* and *The Tale of Tsar Saltan*. These latter pieces, alongside his concert spectacular *Scheherezade*, and his completion and mounting of Borodin's unfinished epic *Prince Igor*, were to prove a fertile

The twelve-note octave as we know it became a firm fixture of Western music after the publication in 1722 of J. S. Bach's forty-eight preludes and fugues for the 'Well-Tempered Keyboard'. The system – which shunted the abundance of naturally occurring notes into twelve equally spaced pitches – was by no means perfect, but it restricted and standardised the concept of 'in tune' and 'out of tune' across all musical instruments.

The MILITARY PROPHET: or A FLIGHT from PROVIDENCE.

Address'd to the FOOLISH and GUILTY, who *timidly* WITHDREW themselves on the *Alarm* of another EARTHQUAKE, *April* 1750.

Two earthquakes struck London in March 1750 and convinced many Londoners that the end was nigh. This contemporary lithograph lampooned the panicked gentry who fled the city – and thus turned Handel's new oratorio, *Theodora*, into a box-office flop.

The Rotunda at Ranelagh Pleasure Gardens, which had a capacity of two thousand and hosted a packed performance by the eleven-year-old Mozart in 1765.

Haydn directing his opera *L'incontro improvviso* at the Esterházy Theatre in 1775.

Niccolò Paganini was one of a new wave of superstar musicians in the first half of the nineteenth century. His extraordinary skills on the violin led many to suspect he had struck a deal with the devil.

Clara Wieck Schumann was the wife and muse of Robert Schumann, and a talented composer and pianist in her own right.

Robert Schumann's *Kreisleriana* (1838), a homage to Johannes Kreisler, the fictional surly musician who featured in the comic novels of E. T. A. Hoffmann, was a musical love letter to Clara.

Franz Liszt, 'The King of the Piano', was music's first international star. His show-stopping performances encouraged piano builders to adopt iron frames to replace wooden ones, because pianos simply broke under the hammering Liszt gave them on stage.

Liszt spearheaded a shift from orchestral to illustrative music, using this 1850 painting of Attila the Hun in battle as the basis for his symphonic poem *Hunnenschlacht*. Amid the chaotic sounds of battle, a plainsong chant, 'Crux fidelis', introduces the figure at top left with a gleaming cross.

'Whoever wants to understand National Socialist Germany must know Wagner,' Hitler once said, and much of the propaganda surrounding him depicted him as a Wagnerian hero.

Third Reich stamps of 1933 featuring Wagner operas: (*clockwise from top left*) *Tannhäuser*, *Rheingold*, *Siegfried*, *Parsifal*, *Lohengrin* and *Meistersinger*.

In 1873, a group of African-American students from Fisk University in Nashville brought the spiritual to Europe. In London they sang for Queen Victoria and the Prime Minister, William Gladstone, who invited them to breakfast with him. They greatly impressed the mixed-race British composer Samuel Coleridge-Taylor, whose 1905 *Negro Melodies* were arrangements of the Jubilee Singers' best-known spirituals.

Claude Debussy was so intrigued by the Javanese dancers and musicians at the 1899 World's Fair in Paris that he developed techniques for evoking the exotic sounds of the gamelan on a Western piano.

Impresario Sergei Diaghilev wowed early-twentieth-century Paris with his Ballets Russes, featuring music from Stravinsky, Debussy and others and dance by such renowned figures as Vaslav Nijinsky (*right*) and Anna Pavlova.

The Beatles borrowed sounds and techniques from both past musical traditions and cutting-edge advances – from ancient folk modes to electronic experiments – to become the most famous band in the world.

Steve Reich exemplified the minimalist movement that bridged the chasm between classical music and pop in the 1970s. His hypnotic drum beats may have sounded repetitive but were in fact comprised of endlessly modifying patterns.

Paul Simon, a master of melding unrelated musical genres, flouted an embargo on Apartheid South Africa in 1986 to record *Graceland* with Ladysmith Black Mambazo, mixing the exuberance of the townships with folk from the Southern United States.

starting point for his – then unknown – protégé Stravinsky's first forays into a new breed of Russian ballet to be shown by Diaghilev in hyper-sophisticated Paris.

The enormous critical success of Diaghilev and Benois's 1908 production of *Boris Godunov* at the Paris Opéra (Palais Garnier) – its first performance outside Russia and starring the legendary Russian bass Feodor Chaliapin – encouraged Diaghilev to plan further Russian spectacles in the French capital, which also had a promising community of wealthy Russian émigrés who had fled their homeland after the 1905 Revolution. Diaghilev was invited to return to Paris the following year; this time he presented five ballets and created a bespoke company of top dancers, including Vaslav Nijinsky and Anna Pavlova, recruited from various Imperial ballet companies for the purpose: the Ballets Russes. Their first season from May 1909 included the Polovtsian dances from Borodin's opera *Prince Igor*, *Le Pavillon d'Armide*, based on the tales of E. T. A. Hoffmann, with music by Nikolai Tcherepnin, and *Les Sylphides*, choreographed by Michel Fokine to music by Chopin – these last two being revivals of earlier Fokine productions for the Imperial Ballet at the Maryinsky Theatre in St Petersburg. Well received though the 1909 season undoubtedly was among the French – the Russians at home were surprised to see it greeted as so 'new', when it was in essence a compilation of what Russian ballet companies had been doing for a decade or more – Diaghilev made a huge loss of 76,000 francs, over £350,000 in today's money. Consequently the expectations placed on the 1910 season were considerable: he needed to balance support from patrons in the West, hoping to be associated with something daring and novel, with the approval of Russian dance critics, especially the influential André Levinson, so that the best dancers would be happy to join his troupe. In the end, he opted to please the Westerners.

Diaghilev took one serious risk with his second season. He commissioned the unknown, untested Igor Stravinsky to provide music for one of the new ballets, *The Firebird*. It was a hunch, but an inspired one. Stravinsky hadn't been Diaghilev's first-choice

composer for the proposed ballet, in fact – the more experienced
Russians Nikolai Tcherepnin and Anatoly Lyadov both withdrew
– but in one important respect the young Stravinsky was a better
idea: namely that the Parisian press had criticised Diaghilev's first
season for the lack of adventure shown in the music. By commis-
sioning Stravinsky for the 1910 season, no one could accuse
Diaghilev of being sheepish with his choice of composer.
Stravinsky's first spell of collaboration with Diaghilev comprised
three ballets: *The Firebird* in 1910, *Petrushka* in 1911 and *The Rite of
Spring* in 1913. When he was commissioned to compose the first
of these he was a nobody; by the morning after the première of
the third, he was both the most notorious and the most eagerly
championed composer in all Europe, seizing the crown from
Richard Strauss in one fell swoop.

The Firebird's scenario, an amalgam of several versions of folk
tales about a magical bird, combined supernatural characters and
beasts with the natural, the fantastical world with the human, and
Stravinsky enhanced the contrast between the two by giving the
two worlds different styles of music. This was a technique he had
learnt from his teacher, Rimsky-Korsakov. Human characters such
as the twelve princesses, or Prince Ivan Tsarévitch, were given
folk-song-derived melodies based on the common Western musical
scale. The fantastical creatures and characters, on the other hand,
were allotted a much more exotic and complex musical palette,
often based on the so-called 'Octatonic' scale. This Persian-inspired
scale – which has nine notes rather than the eight that make up
Western major and minor scales – had been a feature of the music
of Rimsky-Korsakov, especially when depicting the magical, malev-
olent or the mysterious. In Stravinsky, the appearances of the
mythical Firebird itself combined octatonic flavours with frantic,
wing-flapping, fluttering rhythms.

Even when Stravinsky borrowed from Russian ethnic folk music,
which he did in several of his Diaghilev ballet scores, he did so in
order to distort it through some mischievous prism. He was deeply
impressed by field recordings of peasant folk music he had heard

in the years before he began composing *The Firebird*. They had revealed to the educated, bourgeois Stravinsky a distant, ritualistic world and his instinct to repackage Russian folk melody for a Parisian audience, surrounding what they might deem its vulgarity with the dazzling colour at his disposal in a large modern orchestra, was brilliantly provocative. In a cruel irony, ballet commentators back in Russia were irked by Western reviews of the Stravinsky–Nijinsky ballets, which used adjectives such as 'barbaric', 'primitive', 'wild' or 'savage' in almost every paragraph. The St Petersburg ruling elite of the Russian Empire, which had been expanding its Asian dominions greedily for most of the nineteenth century, had been enjoying their own version of Orientalism – celebrated, for example, in Borodin's symphonic poem *In the Steppes of Central Asia* of 1880, his opera *Prince Igor* and in all Rimsky-Korsakov's operas. Now, it seemed, Russia itself was being portrayed as a 'primitive' society, lodged in the Western mind as an archaic peasant culture. Given that Russia was at this point at the very vanguard of modernism it was a bitter pill to swallow, and understandably so.

In their own different ways, all the radicals in the post-Wagner meltdown – Mahler, Debussy, Strauss and Stravinsky – were dismantling the previous system of musical organisation, whereby ideas carefully unfolded, one developing into the next. The new approach, to the ears of many at the time, was bewildering and anarchic.

Even though *The Firebird*, *Petrushka* and *The Rite of Spring* ballets all have narrative threads, Stravinsky played against this tendency in his scores for them. Instead, he assembled a montage, an aural jigsaw, something perhaps closer to what we nowadays expect from a film score, so ballet's short, kaleidoscopic episodes and restless, physical slideshow proved an ideal workshop for his remodelling of musical structure. In our hurried, twenty-first-century way of life, we find the idea of musical collage – the mix, the remix, the iPod shuffle and the mash-up – familiar and unthreatening. But we shouldn't forget how bafflingly *unfamiliar* an idea this was to the musical establishment of the early 1900s. When the Ballets Russes toured Stravinsky's second ballet, *Petrushka*, to Vienna in 1913, the scandalised musicians refused to play it, describing it as 'dirty music'.

Stravinsky's ballet style brought together the legacy of his Russian training, especially that learnt from his revered mentor Rimsky-Korsakov, and his fascination for the new sound palette being pioneered by Debussy, who for a while became his friend. There is a seductive, hallucinogenic quality to much Debussy, though, in contrast to the forceful physicality and ritualistic hypnosis of Stravinsky. Stravinsky, like all Russians, was turned on by the rhythmic urgency of dance. It is often overlooked that *Jeux*, a ballet score Debussy wrote for Diaghilev, which premièred a fortnight before Stravinsky's *Rite of Spring*, was almost as harmonically disorientating as the latter, but it was the primal violence captured in the rhythm and orgiastic pounding of the Stravinsky that caused *The Rite of Spring*'s first performance to descend into a shouting match.

The audience disturbances that undoubtedly did occur during the ballet's première in Paris in May 1913 have been the subject of much colourfully exaggerated language in classical music's collective retelling of the event, habitually being referred to as a 'riot'. Some caution needs to be exercised in repeating this version of the drama, since (a) we are referring to a small gathering of well-to-do people in evening dress, some loudly complaining, others applauding, not a mob of looting thugs: no one was hurt and no property was damaged; (b) a further week of performances passed in Paris without incident and a London run two months later was received politely; and (c) contemporary reviews focused on the outrage provoked by Nijinsky's radical choreography, which pulled no punches in depicting the abduction and ritual killing of an adolescent girl, rather than on Stravinsky's music. Stravinsky may have been keen, in his recounting of the fateful première years later, to talk up the effect of his (undeniably brilliant) part in the collaboration, especially as within a year Nijinsky's groundbreaking contribution had been dropped, not to be reunited with the music on stage until the 1980s.

Whatever may have happened in that small theatre on the Champs Élysées, *The Rite of Spring* is the twentieth century's most thrillingly explosive, iconic piece of orchestral music; it is still astonishing a hundred years later. It is a rebellion in sound. While Mahler had layered melody on melody, tangled together like a twisted knot, and Debussy had manipulated blocks of adjacent sound melting into each other, Stravinsky went one step further, superimposing simultaneous rhythms on top of each other.

Polyrhythm, as it has since been dubbed, had long existed in African tribal drumming, improvised on the spot by highly intuitive, skilful players, often in various states of trance. But polyrhythm conceived from scratch by a composer, written down on the page, imposed on the Western symphony orchestra, player by player, was an utterly novel concept. Stravinsky reported that the idea for a piece based on an ancient pagan dance of ritual human sacrifice came to him in a dream and that the scenario suggested such a deliberately layered sound. It was as if he wanted the past and the present to coexist in one dimension, the prehistoric ritual of his dancers and the modern cacophony of the industrial world, and the only way he could conceive it was to make parallel, competing rhythmic patterns fight for the same space. It's complicated, but it's magnificent.

The Rite of Spring was the zenith of musical modernism in the early twentieth century. But that music had already reached such a point by 1913 presented progressively minded composers of symphonic orchestral music with a dilemma: where to go from here? It was a question that had already begun to be answered, but neither Stravinsky nor Debussy, in 1913, would have guessed just how massive the forces of change were going to be. The signs were all there, though, and had been for a while.

The agent of change was, to begin with, a humble strip of waxed paper from the year 1860. Scratched on the paper is the voice of a woman singing the French folk song 'Au clair de la lune, mon ami Pierrot'. Made on 9 April 1860, it is the oldest surviving evidence of the technology of recording, pre-dating Thomas Edison declaiming 'Mary had a little lamb' on his tinfoil phonograph by seventeen years, and making the man who created it, Édouard-Léon Scott de Martinville, the true inventor of the new technology.

Scott de Martinville had patented his machine, the phonauto-graph, in 1857. It worked by making impressions on the paper, which had been blackened by an oil lamp, using a stylus that vibrated when someone sang or spoke into a large barrel-shaped horn. But Scott de Martinville had no way of playing the recording back: running a stylus back over the indentations in the paper would destroy them. The paper rolls with his recordings were stored with his patent instructions at the Academy of Sciences at the French Institute, silent as the grave, until 2008, when a group of American audio historians and engineers used digital scanning technology to convert the markings back into sound. The French folk singer of 1860, miraculously, sang again.

The phonautograph began a process that would totally trans-form music. Very soon, in 1877, Thomas Edison invented a machine that could play recordings back, and a new breed of musician-researcher popped up, travelling around remote rural areas recording and preserving the folk songs that doubtless bemused locals were persuaded to perform. It is thought that the oldest surviving field recordings are those made in 1889 among the Passamaquoddy Indians in Maine, by American anthropologist Jesse Walter Fewkes. From the 1890s onwards, Edison's wax-cylinder recording devices were being used all over the world, capturing for ever the oral and musical culture of communities now long disappeared. Those made by Evgeniya Lineva, for example, at the turn of the twentieth century in outlying parts of the Russian Empire, were the ones thought to have impressed Stravinsky while he was researching for The Firebird.

Hot on the heels of these philanthropic, documentary-style recordings came those intended to part a paying public with their money. The speed with which the gramophone took off is astonishing, considering how expensive a piece of gear it was in the early days (the equivalent of $550 at the turn of the century): the first million-selling record was of Italian tenor Enrico Caruso, the tearful clown, singing 'Vesti la giubba' from Leoncavallo's opera *I Pagliacci*, in 1907. That *I Pagliacci* was only fifteen years old when Caruso popularised it on record – young in relation to opera's extensive back catalogue – is, with the benefit of hindsight, strangely significant. After all, the record market would be overwhelmingly driven in the years to come by music that was new and that appealed to the young. When radio broadcasts of recorded music began from 1920 onwards, public interest in having one's own record collection accelerated; what had been a trickle turned into a flood.

The advent of recording made the huge wealth of music already written by 1900 increasingly available to millions of people across the world, vastly expanding their musical horizons and turning something hitherto costly and rare into an ordinary commodity. This was a very good thing. But it was also the start of a process whereby, in classical music, the old soon far outweighed the new. Old music, thanks to repetition and familiarity gained through broadcasting and recording, and because there was, unsurprisingly, much more of it, was more comforting and pleasing. It challenged its listener less, required less effort and, as a non-threatening background accompaniment to other activities, it became ubiquitous in a way it could never have been before. Perhaps most significantly, this great wave of 'rediscovered' older music was being offered to the public just as modern music was embarking upon a journey towards greater difficulty, confrontation and experimentation. By the mid-twentieth century, even live concerts reflected this imbalance: whereas audiences in the nineteenth century *expected* to hear mostly brand-new music, as they do by and large in the popular field today, twentieth-century audiences had grown fearful and reluctant to hear new music. They began to prefer old music over new; this was, in many ways, not such a good thing.

Certainly, for popular music, recording was an unqualified blessing. It empowered and spread forms of music that had developed without notation, making available to a mass audience folk and ethnic music that had up to then been confined to local communities. For these communities, music was not just an entertainment. It was a refuge. But the music they had nurtured and were now able to share with the wider world was to have a profound, revolutionising impact on the twentieth century's musical story.

African-American slaves and their descendants, living in conditions of oppressive poverty, developed over time a form of religious song, the spiritual, an amalgam of archetypal African call-and-response song forms and revivalist hymns, particularly those penned by the eighteenth-century English nonconformist writer-preacher Isaac Watts. Spirituals were rich with Old Testament references to the slavery of the Israelites, visions of redemption and heavenly justice – and there have been repeated, anecdotal claims that their texts also included coded references to escape routes and safe houses for endangered slaves in the Deep South.

The existence of the spiritual was for a long time mostly unknown to the white population, a situation that changed in 1871 when a group of African-American students from Fisk University in Nashville, the children of slaves themselves, formed a choir called the Jubilee Singers. Their repertoire included arrangements of spirituals, interest in which subsequently spread rapidly. That same year, they embarked on a series of fund-raising tours, first of the eastern seaboard of the United States and subsequently in Europe, particularly Great Britain, where their first private performance on 6 May 1873 was warmly reviewed in *The Times*, the *Telegraph*, the *News* and the *Standard*, and followed a few days later by a performance of 'Steal away to Jesus' and 'Go down, Moses' for Queen Victoria. Days later the Jubilee Singers were performing for the Prince and Princess of Wales, and Mr and Mrs Gladstone at the Prime Minister's Carlton House Terrace residence. Their journal of the first British tour reveals a touched and amazed response to these events and to the respect they were shown, and includes a letter from Gladstone himself:

> I beg you to accept the assurances of the great pleasure which the Jubilee Singers gave on Monday to our illustrious guests, and to all who heard them. I should wish to offer a little present in books in acknowledgement of their kindness, and in connection with the purposes, as they have announced, of their visit to England. It has occurred to me that perhaps they might like to breakfast with us, my family and a very few friends, but I would not ask this unless it is thoroughly agreeable to them.

The Jubilee Singers stayed in London for three months and then travelled north, arriving in Hull – the birthplace of William Wilberforce – on the fortieth anniversary of the abolition of slavery, followed by Scarborough, Newcastle, Glasgow, Edinburgh, Ayr, Aberdeen, Perth and other Scottish towns. At Greenock they performed two concerts in the town hall to two thousand people a night. After a year in which they visited most of the cities of the British Isles, the Jubilee Singers returned to Nashville having raised £10,000 (£670,000 today) for facilities at Fisk University.

The mixed-race English composer Samuel Coleridge-Taylor, whose triumphant oratorio setting of Longfellow's *Hiawatha* we encountered in the last chapter, and whose champions in Britain included Sir Edward Elgar, caused a similar sensation during three trips to the USA between 1904 and 1910. For a black composer-conductor of such conspicuous achievement to be fêted internationally as he conducted his own compositions was still a very rare, and possibly unheard-of, phenomenon in the eyes of the white arts community. While there, Coleridge-Taylor met the former leader of the Fisk Jubilee Singers, Frederick J. Loudin, and in 1905 he made piano arrangements of twenty-four of the spirituals that the Fisk Jubilee Singers had popularised so successfully, calling them *Negro Melodies*.

But Coleridge-Taylor had previous experience of adapting African-American folk tunes. One of them, 'A Negro Love Song', from a collection of 1898, is early notated evidence of the melodic style of what came to be known as the Blues. The clues here are the so-called 'flattened' degrees of the musical ladder, or scale, at the third and seventh positions. The flattening of these degrees – that is, the slight lowering in pitch – betrays the origin of Blues melodies in older, modal key-families. It may well be a coincidence, but the rules governing melody in English Tudor music – 'Greensleeves', say – operate in a remarkably similar fashion: if the tune's direction of travel is upwards (getting higher), the seventh position *sharpens* (raises its pitch); if the direction of travel is downwards (getting lower), the seventh flattens. This too is a function of the older modal scales that were not confused by the ambiguities thrown up by harmony (that is, before there was Equal Temperament or a distinction between major and minor versions of any given key-family). The flattening of the third and seventh notches on the scale is consistent with centuries-old African melody modes, memories of which had clearly not been lost among the children and grandchildren of slaves. The Blues, as it developed slowly and in a piecemeal fashion among former slave communities in the final decades of the nineteenth century, clung resolutely to the flattened thirds and sevenths, and has done so to the present day, passing on the modal melody shapes to hip-hop. Indeed, after the 1930s the thirds and sevenths actually became known as 'blue' notes.

Modal melodies, revivalist spirituals, the call-and-response or 'holler' songs of African slaves: all of these went into the mixing pot of the early Blues. Early Blues singers moulded tunes with African inflexions in them on to chords borrowed from American hymns, parlour, folk and vaudeville songs. But there were other African ingredients, too, such as use of the Akonting, the plucked folk lute used for accompanying solo singers, and which, alongside the Arab-inspired Spanish guitar, is a parent instrument of the banjo.

The fact that there were European elements in the DNA of the Blues should not surprise us: it had been nearly a century since new slaves had arrived in America from Africa, and the music that Americans of all backgrounds heard and shared in the second half of the nineteenth century was already well blended. There has been considerable research into song forms of the poorest Americans of all ethnic groups, particularly in Peter Van Der Merwe's seminal *Origins of the Popular Style*, which has revealed the extent of the influence of Anglo-Celtic folk music on song types in the growth of the Blues. Not only had the distinctive flattened thirds and sevenths been a feature of Anglo-Celtic folk music since long before the Tudors, but Anglo-Celtic song types, picked up from the slaves' and emancipated slaves' co-workers, vast numbers of whom were from the British Isles, are also known to have been influential. Among these song types are hundreds that lament the burden and misery of underclass life, as became the standard Blues format. The particular lyrical stanza shape of what became the 'twelve-bar Blues', for instance, has been traced to templates derived from the seventeenth-century folk songs 'The Cruel Ship's Carpenter' and 'Pretty Polly', via a nineteenth-century work song called 'Po' Lazarus' (also known as 'Oh Brother, Where Art Thou?'). Likewise the iconic nineteenth-century American work song 'The Ballad of John Henry, the Steel-Driving Man', which itself became a Blues standard, and which commemorates the futile battle between a black railroad worker and a new machine designed to replace him, can be traced back as a pattern to the much earlier British ballad 'The Birmingham Boys'.

It is entirely understandable that there should be sensitivity about the non-African elements in the origin of the Blues, since the music of the slaves from which it sprang was so often a lament or protestation against the harsh treatment they received. But music does not observe racial or national boundaries; it is, as we have seen repeatedly, open and available to all cultures, owned by none. Whatever elements went into its kit of parts, the early Blues musicians made something unique and lasting of their own. The issue of ownership in the breakneck speed of growth and dissemination of popular music styles was to recur time and time again in the twentieth century, with the poorest, least visible musicians often finding their creativity swallowed up in the commercial exploitation that went with it.

The intermingling of styles and traditions that gave birth to the Blues can be seen in the arrival, at around the same time, of 'rag' or 'ragtime' music, which reached its apogee in the sheet-music publications of Scott Joplin (1867–1917). It had originated in the bars and brothels of St Louis and Chicago, where house pianists copied the marching-band style popularised in the 1880s and '90s by bandleaders such as John Philip Sousa. In order to emulate a whole band – bass, accompanying chords and tune – the solo pianist had to leap about the keys frantically, resulting in a rather virtuoso left-hand motion from bass to chord and back. On top of this accompanying oompah the rag pianists wove a catchy tune that pulled the rhythm around, a technique called syncopation. Syncopation is like talking with the emphasis on the wrong words to create a jerky sound.

Ragtime picked up this playful jumping ahead of the tune from the banjo or piano accompaniments for 'cakewalks', also called 'chalk-line walks': parodic dancing competitions held by African-American communities, during which coconut cake may have been offered as a prize. Debussy, in Paris, cashed in on the popularity of cakewalk piano rags, with his 'Golliwogg's Cakewalk' of 1908 – which incidentally also includes a jokey musical quotation from Wagner's *Tristan und Isolde*.

Ragtime's syncopation fed directly into an energetic, driving piano style of the 1920s known as 'stride'. The style was made famous in Harlem by the pianistic wizard James P. Johnson, a quintessential stride performance of his being 'Harlem Strut' of 1921. Ragtime's revolutionary lovechild, though, was a hyper-syncopated form of piano and band playing that flickered into life in the 1910s in the Storyville district of New Orleans and which charismatic performers like Jelly Roll Morton took on tour around the Southern States in travelling vaudeville shows. Though Jelly Roll called a lot of his numbers 'Blues', we now know this as the beginning of a distinct genre of its own: jazz.

The etymology of the term 'jazz' is hotly debated but the most likely derivation is from a non-musical nineteenth-century slang word, jasm, meaning energy, vigour or liveliness. Its choice of instruments – cornet, trombone, clarinet and tuba, supported by banjo, drums and sometimes piano – was heavily influenced by the practical windfall of an injection of cheap, ex-military band stock at the end of the 1898 Spanish-American War. Some elements of the marching-band style remained in the formation of street bands for funeral processions and for dancing, though these bands had a cheerful anarchy to them, each lead instrument taking its turn to improvise solos around the established chordal pattern or tune. The New Orleans prototypes acquired the generic label 'Dixieland', after the huge success of a band called the Original Dixieland Jazz (or 'Jass') Band, whose 1917 hit, 'Livery Stable Blues', sold a million copies.

Despite jazz's African-American origins in the Blues and in New Orleans's funeral procession bands, the members of the Original Dixieland Jass Band itself were the children of white European immigrants. But as jazz spread from the red-light Basin Street area of New Orleans to the clubs of Chicago and New York, thriving in Prohibition-era speakeasies, it provided mobility most of all to black musicians who made up the critical mass of its player pool. Indeed, the spread of jazz into northern and Midwestern cities had coincided with the massively increased availability of wartime factory work, which had encouraged mass black migration in the same direction. Soon, the urban black working class would also have money in their pockets to buy the records of the jazz artists whose success for the first time proved that the American Dream might yet have some meaning for African-Americans after all.

Up to this point in musical history – the first few years of the twentieth century – ethnic folk elements had been co-opted into classical music as subsidiary exotic flavouring. With the emergence of jazz, all this was to change. The unavoidable historical truth is that, despite their best efforts – and they were damned fine efforts, make no mistake – the classically trained composers of the early twentieth century were to be totally outflanked by the newer genres of Blues and jazz, which, as they made common cause with popular songwriters of exceptional skill and panache, swept all before them. Once the choice of which music thrived passed into the hands of an audience of millions through recording and later broadcasting, new priorities very rapidly started to prevail: popular music was taking centre stage while classical music began to move into the slipstream. How was classical music going to respond to this new, potentially fatal relationship between mass audiences and new genres that were irresistible to them? Was this a schism too far for the already reeling Western tradition to handle?

Not quite. Faced with the twin rebellions of dissonant modernism and the mass market, the classical tradition found an ace up its sleeve and played it with impeccable timing. In a world of turmoil and change, its response was nostalgia. A work like Elgar's *Enigma Variations* of 1899 typifies this response, self-consciously backward-looking in its thematic intentions, comprising as it does a series of affectionate portraits of his friends and family, as well as its musical character, with its homages to Beethoven, Mendelssohn and Brahms. Other interpretations of the nostalgic impulse abound as the nineteenth century slipped into the twentieth: Edvard Grieg's *Holberg* suite (1884), Isaac Albéniz's *Tres Suites antiguas* and *Suite española* (1886), Reynaldo Hahn's *Caprice mélancolique* (1897), Maurice Ravel's *Pavane pour une infante défunte* (1899), Jean Sibelius's *Finlandia* (1899), Carl Reinecke's *Serenade in G minor* (1900), Max Bruch's *Serenade in A minor* (1900), Hugo Alfvén's *Swedish Rhapsody no. 1 – Midsommarvaka* (1903), Enrique Granados's *Escénas romanticas* (1904), Elgar's *Introduction and Allegro for Strings* (1905), Amy Beach's *Suite française* (1907), Gustav Holst's *A Somerset Rhapsody* (1907), Frederick Delius's *Brigg Fair* (1907), Ralph Vaughan Williams's *Fantasia on a Theme by Thomas Tallis* (1910), Fritz Kreisler's *Liebesfreud* and *Liebesleid* (1910) and Max Reger's *Eine Romantische Suite* (1912). As the world began to slide towards a final showdown of the

European empires, this kind of music increasingly reminded people of the way of life they were about to lose.

'Light after light goes down. England and the Kingdom, Britain and the Empire, the old prides and the old devotions, glide abeam, astern, sink down upon the horizon, pass – pass. The river passes – London passes, England passes.' So wrote H. G. Wells, somewhat prophetically, in the conclusion of his semi-autobiographical satire, *Tono Bungay* (1909). This chapter, describing a warship heading down the Thames, past London's familiar shoreline landmarks towards the open sea, inspired the final, elegiac movement of Vaughan Williams's majestic *London* symphony, first performed in March 1914 in London and dedicated to his friend and fellow composer George Butterworth. In what could be described as the first cultural casualty of the Great War, Vaughan Williams sent the score to the conductor Fritz Busch in Germany following this performance, where it was promptly lost in the turmoil of the outbreak of war. It subsequently had to be reconstructed from the orchestral parts.

Without doubt, the impending and actual sense of loss motivated British composers in the period before and during the First World War to compose music of outstanding beauty – from Vaughan Williams's heartbreaking 'The Lark Ascending' to Parry's 'Jerusalem' and *Songs of Farewell*, to Holst's *Planets* suite (which begins with 'Mars: The Bringer of War'). Added to the 1914–18 list should be, by dint of his association with the war, George Butterworth's *The Banks of Green Willow* of 1913; he was killed by sniper fire on the Somme in July 1916. The tragedy of the war, on so many levels, and the apparent unravelling of the certainties of the previous century, elicited an unprecedented collective response from British composers. Charles Hubert Parry viewed the war, as did Elgar, from an older generation's perspective, composing a cycle of choral songs of mature, eloquent poignancy in *Songs of Farewell*. (Although Parry survived the war, he died in the influenza epidemic that took twenty-two million lives worldwide in 1918.)

There was no shortage of patriotic, empire-extolling music

provided by home-front composers during the Great War, including Elgar's 'The Spirit of England' and 'The Fringes of the Fleet', and Ivor Novello's 'Keep the Home Fires Burning'. But the two greatest national songs that were the fruit of the conflict, Parry's 'Jerusalem' and 'Jupiter' from Holst's *Planets* – the big tune from which was adapted by him to become 'I vow to thee, my country' in 1921, using Cecil Spring-Rice's poetic response to the human sacrifice of the war – were not traditional, jingoistic anthems as one might expect. Rather they were thoughtful challenges to conscience and faith that asked as many questions as they provided answers.

While the Franco-Prussian War of 1870–71 had provoked in its wake a defensive, nationalistic reaction from composers in France and hundreds of pages of Teutonic vitriol from Wagner, the growing internationalism of music, the intermingling of genres, the easier availability of travel and the growing mass market for records ensured that the great broadening of horizons that had begun before the Great War was, this time, unstoppable, even in the face of such devastation and loss. The twentieth century's musical adventure was just getting into its stride.

7

The Popular Age I
1918–1945

On Christmas Eve 1906, from a wind-lashed transmitting station overlooking the Atlantic Ocean at Brant Rock, Massachusetts, a momentous sound was heard. It was the first ever wireless broadcast of a piece of recorded music: 'Ombra mai fu', Handel's 'Largo', transmitted by an intrepid radio pioneer named Reginald Fessenden.

The intended recipients of this 'broadcast' – a term not yet coined for radio transmission, and subsequently borrowed from farming – were Fessenden's colleagues at a specially constructed receiving station on the west coast of Scotland, but this had recently been destroyed in a storm. Consequently the programme was picked up, to their amazement, by ships at sea. The test broadcast went unreported for some time, but it was nonetheless the first tentative step towards a new age for music.

By 1922, ten million American households owned a radio receiver – up from just sixty thousand in 1919 – many of which were home-made 'crystal' sets. Six hundred broadcasters fuelled the boom, with Chicago's KYW broadcasting nightly operas from 1921 onwards, and lighter fare outside the opera season. Meanwhile, in Argentina, a radio station had in August 1920 transmitted a live performance of Wagner's *Parsifal* from the Teatro Coliseo in Buenos Aires, to the fewer than thirty households in the city with radios able to hear it. Over in Britain, the world's first national broadcaster, the BBC, came into being in 1922, ushering in an age when music would come to belong to everyone, everywhere, often enjoyed completely for free. (In the USA, advertising was in fact paying for radio broadcasting from the mid-1920s; in the UK, a radio licence fee was charged by the government to fund the BBC.)

The advent of free-to-air music for the world's grateful millions would change the value, purpose and style of music more dramatically than any other development in its history. And the dramatic advances in technology in the twentieth century affected popular and classical music in very different ways.

For pop, broadcast technology stimulated a thirst for new sounds and new voices that proliferated vigorously across the world. The explosion of popular songwriting – from George Gershwin and Cole Porter in the 1920s to Dylan and Lennon and McCartney in the 1960s, Stevie Wonder in the 1970s, Michael Jackson in the 1980s, Prince in the 1990s, and Bruno Mars and Adele in our own time – is a glorious, life-affirming phenomenon. The popular age, as it rapidly became known, brought undreamed-of musical benefits and rewards to humankind.

But pop's success also provoked a concern, voiced in every decade since 1900, that it had wittingly or unwittingly brought about the near extinction of other, older forms of music – an accusation specifically levelled at jazz by the writer, conductor and composer Constant Lambert, musical director of the Vic-Wells, later Royal Ballet, in his widely read book *Music Ho!* (1934). It did not help that 'non-popular' music was generically becoming known as 'classical' music, a term that began circulating in the 1930s as a marketing distinction used by record companies hoping to target listeners through the genres they preferred. The label was, initially at least, intended to grant the Western art music of approximately 1600 to 1900 a deferential sheen of permanence and class, but by the 1960s it had come to mean, for many millions, simply 'old-fashioned'. That a whole genre of music acquired a description that said 'antique and formal' when it was often startlingly new, young or *informal* was indicative, so many believed, that the music they loved was being deliberately sidelined in mainstream culture. (To be fair, as many if not more disliked what they saw as the ghetto of the genre term 'folk' music.) That one branch of the family tree had begun to own the term 'popular' was to many classical music aficionados in itself a revealing and disturbing fact of life.

Is it true that classical music has been slowly suffocated in its sleep over the past hundred years? I would say emphatically not. I hope to show in these final two chapters that, despite taking the odd experimental cul-de-sac on its journey, classical music has been alive and well since Reginald Fessenden's test broadcast. It has changed, certainly, and it is now experienced in all sorts of ways that would have surprised, for instance, Edvard Grieg, the Norwegian composer who died a few months after that historic transmission. But classical music's DNA is also embedded everywhere in the popular mainstream, whether in the stage musical, the cinema or in the albums of, say, The Beatles, Paul Simon, The Verve or Alicia Keys.

Of course, music has always had its tribal loyalties and its audience stratification. It is conceivable that a few people in 1875 would have sought out tickets for, and relished with equal pleasure, the openings of Bizet's *Carmen* in Paris, Gilbert and Sullivan's *Trial by Jury* in London, Richard Wagner's concert version of *Götterdämmerung* in Vienna, Ponchielli's cantata *Omaggio a Donizetti* in Bergamo, or squeezed themselves into one of Greater London's three hundred and seventy-five music halls, but in general the audiences at these events would mostly have been people of different tastes and classes. The stylistic parting of ways that started to become evident in the early twentieth century, though, was on an unprecedented scale. This wasn't just about record-buying preferences, either: being a composer in the twentieth century meant making career-defining choices that simply were not relevant to earlier generations. A highly skilled, celebrated musician of the 1920s such as Cole Porter interacted with his (vast) public in clubs, bars, theatres, cinemas and dance halls – a party to which everyone was, in effect, invited – in a manner that was a universe away from the invitation-only aristocratic salons of Vienna's Imperial palaces, where Mozart and Haydn were compelled to ply their trade.

The inheritors of Mozart's legacy in the twentieth century – classically-trained, self-styled 'serious' composers – struggled desperately with this challenge. After all, if you are not popular in a popular age, what are you for? The anxiety that underpins such a question can be seen playing itself out time and time again, and it is an anxiety that has often led classical musicians and their fans to look with disdain upon their counterparts in the popular field.

The awkward exchange between the two worlds was addressed with (unintentionally) prophetic poignancy at a concert given at the Aeolian Hall in New York in February 1924. Indeed, the event was something like a musical equivalent of nuclear fusion. The point of the concert, *An Experiment in Modern Music*, whose programme had an exhausting twenty-six different items, was educational, the third of three concerts designed to convince critics and the concert-going public that jazz was America's modern music and worthy of serious consideration. Led by the (classically trained) jazz bandleader Paul Whiteman, the concert was designed to bring about some kind of rapprochement between the two genres, and to show that jazz would develop from the rougher New Orleans 'Dixie' style towards an orchestral milieu in the near future. The highbrow world of classical music would be presented with examples of how various forms of jazz might work in a 'proper' concert hall setting, as if to say, 'One day jazz will grow up and will be respected like Beethoven.' At the same time, Whiteman hoped the kind of people who liked jazz might discover that a formal concert hall wasn't so scary and unapproachable after all, and might be encouraged to come again to a more conventional symphony concert.

In the event, the concert became famous for one reason only. One of the composers Whiteman approached to compose something hybrid that straddled jazz and classical was George Gershwin, who, just before the final item (Elgar's *Pomp and Circumstance* marches), premièred a work he had composed in just five weeks, *Rhapsody in Blue*. By the end of its fourteen minutes, the world of music had changed for ever.

In one sense those fourteen minutes tell the story of the next fifty years. The upstart popular musicians, invited to bow at the altar of High Art, were at first dismissed by critics despite having delighted the audience. A typically snooty review of *Rhapsody in Blue*'s première appeared in the following morning's *New York Tribune*: 'How trite, feeble and conventional the tunes are; how sentimental and vapid the harmonic treatment . . . Weep over the lifelessness of the melody and harmony, so derivative, so stale, so inexpressive!'

But great music has a way of finding its voice whatever snobbery throws at it, and what happened next is that Gershwin's first recording of *Rhapsody in Blue*, made three years later in 1927, sold a million copies within a year. It is now one of the standard pieces in every orchestra's repertoire, an out-and-out modern classic. In the thirty-odd years between December 1893, when Czech patriot Dvořák's *New World* symphony had its première at Carnegie Hall, conducted by an eminent Hungarian, and Paul Whiteman's *Experiment in Modern Music* at the Aeolian Hall in February 1924, the status of home-grown music in the United States had changed beyond recognition, largely due to the country having become the crucible of vibrant new forms of popular music. Race issues still scarred civil society, certainly, but one problem that Americans were happy to live without was the blight that ravaged Europe in the 1920s, '30s and '40s: militant nationalism. So many American composers of the early-twentieth century were immigrants or the children of immigrants whose (prior) national identities were wilfully abandoned in the rush to find an 'American' sound in their music.

It was quite another story over in Europe, where one gruesome incident in 1927 – the same year as Gershwin's frontier-busting *Rhapsody in Blue* sold a million copies – provides a glaring demonstration of the widening gulf between the two continents. It concerns the remains of composer and cellist Luigi Boccherini, a contemporary of Mozart and Haydn who was born in the Italian city of Lucca but who settled in Spain as a young man, marrying (twice) and having six children there. He was buried with his family in Madrid, his descendants putting down roots in Spain that persisted into the twentieth century. Some of Boccherini's most memorable – and utterly enchanting – chamber music is a collection called *Musica notturna delle strade di Madrid* (Musical Nights in the Streets of Madrid). Nonetheless, and sidestepping the details of Boccherini's actual life, Mussolini decided in 1927 that the remains of an Italian-born composer of nearly two hundred years earlier should be dug up and brought back to Lucca. This gesture – forcing a national identity upon someone whose music was filled with the colour, rhythm and spirit of his adopted home – would have been ludicrous and ignorant in any age, but in the twentieth century, when music escaped from its boundaries with a vengeance, it was hollow, petty and meaningless. It may be a cliché but the melting pot of the United States proved, in its domination of twentieth-century music, that leaving behind nationalistic distinctions in search of a collective voice was by far the more fruitful way forward.

In the years between the First World War and the disinterring of Luigi Boccherini's bones, music's family had expanded prolifically. Even before the war, a third of all homes in Great Britain alone had a record player. In 1914, twenty-seven million records were sold; by 1921, that figure had reached a hundred million. A method of synchronising sound with film was unveiled in 1922, the year the BBC was founded, and in 1926 Warner Brothers released *Don Juan*, the first Hollywood film containing a musical score embedded on the film's 'soundtrack'.

Nor was music seen as a background supplement to films. In big cities, before musical sound could be integrated into the film itself, cinema audiences would be treated to the lavish sight and sound of a live orchestra playing a score composed specially for the action on screen. For many people this would have been their first experience of a live orchestra playing what was, in all but name, classical music. In smaller cinemas a pianist or organist would provide a similarly live accompaniment; Russian classical composer Dmitri Shostakovich supported himself in Leningrad in 1924–5 by doing just that. It is worth noting that the man who more than anyone launched Hollywood's worldwide success, Charlie Chaplin, was also composer for his films, with and without sound; his first commercial venture after moving to the United States as a music hall performer was to set up a music publishing company. Chaplin's first film with a synchronised music soundtrack was *City Lights*, released in 1931, for which he also composed five songs in addition to the score. Thereafter, as well as composing for all his subsequent films, Chaplin wrote and recorded retrospective scores for his earlier silent films, continuing to do so well into the 1970s.

In 1921, Eubie Blake's *Shuffle Along* became the first musical comedy written by African-Americans and starring African-Americans to run successfully on Broadway. Its hit song, 'I'm Just Wild about Harry' (lyric by Noble Sissle), challenged a racial taboo of the time by featuring a romantic duet between two black characters. Blake, who was from Maryland, was the only surviving child of eight born to former slaves, and like Chaplin he had learnt his trade as a vaudeville performer. He made his name with ragtime but this style, as we saw in the previous chapter, was in the early 1920s being superseded all over America by jazz.

Indeed, the jazz stars of the 1920s – among them James P. Johnson, Fats Waller, Bessie Smith, King Oliver, Fletcher Henderson, Count Basie, Louis Armstrong and Duke Ellington – were, alongside Hollywood's biggest names, becoming the best-known celebrities in America. That they had virtually all come from lives of obscurity and poverty is in itself remarkable and a phenomenon rarely witnessed in Western music before the twentieth century. When such an incredible change in fortune *had* occurred in the past, it had typically taken composers and performers a lifetime to achieve a position of prestige, usually among a privileged cognoscenti, and even then their status was rarely recognised by the public at large. The boy Mozart was 'famous' as a child prodigy, to be sure, but famous in this context meant 'attracting comment and wonderment for brief spells at various royal courts of Europe'. Ordinary working-class Europeans would not have known who Mozart was either during his life or for a long time after it.

The fame enjoyed by the first jazz celebrities, however, was of an unheard-of scale both in terms of the rapidity of their ascent and the millions of listeners who became intimately familiar with them and their music, thanks to radio, records and films. Duke Ellington, grandson of a former slave, began with his band a four-year residency at New York's Hollywood Club in 1923. In the same year, Louis Armstrong, born into abject poverty in New Orleans and also the grandson of slaves, was playing cornet for King Oliver's Creole Jazz Band in Chicago, making records, earning good money and living in his own apartment. There were precious few opportunities for young black men in the segregated America of the 1920s, yet through music these two men became icons. The historic transformation of music in the jazz age was enabling an equally historic, admittedly embryonic, social trans-formation. That it was a change on a grand scale is undeniable; historian Eric Hobsbawm, in *The Jazz Scene* (1959), estimated that on the eve of the Great Depression there were a staggering sixty thousand jazz bands containing two hundred thousand profes-sional musicians in America.

Jazz celebrity though he was, Duke Ellington disliked his music being pigeonholed as 'jazz'; he preferred simply to call it 'American music', and he experimented in many forms and genres. He had a point: from the very beginning, jazz as a style thwarted defini-tion, so various were its manifestations in different places. The convergent tendency of twentieth-century music was manifest even in its most infant genre, articulated by its most eloquent spokesperson: jazz was *born* defying categorisation, even as white critics in journals were trying their toxic best to exclude it from serious study. (A *New York Times* editorial of 1924 dismissed is as 'a return to the humming, hand-clapping, or tomtom beating of savages'.) It is hardly surprising that a genre that consciously eluded form, which chose improvisation over the printed page, which allowed maximum freedom and looseness in its harmony, its interpretation of melody and its rhythm, should have splintered into a hundred colourful shards on impact with the world.

In all fields of music, the do-as-you-please freedom of the roaring twenties gave way to more organised, ordered forms in the 1930s. It is tempting to link this move towards greater organisation and a curbing of carefree individuality to parallel developments in the political temperature of the times, with the rise of dictatorships – or, in a benevolent form, the New Deal programmes of state intervention, directed employment and the rise of trade union solidarity – as a response to the fear generated by the meltdown of the Great Depression. More likely, though, conformity of expression gathered momentum because the record-buying, radio-listening public liked it better, and bands reflected the change in fashion for entirely understandable commercial reasons. On top of the demands of radio, the jukebox was another factor in the slimming-down of rambling jazz sessions: by 1937 there were one hundred and fifty thousand jukeboxes in America, further stimulating the market for record buying. In jazz, the shift in emphasis meant bigger bands comprising more structured families of instruments playing well-honed, written-out arrangements, with occasional well-defined solos emerging from the texture.

Greater shape and clarity, of course, was what the fledgling record industry preferred to long-winded periods of virtuoso meandering. It wanted tracks that could be packaged and contained on one side of a '78' shellac, ideas contained in catchy three- or four-minute bursts – as in Ellington's 1928 hit, 'Diga Diga Doo' – a pragmatic consideration that continues to this day, despite the freedom from time constraints afforded by digital technology. The three-minute convention persists thanks in no small part to attention spans and radio playlist imperatives.

The prevailing style of the 1930s and '40s, nurtured initially in the mob-run entertainment hub of the South, Kansas City, was both *called* 'swing' and *had* a swing to it, though nailing down a definition of 'swing' that all its practitioners would have agreed on has always been rather a minefield. Moreover, since swing is a technique that is 'felt' by the player in performance rather than written down and rehearsed methodically like most of music's other rhythmic features, its application is deliberately non-standardised. It is in this respect not dissimilar to the nuance of accent when learning a language: it is relatively straightforward to learn from a book the vocabulary, idiom and grammar of a foreign language, but speaking it like a native is only possible by spending years immersed in the sound and interplay of the language as it is spoken every day.

There are two chief ingredients in swing. One of these is the syncopation we have already encountered in ragtime, whereby the melody – it is usually the melody, though inner parts of the music and even the steady bass line may be susceptible – trips ahead and falls behind the point where the beat is expected to fall. Syncopation was immediately apparent in (and essential to) ragtime style, where just one player provided both the regular pulse *and* the cheeky push and pull against it, the right hand being mischievous with the steadiness of the left. Ragtime's syncopation was drawn from a relatively limited menu of possible variations, and could therefore also be written down and mastered, in time, by any competent pianist. As it was passed from ragtime to early 'Dixieland' jazz bands, though, syncopation became more sophisticated: now, instead of the right hand cheating the left, one instrumentalist was playing against another. The possible variations for errant beats multiplied rapidly and unpredictably. The push and pull of anticipating and delaying notes as manipulated by two, three or four improvising musicians, treating the bass and drums as their governing foundation, significantly complicated the layers of syncopation available, giving early jazz its bubbling energy and sense of fun. Indeed, as jazz reached out beyond its localised street gatherings and sleazy clubs, spreading across

America and thence to Europe during the First World War, it seemed to listeners and musicians alike that it was a playfully anarchic genre; it had an appealing naughtiness that was provided almost entirely by rhythmic syncopation.

The second major component of swing was a lilting effect achieved by subtly shifting the subdivisions of the given four-in-a-bar beat. This effect was not unique to swing, though – it had by the end of the nineteenth century become ubiquitous in music hall, vaudeville and minstrel songs and, separately, in Latin American dance music – but let's look back briefly at how the popular lilt developed into the 'swing' of swing music.

The nineteenth century had seen a rise in popularity of a lilting form of music known as the *habanera* in many Central and South American countries, particularly Cuba with its geographically concentrated, intertwined African, Creole and Hispanic communities. The habanera had been imported by Spain to various of its colonies but the Spanish had inherited it from the earlier French *contredanse* – and the French had in turn inherited it from an even earlier English *country dance* pattern. In fact, the habanera had found its way to Cuba not via the colonial Spanish – who lived very separate lives from the other classes on the island, where slavery was not abolished until 1895 – but rather via French-speaking Haitian refugees fleeing slave rebellions (and retribution from such rebellions) at the very end of the eighteenth century. A notated form of Cuban habanera, a song called 'San Pascual Bailón', survives from as early as 1803. Over in Europe, the proto-type English country dance and its French *contredanse* spin-off, in duple time (two-step), fell from popularity in the nineteenth century and were replaced by the spectacularly successful triple-time (three-step) waltz from Austria, and to an extent the duple-time polka from Bohemia – which, incidentally, was something of a template for Scott Joplin's piano rags. In the later nineteenth century, however, the habanera was reintroduced to Europe as an 'exotic' dance from Cuba, and it began to reappear in European music. The most celebrated example is the habanera from Bizet's opera *Carmen* (1875), in which it forms the accompaniment of the song 'L'amour est un oiseau rebelle' (Love is a rebellious bird). Bizet's habanera was itself an adaptation of a song, 'El arreglito', by the Spanish composer Sebastián de Iradier, who had visited Cuba in 1861 and been enchanted by its dances. (Iradier's other claim to fame is that he wrote 'La Paloma', the most recorded Spanish song of all time.)

The habanera and its *contredanse* antecedents had a highly distinctive accompanying rhythm of four beats, which in musical notation – as in the opening of the Bizet song – looks like this.

The '2/4' designation at the start tells us that there are two principal beats in this bar – they fall on the numbers 1 and 5 – that can, as here, be subdivided into eight shorter beats, known as 'semiquavers' or 'sixteenth notes' in music terminology. The fact that there are two principal beats indicates this is a duple-time (two-step) dance. In this example, the first note (D), with a duration value of three semiquavers, acts as a springboard for the one-semiquaver second note (A), which is followed by two notes (F and A) of two semiquavers each. To let you know that the first note is three semiquavers long instead of two it has a dot added to it, which is why this is called a 'dotted' rhythm. The effect of it is a slightly jerky sound, especially as the first note is in practice not sustained for all of its three beats; rather it is shortened to make it spikier and more accented, leaving a little gap between the first and second notes.

'Dotted' patterns, with the skipping **rum**-tah-tum emphasis they create, were very common indeed in European music of the seventeenth and eighteenth centuries, especially in France. The royal composers Lully and Rameau, who wrote ballet music for the courts of Louis XIV and XV, were obsessed with dotted rhythms – so much so, in fact, that they favoured a performance practice known as *notes inégales*, whereby even notes written out as equal (undotted) were *assumed* to be dotted. We shall return to this assumption very shortly, because its application finds a direct parallel, believe it or not, with swing in the 1930s.

By the nineteenth century, though, a dotted rhythm was only played if the composer had specified it with a dot in the notation. Here, though, a new oddity arose, which I shall demonstrate with the help of a rousing abolitionist song from the American Civil War, 'John Brown's Body', which was adapted into a thousand other versions, including 'The Battle Hymn of the Republic'. Its catchy tune is in 4/4 time – that is, it has a steady marching pulse of four principal beats per bar – and it would be written or printed out thus. (Note the prevalence of 'dotted' pairs.)

Here is the oddity. 'John Brown's Body' is a march, and as such you would expect its rhythm to be regimented and precise, with drummers keeping everything in strict order. But when sung, the very precise-looking rhythm notated above is not what is heard.

What is in fact performed and heard is a more lilting version of this rhythm, the lilt produced by a subtle reapportioning of the beats. Thanks to recordings, we know that this has been the case since at least the late-nineteenth century.

In the above example, there are two notes on the word 'body', E and G; the first note, E, like the first note of our habanera example, is dotted, so instead of being two semiquavers it is three. The next note, G, is just one semiquaver. This makes the two notes rhythmically identical to the first two notes of our habanera example: $3 + 1 = 4$ semiquavers. The four principal beats of our bar are known as 'crotchets' – each crotchet is made up of four semiquavers – and we can use these crotchets to track where the strong, or accented, beats fall. The highlighted words are the beats on which our feet would step, if we were marching to the song.

John
Brown's
Bo-dy
Lies a-
Moul-drin'
In his
Gra-ave

But although '**bo**-dy', for example, is marked as being $3 + 1$ semi-quavers, the lilting variation of this song that became the norm in performance – and which you are playing in your head as you read this – does not divide each of the crotchets into four subdivisions but rather into three. Subdividing a beat by three instead of four naturally makes each of the new smaller beats slightly longer. Now the mathematical value for '**bo**-dy' is $2 + 1$. The audible result of this slight increase in length of each subdivision is that the rhythm feels more relaxed, smoother and less rigidly precise. If the audible version were written out in musical notation it would read like this, with all its 'dots' gone:

This 'triplet' reorganisation of what might otherwise have been a 3 + 1 pulse underpins an enormous number of popular parlour and music hall songs of the turn of the twentieth century, from 'I do like to be beside the seaside' to 'Daddy wouldn't buy me a bow-wow' and 'Hinky-Dinky Parlay Voo'. It runs through all those songs because it is a natural pattern of rhymed, spoken English: it is the rhythm, for instance, of 'Humpty Dumpty sat on a wall, Humpty Dumpty had a great fall', which dates from the English Civil War. This lolloping rhythm also became a major component of swing rhythm – and the funny thing is that it still isn't written down: all songs, however jazzy, are transcribed with the archaic 'dotted' version, but 2 + 1 instead of 3 + 1 is *always* implied. In this respect the 2 + 1 triplet has become as habitual to post-jazz popular song as the unwritten *notes inégales* were to the dance music of Lully and Rameau.

The 'swung' triplet is absent from the surviving recordings of Scott Joplin playing in ragtime, but it can be heard tentatively in early jazz, its swagger detected in the Original Dixieland Jass/zz

Band's 'Soudan' (also called 'Oriental Jass' and 'Oriental Jazz'), which was recorded and released in London in May 1920. By the time of Bennie Moten's 'Kansas City Shuffle' of December 1926, the triplet-driven beat has acquired a new name, 'shuffle', and is heading towards absolute universality in the 1930s swing craze: Art Tatum's dazzling, acrobatic solo piano version of 'Tea for Two' (March 1933) demonstrates how one man could syncopate, swing, shuffle and solo without the need for drums, bass and guitar to provide the rhythmic foundation. A particularly clear example of the swing dynamic can be found in Count Basie's 'One o'Clock Jump' of July 1937, in which the discreet brushed drums and rhythm guitar initially provide reliably straight four-in-a-bar beats, while the piano tumbles about tripleting and syncopating against this framework. Then other instruments, notably sax, trombone and trumpet, perform similarly athletic interludes atop the structure.

Swing, which was all-conquering in the 1930s and '40s, and which Duke Ellington, doubtless tired of explaining what made jazz tick, coquettishly refused to define in his mammoth hit of 1931, 'It don't mean a thing if it ain't got that swing', subsequently bequeathed its shuffling triplets to rock and roll. The handover can be plotted in stages, starting with a slow, dreamy triplet shuffle in jazz violinist Joe Venuti's 1929 track 'Apple Blossoms', then in a more frantic version in his 'Really Blue' of 1930. The third stage in its journey to world domination has it transferred into the chordal texture provided by piano and guitar, which had hitherto been the home of the steady four-crotchet beat, as in 'One o'Clock Jump'. This shift was in evidence as early as 1931 in Venuti's 'Tempo di Modernage', in which the seeds of rock and roll were truly sown: it was precisely this triplet pattern, the one we have tracked from 'Humpty Dumpty' in the 1640s, which became the bedrock of the rock and roll shuffle style. The triplet configuration of chords driving the four-beats-in-a-bar rock shuffle can be heard in songs as diverse as Fats Domino's monster hit 'Blueberry Hill' of 1950 and Leonard Cohen's 'Hallelujah' of 1984.

A footnote to the riotously successful triplet shuffle of swing is that the one style it did not fully colonise was – perhaps ironically – the family tree of dance forms that began with the *contredanse* and habanera. The habanera's strict dotted 3 + 1 pattern was handed down to the Spanish *zarzuela*, the Cuban *danzón*, the Brazilian *maxixe* and the Argentinian and Uruguayan *tango*. For the tango, with its abrupt, machismo movements, its upright body posture, tight physical language and the participants' high-heeled shoes, the more rigid definition of the dotted pattern was much more suitable than the deliberately casual atmosphere of the more liquid, loose triplets. We shall return to the far-reaching influence of Cuban *danzón* and other related forms in the next chapter.

The transition from the chaotic, individualistic, rough-and-ready nature of 1920s jazz to a more streamlined form of swing in the 1930s was mirrored in other musical genres. A new breed of 'book-based' musical emerged on Broadway – that is, shows with a clear narrative and dramatic shape, not just vague showbusiness storylines on which to hang unrelated songs – and hastily cobbled-together revues with random extravagant dance routines were shown the exit signs, at least temporarily. Jerome Kern and Oscar Hammerstein II's *Showboat* of 1927 was a turning point in this respect, demonstrating what a well-written, clearly structured musical with a thought-provoking plot could be.

Showboat is many things – full of memorable tunes, daring (for the 1920s) in its confrontation of racial issues, emotionally rich, inescapably enjoyable and utterly sincere – but what it is not is a reflection of the jazzy, popular song style of the day. Its songs, with the one exception of 'Can't Help Lovin' Dat Man', are firmly grounded in a sentimental operetta and music hall milieu; they could all have been composed at any time in the previous fifty years. It's as if Duke Ellington, Fats Waller and Louis Armstrong simply had never existed.

Much of *Showboat*'s attitude to poverty and racial stereotypes seems to us somewhat patronising, but this was the 1920s and at its core is a well-intentioned heart. Call it sentimental, but the twentieth-century Broadway musical was created by Jewish men and women whose families had – almost universally – been offered a lifeline of opportunity via immigration from Europe to the United States. Their unflinching belief in the transformative effects of populist American art forms such as the musical and the movie was heartfelt, and audiences then as now knew that a Kern and Hammerstein or Rodgers and Hammerstein musical was a cynicism-free zone.

The 1930s saw some giants of 'musical comedy', as it mostly was at that time, straddle the twin worlds of Broadway and Hollywood – among them George and Ira Gershwin, Cole Porter and Rodgers and Hart. But the growing commercial confidence of Broadway and Hollywood musicals and of their songwriters blossomed at a time when classical music was struggling to find a sense of purpose beyond mere experimentation.

While classical composers may not have felt in direct competition with the glitz of 1920s Broadway or 1930s Hollywood, it cannot have escaped their notice that the marketplace for new music was increasingly crowded and competitive. In a handful of decades, new media had entered the fray: one can't help wondering whether the stage spectacles of underwater Rhine maidens in Wagner's *Rhinegold* in Munich (1869), or of a glass palace on the moon in Offenbach's *Voyage dans la lune* in Paris (1875), would have attracted as much excited attention had the audiences had the option of seeing the same wonders evoked on film. Added to classical composers' discomfort was the prospect of some of their most conspicuously successful 'popular' counterparts, such as Gershwin and Porter, threatening to set up shop in the 'serious' field: Gershwin's *Rhapsody in Blue* was followed by a string of orchestral commissions, including a piano concerto, and Cole Porter composed a fine ballet score, *Within the Quota*, for the Ballets Suédois in Paris in 1923. The twentieth century put enormous pressure on classical composers to carve out a new role for themselves. One route open to the advance guard was to play with the musical possibilities of the surreal and the absurd.

The term 'surrealist' was first used to describe a ballet, specifically one infamous collaboration between composer Erik Satie, painter

Pablo Picasso and writer-dramatist Jean Cocteau, a clownish concoction called *Parade* that had its first performance in Paris in May 1917. Its series of street entertainers in jesting, facetious mood was not without its innovations, from the bizarre juxtaposition of seemingly unrelated scenes and the disruption of any expectation of a narrative to Picasso's cardboard costumes that made dancing all but impossible and in-joke mockery of impresarios and audiences who would put on (or watch) any old tat without discernment.

Parade's innovations, though, ought to be seen in the context of the times. Its buffoonish hooey and end-of-the-pier music may have amused its creative team and some critics, but with the benefit of hindsight its timing seems tasteless and incomprehensible. Just a hundred miles away from the sumptuous Théâtre du Châtelet in Paris's fashionable first *arondissement*, the catastrophe of the Second Battle of the Aisne, which claimed a hundred and twenty thousand French lives in two weeks on the notorious *Chemins des dames*, was turning into a rout and a wholesale mutiny with mass desertions. How cut off from reality had the arts world become that Cocteau and his colleagues deemed the up-yours camp of *Parade*, which had all the hallmarks of a hastily thrown-together student revue, an appropriate public offering in May 1917? The Parisian arts clique at whom it was targeted were both scandalised and offended by it – and the very fact that it was targeted at them rather than at, say, soldiers on leave from the front, precludes it from any defence that it was intended as harmless escapism, like the contemporaneous, tuneful smash-hit hokum that was Oscar Asche and Frederic Norton's *Chu-Chin-Chow* in London's West End.

It is not that slapstick distraction in itself was necessarily out of place between 1914 and 1918 – Charlie Chaplin made over forty films during the First World War, after all – but attempts by musicological and arts commentators to justify the 'meaning' of staging *Parade* in the midst of a devastating war have never ceased to sound tenuous and desperate. Daniel Albright, Harvard Professor of Literature, described it as 'one of the profoundest responses to the Great War', precisely *because* it flew in the face of current events, cocking a snook at the solemnity of the 1917 mood, striking a pose he described in his *Untwisting the Serpent: Modernism in Music, Literature and Other Arts* (2000), as 'cultivated apathy'. But explanations of the fiasco by Jean Cocteau and poet Guillaume Apollinaire, who wrote the programme note as well as coining the expression '*surréalisme*', do not indicate that thought anything like as deep as Albright suggests went into *Parade*. Apollinaire claimed half-heartedly that there was a patriotic aspect to the endeavour, celebrating the new simplicity and clarity of French style in opposition to the complicated pretension of the German – but this observation came far too late to be taken seriously: Satie had begun his move towards 'simplicity and clarity' thirty years earlier with his *Gymnopédies*, Fauré had started writing songs in the newly purified sound ten years before that, and Saint-Saëns's decidedly un-German, playful mockery of musical pretension, *The Carnival of the Animals*, was composed in 1886. Cocteau's main aim, it would seem, was to shock *Parade*'s de facto producer, Sergei Diaghilev, who had challenged Cocteau to 'astonish' him.

Though music's flirtation with surrealism was short-lived – how can such an unreal art form ever really have had any relationship with surrealism? – one controversial aspect of *Parade*'s score had some coincidental forward momentum. This was its integration, against the composer's wishes, as it happens, of non-musical sound effects into the score. The rhythmic qualities of these sounds, from typewriters to factory sirens, were exploited time and time again as the twentieth century wore on, though it has to be said that the little-known *Parade* was not directly responsible for inspiring subsequent experiments. The most extreme early example of this 'industrial' sound texture, premièred in 1922, was the *Simfoniya gudkov* (Symphony of Factory Sirens) by Russian composer and sound technician Arseny Avraamov. As well as factory sirens, his symphony featured bus and car klaxons, the foghorns of a Soviet flotilla in the Caspian Sea, artillery guns, cannon, machine guns, pistols (supplied and 'played' by an entire infantry regiment), ship's sirens, various steam whistles and massed military bands and choirs. Aptly, it had its first performance in Baku, capital of Soviet Azerbaijan and home to the Caspian fleet. Other machine, or 'found-sound', works of the period included 'Zavod, Symphony of Machines' by another Russian, Alexander Mossolov, the soundtrack to a Soviet film *Entuziazm: Simfoniya Donbassa* in 1931, and solo typewriters joined the orchestra for Leroy Anderson's *The Typewriter* (1950) and Krzysztof Penderecki's *Fluoresences* (1962).

Musical surrealism and attempts at finding what the future of sound might be ran, somewhat surprisingly, alongside another avenue being explored by classical composers in the 1920s: rummaging around in music's attic. Led by Stravinsky and Sergei Prokofiev, both composers disorientated by the year-zero politics that followed the Russian Revolution and Civil War, they took to resurrecting antique musical forms and sometimes actual pieces by long-forgotten seventeenth- and eighteenth-century composers, and adding their own twentieth-century slant to them. In a sense this process, given the fancy title 'neo-classicism' by music historians, was at times nothing more elaborate than plagiarism. Stravinsky and Prokofiev, though, were engaged in something more than simply regurgitating old styles: they tampered with them along the way, as if to modernise the originals, inserting into them, for example, unexpected and anachronistic dissonances. Playing merry havoc with the styles of previous eras was a perfectly legitimate game to play, but it is hard not to draw the conclusion that experimental modernism was running out of steam, to be replaced with the musical equivalent of repro furniture.

Stravinsky had mischievous fun pillaging music's dusty back catalogue with the ballet *Pulcinella* for Diaghilev's Ballets Russes company in 1920. It coquettishly combines 1920s chutzpah and eighteenth-century courtly dance, quoting along the way actual music by eighteenth-century Italian composers. Diaghilev and Stravinsky believed the manuscripts – from a Naples library – to be the work of Giovanni Pergolesi (1710–36) but it has since transpired that they were in fact mostly by the more obscure Carlo

Ignazio Monza and Domenico Gallo, who died in 1739 and 1768 respectively. *Pulcinella* is sparklingly inventive with its source material but it is nevertheless the musical equivalent of placing the Art Deco spire of Manhattan's Chrysler Building on top of Christopher Wren's Greenwich Hospital. Prokofiev, for his part, wrote a pastiche symphony in the style of Haydn, known as *The Classical*, and had his own stab at clownish knockabout in the ballet *Chout* (The Tale of the Buffoon), also for the Ballets Russes. Though Diaghilev and Prokofiev first put it together in 1915 it was not deemed ready for production until 1921 – and even then, amid post-war euphoria and forgetfulness, *Chout*'s black comedy of serial wife-murdering was lost on the audience. Francis Poulenc's Ballets Russes commission, *Les Biches* (1924), also plundered the Old Curiosity Shop of dance styles, mixing and matching with more recent fashions and unashamedly giving movements names like 'Rag-Mazurka'.

There is something laudable in the attempts of these sophisticated, well-heeled composers and their fellow Ballets Russes artists to capture the popularity of Keystone Kops-style entertainment of the time, but also something rather desperate and even embarrassing about the results. It was rather like someone's dad turning up at the school disco and jiving awkwardly with the kids. Comparing *Chout* with Chaplin's *The Kid* of the same year sheds a cruel and amateurish light on the former. Chaplin went on to make (and compose music for) a series of truly outstanding full-length films – *The Gold Rush* (1925), *City Lights* (1931), *Modern Times* (1936) and *The Great Dictator* (1940) – all of them notable for being knockabout fun with consummate physical skill, contemporary resonance, social insight and considerable emotional power. Most important, and this is often conveniently glossed over, they were popular throughout the world because they were actually *good*.

It was no coincidence that an urge to disinter elements from music's past should have come about at a time when – invigorated in large part due to recording technology – scholarly interest in earlier music was enjoying a new lease of life. French composer-academic Vincent D'Indy (tutor of Cole Porter, among others) put on a performance in Paris in February 1913 of Monteverdi's opera *The Coronation of Poppea* using an edition of the score he had painstakingly reconstructed from surviving but neglected manuscripts. The opera had not been heard in its entirety in public since 1651. Monteverdi's earlier 1607 opera *L'Orfeo* was produced on stage at Oxford University in 1925 for the first time since its composer's death nearly three hundred years earlier. In 1926 in a monastery in Piedmont, north-west Italy, a huge treasure trove of Vivaldi manuscripts, thought lost in the Napoleonic Wars, was rediscovered, including the scores of three hundred concertos, nineteen operas and over a hundred other works. This haul was in effect the start of the twentieth century's Vivaldi revival and a great flowering of musicological interest in this hitherto all but forgotten master.

Though Stravinsky had been, and continued to be, one of the standard bearers of the new-from-old trend in such works as his magnificent *Symphony of Psalms* (1930) and his Hogarth-inspired opera *The Rake's Progress* (1951), he was instrumental in breaking away from its strictures too. Having detonated a modernist explosion with his *Rite of Spring* in 1913, his name subsequently becoming a byword throughout the world for the edgy, contemporary classical composer, he was not yet ready to retire from the front line.

As is so often the case in music's rich history, the most original, daring and influential works – Beethoven's *Eroica* symphony, Richard Strauss's *Salome* – are ones that creep up on the world, apparently out of nowhere. Stravinsky's complicated 1923 masterpiece *Svadebka*, known mostly by its French title, *Les Noces* (The Wedding), is another such smoking gun.

The basic premise of the work, which was first conceived ten years earlier in the aftermath of Diaghilev and Stravinsky's *The Rite of Spring*, is the recreation of an Orthodox Russian peasant wedding ritual, using spoken and sung fragments of speech. Stravinsky, who had by 1923 emigrated from his homeland, later reflected on the

bride's loss of virginity being to some extent a metaphor for what
he saw as the 1917 Revolution's rape of Mother Russia. At any rate,
there was a brutal vigour and anonymity to the conjugal proceedings in the piece. At times the role of the voice is akin to the
modern technique of rapping. The hybrid keening-singing-
declaiming style Stravinsky adopted was like no sound ever before
heard in a concert hall or theatre. It is an extraordinary noise, even
to tired, over-bombarded modern ears. The use of voices – chorus
and soloists – as quasi-instrumental sound-effect texture was revolutionary enough in itself, but the nature of the rest of the ensemble
is equally startling: a large battery of percussion instruments,
including four pianos. Stravinsky had at various points in the genesis
of the work toyed with the inclusion of synchronised pianolas
(mechanical roll-operated pianos), harmoniums and keyboard-
controlled cimbaloms (a hammered-string folk instrument prevalent in Eastern Europe and Russia). The resulting jangling,
sparklingly dissonant sound, which is brittle, full of edgy attack
and a kind of out-of-tune resonance, would have been – literally
– unimaginable, even terrifying to audiences of the day. One
contemporary critic described *Les Noces* as 'enough to convert
intending brides and bridegrooms to celibacy'.

To other composers, though, as they gradually came across *Les
Noces*, its peculiar, faux-primitive, fierce sound proved irresistible.
To them its assault on the senses was startlingly fresh, as if someone
had uninvented the symphony orchestra and started again from
scratch. The sound world of *Les Noces* is, quite simply, the most
imitated of all twentieth-century combinations outside the fields
of jazz and popular music. The auditory sensation of the piece is
faithfully imitated, to a greater or lesser degree, in works as
different from each other as Carl Orff's *Carmina Burana* (1937),
Béla Bartók's 'Sonata for 2 Pianos and Percussion' (also 1937),
Olivier Messiaen's *Turangalîla-Symphonie* (1948), Leonard Bernstein's
West Side Story (1957), Steve Reich's *Music for Mallet Instruments,
Voices and Organ* (1973), John Adams's *Grand Pianola Music* (1982),
James McMillan's *Veni, Veni, Emmanuel* (1992), and a gallimaufry

of film scores, of which Bernard Herrmann's for 1963's *Jason and the Argonauts*, particularly the coming alive of the skeleton army, and Hans Zimmer's *Angels and Demons* (2009) – the least believable film ever made – are but two randomly plucked examples. In all of the above, it is the metallic, kitchen-utensil-like sense of attack and attrition of the percussion, combined with the high-frequency, bell-like penetration of the tuned instruments, that so effectively assaults (and enchants) the listener: the impact of this orchestrational colour is, literally and historically, inescapable.

While Stravinsky's notoriety as classical music's Lord of Misrule afforded him the kind of profile that encouraged wealthy philanthropists to be generous in their support of him, especially after his move to America in 1939, in many ways he was an anomaly. For classical music as a whole, the 1920s were marked by deep fissures in the previously unchallenged prestige of Western 'art' music. The writing was certainly on the wall.

The unveiling in 1926 of a new opera by the last great Italian composer in the genre, Giacomo Puccini, could fairly be described as a media event on a global scale. *Turandot* was performed to huge audiences from Milan to Buenos Aires in short succession. Its biggest tune, 'Nessun dorma', was incredibly popular, not just with a few diehard fans but rather with just about everyone who heard it. It became an instant classic, but *Turandot* was to be a last hurrah. With the exception of a handful of later works by American composers John Adams and Philip Glass, newly written operas gradually became more or less invisible to the population at large, even as the audience for revivals of *old* operas grew and grew. A newly composed classical opera in the late-twentieth century was like Beluga caviar: a shockingly expensive commodity from an endangered species, accessible to a very privileged few but an inconceivable luxury to the rest.

The knee-jerk reaction of many classical music commentators to this flight from opera is to find causes in changing social habits, in education, in broadcasting priorities and the grip of the marketplace, but this conceals one important reality: composers *themselves* were drifting towards alternatives to long-established musical forms and traditions. Audiences may well have flocked to new, younger Puccinis, had they come along, but composers didn't want to *be* new Puccinis any more.

A bracing example of how the landscape was changing can be seen in the unfolding career of the classically trained son of an orthodox Jewish cantor, Kurt Weill. Weill's early exposure to music would have been envied by many classical composers: his parents actively encouraged interest and funded formal studies in music, and he received training both at his local opera house in Dessau and at music academies in Berlin. His early compositions place him squarely in the post-Mahler European classical tradition, a skilfully constructed first symphony of 1921 and his first full-length opera *Der Protagonist* showing him to be not so very different from his contemporaries: Samuel Barber in the USA, Shostakovich in Russia, Arthur Bliss in the UK or Paul Hindemith in Germany. Then he made a stylistic leap that dramatically transformed his career and the course of music history with it.

As Germany's vulnerable but well-meaning Weimar Republic of the 1920s and early '30s grappled with hyper-inflation, unpay-able war reparations, rioting and the rise of extremism to left and right, a remarkable cultural scene emerged in Berlin. It was, to some extent, the European equivalent of what Gershwin was doing in America: finding a hybrid style that existed in the no-man's-land between jazz and classical, a no-man's-land that was ultimately to become everyman's-land, though its protagonists didn't know it at the time. Unlike the frivolous goings-on in Paris or New York, though, the cabaret style of Weimar Berlin had a deadly serious undertow.

In the cultural soup that was Weimar Germany, Kurt Weill teamed up with Communist playwright Bertolt Brecht in the making of a piece of musical theatre that was neither strictly speaking an opera, a play with songs nor a musical, though it contained elements of all of these. Its vocal ranges were operatic, its naturalistic acting style more like that of a play, its structure of spoken plot-carrying scenes interspersed with verse-chorus-designed songs akin to those in musicals. *The Threepenny Opera* was the Berlin stage hit of 1928.

The Threepenny Opera wasn't intended just as escapist fun in hard times, but also as a piece of biting Marxist satire critiquing the corruption of capitalism. It was based on John Gay's eighteenth-century mock-opera *The Beggar's Opera*, which had, in 1920, been revived to great acclaim at the Lyric Theatre in Hammersmith, a production known to Brecht, Weill and their translator Elisabeth Hauptmann. Its musical texture deliberately mined the sleazy Berlin cabaret style of the moment, as it did popular dance idioms like the foxtrot and tango, but it was written with a knowing wink towards operetta and sentimental romanticism – especially in Weill's setting of words of hard-hearted irony. Macheath (Mack the Knife) and prostitute Jenny, for example, share a genteel duet, the tango-spirited 'Zuhälterballade', about their previous times together, he the abusive pimp, she the put-upon sex worker who, while going along with the mock nostalgia of the song, betrays him to the police. The most memorable song of the show, 'The Ballad of Mack the Knife', acts as a prelude to the unfolding fable, a laconic but immediately catchy melody that, were it not for the lyrics, could be mistaken for a Berlin tea-dance song, with a piano accompaniment that becomes increasingly like something from a 1920s Shanghai opium den. The lyrics, by deliberate, sharp contrast, speak graphically of Mackie Messer's appalling catalogue of crimes.

In Depression-era Europe, *The Threepenny Opera* clearly struck a chord: by the time Weill left Germany for the USA in 1933 it had been translated into eighteen languages and performed several thousand times. It was one of three collaborations Weill put together with Brecht, alongside *Happy End* and *The Rise and Fall of the City of Mahagonny*, a triptych whose tone is a world away from the wacky tomfoolery of Satie's *Parade* and Prokofiev's *Chout* of the previous decade.

All three Brecht–Weill pieces address the social inequalities of the day head-on, in a deliberately non-arty, low-budget way. *The Threepenny Opera* was a kind of *Trainspotting* for the late 1920s, presenting the middle classes with a grimy, warts-and-all vision of the alienated, nihilistic underclass. Some measure of the political sensitivity and topicality of the Brecht–Weill musicals is apparent when compared with Stravinsky's notoriously controversial *Rite of Spring*. While the latter had had a few people in black tie and tails heckling its first performance in 1913 in Paris, *The Rise and Fall of the City of Mahagonny*'s first night, in Leipzig in 1930, was invaded by brown-shirted Nazi thugs who intimidated audiences so much that the show was pulled after a few days.

At a time when the inventor of serialism, Arnold Schoenberg, was pompously describing his music as 'produced on German soil, without foreign influences' and therefore 'able most effectively to oppose Latin and Slav hopes of hegemony', Weill was deliberately mixing and matching a range of styles and trends that were around in the 1920s and 1930s. He added little touches of whatever took his fancy, from a chorus that sounded like a German Lutheran hymn ('Schluss-Choral') to a quick-stepping Dixieland rag ('Ballade vom angenehmen Leben' – The Ballad of Good Living). Musically speaking, *The Threepenny Opera* would have sounded to people of the time like a distorted jukebox of contemporary sounds, filtered by the razor-sharp mind of a man who had already composed an opera and a symphony. It was nevertheless a style that found immediate favour with the theatre-going and record-buying public, and its jerky, broken-glass catchiness was to insinuate itself into two or three generations of music theatre composers' work, from Marc Blitzstein's controversial 1937 musical *The Cradle Will Rock* to his friend Leonard Bernstein's *West Side Story* (1957), thence to Sondheim's *Sweeney Todd* (1979), Kander and Ebb's *Flora the Red Menace* (1965) and *Cabaret* (1966), and even, dare I venture, my own 1984 collaboration with Melvyn Bragg, *The Hired Man*. Weill and Brecht's theatre songs further cast their spell on later artists as diverse as Frank Sinatra, Louis Armstrong, Bob Dylan, David Bowie, Sting, Lou Reed, Marianne Faithfull, Tom Waits, Dagmar

Krause and Martha and Rufus Wainwright, all of whom produced cover versions. What binds these cover versions (except for the unrhythmical braggadocio of Sinatra, imitated more recently by Robbie Williams, and the loose, growling swing style of Satchmo) is a quality of acerbic detachment, a serrated edge that could strip one's emotional defences, or wallpaper.

The Threepenny Opera ends with Mack the Knife, a low-life criminal absolutely devoid of morality and remorse, about to be hanged, when Queen Victoria instead grants him a pardon, a title, a castle and a pension. The absurdity of this reversal of fortune may not have struck millions in the industrialised world after the Wall Street Crash of 1929 as all that implausible. Life had become unpredictable and harsh. As the world descended into anxiety, paranoia and financial meltdown, not to mention Fascism and Stalinism, increasingly it was composers embracing popular forms who became the voice of conscience. This subterranean shift could not have been anticipated at the start of the century. Nor were the fruits of the voice of conscience without controversy and complication, particularly where questions of race came into play.

Take the 1935 'American folk opera' *Porgy and Bess* by George Gershwin, with lyrics by his brother Ira and playwright DuBose Heyward. Set in a poverty- and drug-stricken African-American fishing community in the South, *Porgy and Bess* was notable for its sympathetic but clear-eyed portrayal of underclass life.

The fact that three white men wrote *Porgy and Bess* caused unease at the time and has stirred a certain amount of discomfort ever since. That the characters in the opera, which was based on an earlier play by DuBose and Dorothy Heyward, may be unflattering racial stereotypes that 'ghettoise' African-Americans is a legitimate subject for debate, even if *Porgy and Bess* has paradoxically only attracted this criticism because it has, on account of its great quality, outlived the many other artistic portrayals of earlier, less enlightened times. Its genius and consequent longevity have in effect caused it to be penalised, whereas a once popular parlour song like Ernest Hogan's 'All Coons Look Alike to Me – A Darkie Misunderstanding' (1896) has quite rightly been forgotten by most. *Porgy and Bess* suffers from much the same problem as Shakespeare's *The Merchant of Venice* or Wagner's *Parsifal*, both of which arouse discussion of perceived anti-Semitism because they are both still performed today. Whether it is fair to charge the Gershwin brothers simply because they were white Jews writing about African-Americans per se is a much less clear-cut accusation. What has never been contested is the beauty and timeless power of the songs the Gershwins created for *Porgy and Bess* and which have been covered uncomplainingly by most of the great African-American recording artists of the twentieth century, including Louis Armstrong, Ella Fitzgerald, Oscar Peterson, Miles Davis and Aretha Franklin.

In tackling the inequalities and injustices of the Great Depression, popular song of the 1930s proved it was already light years ahead of 'All Coons Look Alike to Me', even if groundbreaking songs that provoked serious thought were still rare. In the frothy 1930 Broadway revue *The New Yorkers*, Cole Porter made his well-to-do audience sit uneasily through a sympathetic portrayal of a prostitute in the piercingly sultry song 'Love for Sale' – though initial resistance by censors was relaxed when the character was changed from white to black: race relations were still lagging shamefully behind gender politics. Even relatively liberal-minded Porter, though, could not match the devastating impact of the Abel Meeropol song 'Strange Fruit', recorded by Billie Holiday in 1939. The song, which began as a poem, is thought to have been prompted by the shocking – and sadly iconic – newspaper photograph by Lawrence Beitler of the lynching of Thomas Shipp and Abram Smith in Marion, Indiana, in August 1930. Despite the undoubted inspiration it provided for the leaders of the subsequent Civil Rights movement in the United States, the birth of 'Strange Fruit' was by no means easy: Holiday's usual record company, Columbia, refused to release it and a small independent label had to take it on instead. Radio stations likewise gave it a wide berth.

Some concert venues objected so much to this signature song being included in Holiday's set that white staff would deliberately create noise with the cash tills or bottle crates while she was singing it.

Two years after the recording of 'Strange Fruit', Meeropol was summoned to appear before New York State's Rapp-Coudert committee investigating alleged Communist infiltration of the state's high schools. He was accused of having been commissioned by the Communist Party to write the song. That it became well known against such odds is testament both to its simple power and to the fact that it was still extremely difficult in 1939 to challenge publicly the inequality of the race divide in America.

Holiday's performance and the disturbing images of the poetic text mark the moment in the development of popular song when it could no longer be dismissed as mere frivolity. In the troubled 1930s, escapism and harmless entertainment were the principal domain of popular music, but – as Chaplin's *Modern Times* and *The Great Dictator* showed – being commercially successful was no longer synonymous with a lack of serious purpose. That the Nazis should have felt threatened enough by American jazz and swing to ban it in the Third Reich, despite or perhaps because of its popularity among the German population, is a telltale indication of its potential to unlock the dangerously unpredictable emotions of whole populations. To the Nazis, American jazz was racially inappropriate (i.e. African) and decadent, though hypocritically they continued to encourage German recording artists to cover favourite swing numbers for the enjoyment of their master race citizens.

Escapist fun was not, by and large, a route chosen by classical composers in the twentieth century. The final gasp of classical music's contribution to uncomplicated fun was probably Franz Lehár's *The Merry Widow*, which opened in Vienna in December 1905, and Ermanno Wolf-Ferrari's comic romp *I Quatro rusteghi* (The School for Fathers), which opened in Munich in March 1906, though Richard Strauss's *Der Rosenkavalier* (opened January 1911) might just squeeze into the category. After that, seriousness, confrontation and challenge were classical music's guiding stars. Indeed, when Shostakovich wanted to mock German culture in his seventh symphony, to evoke the Nazi invasion of the USSR (which we'll come to shortly), his parody-march was based on a tune from Lehár's *The Merry Widow*. Even today there is no greater venom among hardcore classical music champions than that reserved for so-called 'crossover' artists who dare to pollute the pure waters of the classical repertoire by appealing to the masses. For Lehár and Wolf-Ferrari in the early twentieth century, read Il Divo and Andre Rieu in the twenty-first.

As European nation-states descended into industrial-scale barbarism in the second half of the 1930s, musicians in these countries were placed in a difficult position. Jewish artists and intellectuals of all kinds fled Nazism, and music by Jews, Communists and Blacks was banned in the Third Reich and its occupied territories. A touring exhibition called *Entartete Musik* (degenerate music) opened in 1938, ridiculing these minority composers, as well as non-Jewish French composers Ravel, Satie and Saint-Saëns, who were deemed for the purposes of the exhibition to be Jewish. What, though, were the non-Jewish composers left behind expected to do? Collaborate or resist?

Composers who remained in Germany and wanted to have their music performed had no option but to stay on the right side of the regime. Orchestras and opera houses thrived under the Nazis, supported by generous state funding. Musicians and singers were granted privileges and perks denied the rest of the population in wartime. Indeed, the only adult males in the whole of Berlin's population exempt from defensive duties during its apocalyptic fall to the Red Army in April–May 1945 were the members of the Berlin Philharmonic. In the first hours after the guns fell silent in the ruined city, one of the most horrifying sights reported by civilians and Russian soldiers emerging from the rubble were the corpses of young boys hanging from lamp-posts in the city centre with signs round their necks reading 'coward' or 'would not fight for his Fatherland'. Yet, as reported in Misha Aster's eye-opening *The Reich's Orchestra: The Berlin Philharmonic 1933–1945*, within days of the city's surrender the players of the Berlin Philharmonic Orchestra were congratulating themselves on being able to convene a rehearsal in a makeshift hall and to keep the flame of their reputation alive in spite of the devastation all around them.

The Nazis accorded music considerable esteem, hoping to shape the course of musical history by manipulative policies affecting the production and reception of music across the vast territories they eventually controlled. Attempting to eradicate Jewish composers and musicians under their jurisdiction was one way of stifling a particularly vigorous community of practitioners in the field, filling the inevitable gaps in Germany's numerous pre-1933 musical institutions with Aryans whose abilities were less important than their racial background. It can only be guessed what future musical riches may have been forfeited from the loss of talent to the Third Reich's programme of extermination. Despite wrapping up their objections to aspects of musical modernism in pseudo-scientific claptrap about 'degeneracy', the Nazi leaders' distrust of certain forms of music was nothing more than crude, beer-cellar racism. Thus, 'atonal' (twelve-tone, or serialist) music was condemned when it was by Schoenberg, its Jewish inventor, but condoned when it was by the Aryan Paul von Klenau.

The most famous living composer in Europe, the now elderly Richard Strauss, had a relationship with the Nazi government that oscillated between polite acquiescence and obstinate stand-offishness, despite its PR-conscious enthusiasm to keep such a high-profile cultural figure happy. He did not openly take the regime to task for its abhorrent racial policies and was involved in a number of prestigious propagandist events – he composed a hymn for the 1936 Berlin Olympics and conducted his 'Festive Prelude' at the 1938 Reich Music Festival, convened by Joseph Goebbels, at which the grotesque *Entartete Musik* exhibition was launched – but mostly Strauss withdrew from public life. Strauss scholars disagree on whether his withdrawal was a rejection of his previous accommodation with the regime, a suspicion that it might not last, or simply an old man choosing retirement.

One composer who had no qualms about cooperating with the Nazi regime was Carl Orff, whose *Carmina Burana* had its tumultuously successful première in Frankfurt in June 1937. Its sequel, *Catulli Carmina*, the second part of a trilogy, was presented at the Leipzig Municipal Theatre in November 1943. (It is surely the only work in the choral repertoire with a repeated chorus of '*Mentula, mentula, mentula, mentula!*' – penis, penis, penis, penis!) Orff had his tetchy criticisms of the regime – not directed at its deranged policies, mind, but because it wouldn't roll out his children's music programme *Schulwerk* into all state schools in the Reich. He did, however, accept the Nazi government's commission to replace the Jewish Mendelssohn's incidental music to Shakespeare's *A Midsummer Night's Dream*, and felt unable to intervene on behalf of a close friend, Kurt Huber, founder of the White Rose resistance group, who was tortured and executed by the regime. After the war Orff claimed falsely at his de-Nazification tribunal that he had himself been involved in the founding of the White Rose movement. All in all, and certainly from a musical point of view, Orff's acquiescence with the Third Reich drove him into a cul-de-sac from which he never really recovered – which is unfortunate if only because *Carmina Burana* was one of the handful of new classical works written between 1930 and 1960 that found genuine popularity with the general public without seeking to be deliberately old-fashioned. (Ottorino Respighi's patriotic paeans to Roman power in Fascist Italy, *Pines of Rome* and *Roman Festivals* of 1924 and 1928, were also newly written and popular then as now, but they sit squarely amid his reliquary of plundered, re-orchestrated musical trinketry of Italy's distant past.)

The nearest thing classical music had to a genuine political dissident in the 1930s was the Hungarian modernist Béla Bartók. By the 1930s, Bartók was eminent as a cutting-edge modernist composer in the Stravinsky mould: his *Music for Strings, Percussion and Celeste* (1936) and *Sonata for 2 Pianos and Percussion* (1937) had already established his reputation throughout Europe and are still regularly performed today. He was also a tireless collector and annotator of East European folk song, and is in fact one of the chief architects of a whole branch of music study known as ethnomusicology. Bartók had serious misgivings about Hungary's slide towards Fascism, concurrent with developments in Germany and Italy, and after the Nazis seized power in Germany he forbade all performances or broadcasts of his music in the Third Reich and Fascist Italy, a gesture that impoverished him, since his publishers and the lion's share of his royalties came from Germany. When, in 1938, Goebbels mounted his *Entartete Musik* exhibition, Bartók asked for his name to be added to the list voluntarily, so disgusted was he with the hate campaign waged against selected modernist music, jazz and anything composed or performed by Jews, Slavs, Romani people or anyone of African origin.

Like most high-profile classical composers, though, Bartók was able to leave Axis-controlled Europe safely. He resettled in the United States in 1940, thereby avoiding any more serious consequences of challenging the totalitarian line.

However difficult the situation in Hungary, however, it was a tea party compared to the nightmare that unfolded in Russia in the 1930s. From 1934 onwards, Stalin rigorously suppressed any sign of 'decadence' (code word for avant-garde) from composers, in line with his general cultural clampdown, a significant U-turn on the previous Soviet policy of encouraging experimentation in the arts. This hardening of official attitudes made life increasingly difficult for Russia's leading composers, Prokofiev and Shostakovich (Stravinsky having emigrated, only to return for one emotional visit in 1962, aged eighty). At times they were in favour and received privileges ordinary Russians would have marvelled at; at others their continued survival as professional composers hung by a thread. Shostakovich, for example, was officially denounced in 1936 and again in 1948, but was also a multiple recipient of State Stalin Prizes for the Arts, a People's Artist of the USSR and holder of the Order of Lenin, the Order of the October Revolution and Hero of Socialist Labour.

He and Prokofiev were both mercifully spared the treatment accorded writer Alexander Solzhenitsyn, whose criticisms of Soviet authority in his books and public statements landed him in a Siberian prison camp.

Analysts since their time have discussed at length whether Shostakovich's and Prokofiev's music somehow 'defied' Stalinism in some surreptitious, ironical or coded manner, even when it was ostensibly toeing the Party line, which variously entailed being optimistic and relevant to the ordinary people (abiding by 'Socialist Realist' principles, in Soviet jargon), not being too Western-sounding ('reactionary'), and not being too modernist ('formalist'). Strangely, it was one of Shostakovich's most instantly admired larger-scale works, and one which was set in the Bad Old Days of Tsarist Russia, that started his problems with the Soviet regime: his opera *Lady Macbeth of the Mtsensk District*, which opened at the Maly Theatre in what was then Leningrad in January 1934.

Lady Macbeth of the Mtsensk District isn't exactly *HMS Pinafore*. It's a hard-hitting, sometimes grotesque, often violent and erotic spectacular. It's exciting and powerful, but you couldn't call it tuneful, or a laugh a minute. Although the story, which concerns a faithless wife who murders her husband, ends up in a Siberian labour camp with her lover, then kills herself, was set in the days of the hated former regime, it must have been crystal clear to its audiences that not much had changed. Indeed, when Stalin, Molotov and a coven of other Party leaders went to the Bolshoi Theatre to see it in December 1935, the same thought occurred to them. They walked out in disgust.

A few days later, the official newspaper of the Party, *Pravda*, published a stinging attack – thought at the time to have been written by Stalin himself – on *Lady Macbeth* and its composer, headlined 'Chaos instead of music'. It described the music as 'fidgety, screaming and neurotic', and as a 'confused stream of sound'. The story was caricatured as 'coarse, primitive and vulgar'. Another venomous article appeared the following week. Shostakovich was denounced by the Soviet Composers' Union, and then came a deluge of public criticism – even from former friends and colleagues. A few months later he was summoned to the 'Big House', the headquarters of the NKVD, the forerunner of the KGB. Many walked through its doors over the course of the 1930s; not many walked out again. (To put this terror in context, between January 1935 and June 1941 official figures claim arrests by the NKVD of just under twenty million people, of which an estimated seven million were executed.) The secret police wanted Shostakovich to answer questions about his friendship with Marshal Tukhachevsky, formerly head of the Red Army, who was being set up for a show trial. He was interrogated on a Friday and told to return on the Monday. In anticipation of his own arrest and almost certain death in the gulag, Shostakovich packed his bags, but in a bizarre twist that was strangely typical of Stalin's looking-glass world, he was saved by the fact that the NKVD official himself had been 'purged' over the weekend.

Clearly, whatever Shostakovich did next was going to seal his fate one way or another. He shelved his newly completed fourth symphony, sensing that its dark modernity might make matters worse, and for a while retreated to the relative safety of film scoring. The work that eventually emerged from all this anguish, his fifth symphony, premièred in November 1937, is now recognised as one of the classical masterpieces of the twentieth century. Shostakovich edged back from his previous gloom and dissonance, composing a more 'traditional'-style symphony of four contrasting movements, progressing in them from grim, layered anxiety in the first to a triumphant conclusion in the fourth. The symphony's first audiences were unanimous in their loud approval of it, with extraordinarily emotional scenes at each performance. To the concert-going public, hanging on desperately to some kind of sanity in the midst of Stalin's murderous, arbitrary repression, the symphony offered a glimmer of hope and, interpreting the music's journey from struggle to resolution, some kind of defiance. Written in the teeth of the terror, it is an astounding testament of its time. It also, miraculously and without doubt, saved his life. The Party endorsed it.

It is easy, from the comfort and distance of our own time, to judge high-profile Soviet-era composers like Shostakovich and Prokofiev for not being more outspoken against Stalin, but they knew well enough what resistance meant in a time of purges. Leaving the USSR between 1936 and the end of the Second World War, in the way Bartók was able to leave Hungary, or film-music pioneers Erich Korngold and Franz Waxman were able to escape the Third Reich, was all but impossible. Whether it is indeed possible to detect a challenge to authority in any abstract piece of music without being given prior non-musical information is debatable, and both Party officials and early audiences of the fifth symphony would have been well aware of Shostakovich's own public description of his forthcoming work as 'a Soviet artist's creative response to justified criticism'. Of course, this did not stop contemporary commentators – nor modern ones – from imputing quasi-narratives to Shostakovich's fifth, as had been the case with Beethoven's *Eroica* and Mahler's fifth (a clear model for Shostakovich's fifth), and hundreds of other pieces whose only descriptive clues lie in their directed performance speeds. Thus one contemporary composer and critic, Boris Asafiev, claimed: 'This unsettled, sensitive, evocative music which inspires such gigantic conflict comes across as a true account of the problems facing modern man – not one individual or several, but mankind.'

Shostakovich himself fuelled speculation as to the 'meaning' of his fifth symphony by saying, cryptically, in later, safer years: 'I'll never believe that a man who understood nothing could feel the Fifth Symphony. Of course they understood, they understood what was happening around them and they understood what the Fifth was about.' That a debate still continues, seventy-five years later, as to whether the 'triumph' at the end of the final move-ment is a genuine triumph or a parody of triumph reveals how tricky analysing abstract music and making assumptions about it can be.

Whatever agonies Shostakovich and Prokofiev may have endured during the Stalinist terror, and however these agonies may have played themselves out in their music, what cannot be denied is the two composers' solidarity for and love of Russia and its people, whoever was in charge. So when Germany invaded the Soviet Union in 1941, the agendas of Stalin and his composers were abruptly realigned. Composers' purpose, and cause, became patriotism.

Perhaps the most extreme example of a large-scale work of patriotic purpose was Shostakovich's seventh symphony, *Leningrad*, premièred in March 1942 and dedicated to the people of his home city, who were at that time enduring an apocalyptic siege by the German Army Group North and their Finnish allies. Shostakovich had composed some of the symphony in Leningrad itself – modern-day St Petersburg – before his evacuation on official orders. It began life as a single, long, exhaustingly forceful movement, but Shostakovich, in a white heat of besieged inspiration, fleshed it out to a further three movements. Although the threat of official denouncement and censure was safely in the past – or so Shostakovich innocently thought – *Leningrad* nevertheless took the accessible, martial masculinity of the final movement of his fifth symphony as its stylistic starting point. Again, Mahler is all-present in the first and subsequent movements, but this time there is no doubt whatever as to the sincerity of the triumph with which the finale concludes.

In more recent years, a reluctant consensus has emerged among musicians that *Leningrad* may not be Shostakovich's best symphony, despite its iconic status. But its third movement, *Adagio*, is its highlight from a purely musical point of view, bringing together influences as diverse as Stravinsky and Bach in a lament that switches between unsettling block woodwind chords and wrought, isolated violins. This symphony too, in the understandably heightened temperature of war, was scrutinised for 'meaning' to within an inch of its life, *Time* magazine's preview for the US première summarising the first movement thus:

The deceptively simple opening melody, suggestive of peace, work, hope, is interrupted by the theme of war, senseless, implacable and brutal. For this martial theme Shostakovich resorts to a musical trick: the violins, tapping the backs of their bows, introduce a tune that might have come from a puppet show. This tiny drumming, at first almost inaudible, mounts and swells, is repeated twelve times in a continuous twelve-minute crescendo. The theme is not developed but simply grows in volume like Ravel's *Boléro*; it is succeeded by a slow melodic passage that suggests a chant for the war's dead.

Whatever its meaning, its musical flaws or merits, *Leningrad* certainly succeeded in its patriotic purpose. In June 1942, a few weeks after its première, a score of Shostakovich's symphony was dropped overnight by plane into the city of Kuibyshev (present-day Samara), well behind Russian lines, and hastily assembled into orchestral parts. In Leningrad itself, in early August, a scratch orchestra of any musician still alive was put together for a performance that was relayed on PA systems throughout the city and out towards the German lines, which had been bombarded comprehensively beforehand to ensure some respite. The gesture of defiance and survival that the broadcast sought to express reverberated around the world. There can be no performance of a piece of music that has had so powerfully symbolic an impact as on that night in August 1942 in Leningrad. The symphony was performed repeatedly in Allied countries in the months that followed.

The Siege of Leningrad did not end until January 1944, almost two years after the première of the symphony dedicated to it. It remains to this day the most deadly battle in human history, in terms of lives lost: over a million civilians and a million Red Army soldiers, with a further two and a half million wounded. So desperate were conditions in the besieged city that, in the winter of 1941–2, police had to form a special unit to combat gangs involved in cannibalism. These were appalling scenes, compounded in January 1944 by the retreating German armies looting and destroying the historic galleries, mansions and palaces of the tsars. A huge haul of art treasure was taken back to Nazi Germany, but there was one cultural item that could never be stolen from Leningrad: Shostakovich's seventh symphony.

In Britain, some classical composers joined the war effort by composing scores for patriotic films, such as William Walton's stirring accompaniment for Laurence Olivier's *Henry V*, but it is fair to say that the orchestral music that most bucked up ordinary people on the home front was Eric Coates's 'Calling All Workers', the theme tune of BBC radio's *Music While You Work*. Benjamin Britten enjoyed an extended holiday in America, while Michael Tippett, a conscientious objector, produced an eloquent and moving wartime plea for unfashionable pacifism in his oratorio *A Child of Our Time*.

A *Child of Our Time* reflects upon real events from 1938: the assassination of German diplomat Ernst vom Rath by a seventeen-year-old Jewish refugee, Herschel Grynszpan, enraged at the deportation of his family and twelve thousand other German Jews. The assassination led to the *Kristallnacht* pogroms across Germany and Austria. *A Child of Our Time* intersperses quasi-operatic narrative passages with arrangements of African-American spirituals, as Bach had done with Lutheran hymn-chorales in his oratorios on the passion and crucifixion of Jesus Christ. *A Child of Our Time* may be classical music's most heartfelt answer, during the 1940s, to the challenge of Billie Holiday's 'Strange Fruit' – to confront the anxieties of the age in a language that could still communicate to the community at large.

For other mid-twentieth-century composers, however, it seemed increasingly as if being complicated and uncompromising was more important than producing something beautiful, entertaining or simply enjoyable. Few of the contemporaries of American composer Aaron Copland heeded his open-hearted declaration in his *Appalachian Spring* of 1944 that "tis a gift to be simple'.

Like Stravinsky's *Firebird*, *Rite of Spring* and *Les Noces*, Debussy's

Jeux, Prokofiev's *Romeo and Juliet*, and Ravel's *Daphnis et Chloé* and *Boléro*, Copland's Pulitzer-prize-winning *Appalachian Spring* was composed as a ballet score. It is hard to imagine what twentieth-century classical music would have done without ballet. It was as if the distraction of telling a story, of reaching a different audience, or of submitting to the structure of another art form, liberated composers from having to deal with the question 'whither music?'. It was a question that ran like an unstable, life-threatening electrical current through the century that followed 1910, the year that had confidently yielded Stravinsky's *Firebird*, Elgar's violin concerto, Strauss's *Der Rosenkavalier*, Vaughan Williams's *Sea Symphony*, Ravel's *Daphnis et Chloé*, Parry's fourth symphony, Puccini's *The Girl of the Golden West*, Scriabin's *Prometheus, the Poem of Fire*, Debussy's *First Book of Preludes*, the première of Mahler's eighth symphony and the completion of his ninth. Such confidence was inconceivable thirty years later.

Audiences adored Copland's *Appalachian Spring*, though, with its touching innocence and optimism, as if America's victory in the Second World War really would usher in a better age, all reflected in the sincerity and uncynical values of the pioneer rural communities it celebrates. (The phrase ''tis a gift to be simple' comes from the Shaker spiritual song, 'Simple Gifts', the melody of which, composed by Joseph Brackett, a member of the Shaker community at Gorham, Maine, is widely quoted in the ballet score.) It is worth noting, though, that Aaron Copland – left-wing, gay and Jewish – might have approached the same commission very differently had it come his way *after* the liberation of the Nazi death camps, or Hiroshima, or during the McCarthyist witch-hunts. Unlike much else composed in the 1940s, it is still popular and regularly performed both in the theatre and on the concert stage today.

Nevertheless, the concert hall success of Copland's *Appalachian Spring*, as with Tippett's *A Child of Our Time*, Shostakovich's symphonies, Stravinsky's ballets and Orff's lusty secular oratorios, should be seen as the 'high end' of public engagement with the arts, belonging to a classical tradition that, by and large, maintained a separate, parallel path from any of the key popular genres. You don't expect to hear rock and roll guitar in Shostakovich or a bluesy sax solo in Bartók, even though these composers would have heard both, often, during their working lives.

But ballet was not the only medium that allowed classical composers to hang on to their distinctive orchestral idiom and appeal directly to a broad audience, freeing them from writing over-complicated, abstract music that a listener might need a PhD to appreciate. Dance certainly had a huge influence on music in the twentieth century, but classical music would surely have continued sleepwalking on the path to oblivion after the war had it not been for another knight in shining, or perhaps silver, armour: cinema.

Following *Alexander Nevsky*, Prokofiev's groundbreaking collaboration with fellow Russian film-maker Sergei Eisenstein in 1938, it was clear that large-scale orchestral music was going to be a powerful component in making films more exciting, more frightening and more emotional. To this day, millions of people who might never set foot in a classical concert hall thrill to the symphonic sound of film scores that are often made up entirely of classical orchestral styles and techniques. If anyone tells you classical music is dead in the twenty-first century, all it means is that they don't go to the cinema.

When European composers fled Nazism in the 1930s, they usually ended up in Hollywood hoping to make a living from film, an opportunity the directors, producers and writers, who were themselves either émigrés or the children of émigrés, were happy to provide. Some, like Erich Korngold, leapt enthusiastically into this new, populist role with skill and seriousness, widening the scope and capability of the film orchestra in the process. His scores for *Captain Blood*, *The Sea Hawk* and *The Adventures of Robin Hood* only seem like clichés to us now because their swashbuckling grandeur has been so comprehensively imitated for so long by so many others.

The truth is, though, that from the 1940s until the 1990s, film composers tended to be a different breed from concert hall composers. Few classical composers made headway in film and many viewed it suspiciously or with condescension, as something only good enough for the paying of bills. How shallow that criticism now seems, with some of the best purely orchestral music from the past half-century being written for film: whether the thrilling, scary power of Bernard Herrmann's *Vertigo* and *Psycho* or Miklós Rózsa's *Spellbound*, the haunting melancholy of Ennio Morricone's *The Mission*, Nino Rota's *Godfather* or Gabriel Yared's *The English Patient*, the expansive drama of John Barry's *Goldfinger*, Maurice Jarre's *Lawrence of Arabia*, or Hans Zimmer and Lisa Bourke's *Gladiator*, the sweeping adventure of Dmitri Tiomkin's *High Noon* or Danny Elfman's *Batman*, the sensuality of Jerry Goldsmith's *Chinatown* or Thomas Newman's *American Beauty*, or the heartbreaking grace of Dario Marianelli's *Atonement* and John Williams's *Schindler's List*. What is remarkable about this tiny, tip-of-an-iceberg roll-call of great scores is that, as I write them down, I know that many of you will be able instantly to recall the mood and themes of these scores in your minds. They are part of a shared cultural inheritance of the past half-century. Of how many other classical works since the Second World War is it possible to make that statement?

For all the scepticism of film music among 'serious' composers, cinema was a lifesaver for classical music. It not only gave the genre a new relevance in the modern age, but also brought it into the lives of people who would never have thought themselves interested in it. And indeed, introducing classical music to the masses became something of a mission for post-war governments. The governments of Third Reich Germany, Fascist Italy, Roosevelt's America, Stalin's USSR and Blitzkrieg Britain had viewed classical music not – like comedy, film and popular music – as a comfort and distraction in grim times, but rather as a way of defining cultural identity among their populations, of saying 'this is what we might lose if the barbaric enemy wins'. After the war they all determined to bring 'high art', as it was deemed to be, to the people, setting up various publicly funded and privately sponsored institutions to make this a reality. The great American conductor and champion of new music Serge Koussevitsky, for example, commissioned Benjamin Britten's gloomily magnificent opera *Peter Grimes*, which, miraculously, was produced at Sadler's Wells Theatre in a bombed-out London just four weeks after VE Day.

Despite the cast of *Peter Grimes*'s first production complaining that the music was difficult, modernist and impenetrable, it presented no such obstacle to opera-goers in the UK and around the world, both at the time and in the decades to follow. This, surely, was because what Britten had written was essentially an old-fashioned, nineteenth-century music drama such as Verdi, or even at a pinch Wagner in *Flying Dutchman* mode, might have concocted – which brings us to one of the (perhaps unexpected) trends that emerged from the post-war promotion of music.

Undeniably the instinct to support the arts went – and still goes – hand in hand with a desire to reach out to larger numbers of people, but the two aims were often contradictory. Orchestras and opera houses, for instance, tended to be presided over by powerful patrons who might well have paid lip service to the notion of introducing ordinary folk to the new and unfamiliar, but who were just as concerned with getting the state to subsidise an expensive minority taste. The fact that the 'new' was narrowly defined as 'contemporary classical' rather than, say, bebop is indicative of this. Public subsidy allowed formats that had become financially unviable – such as the nineteenth-century symphony orchestra – to prosper somewhat artificially in the twentieth century, justified by the preservation of heritage. In previous centuries, forms had come and gone as the 'market' (or aristocratic fashion) changed; nobody, after all, had tried to keep Louis XIV's lavish opera-ballet spectacles going after he lost his head.

But what subsidy and philanthropic patronage of classical music in the post-war years made possible were two somewhat para-doxical outcomes: the preservation of a musical idiom that was obstinately fixed in the mentality of the nineteenth-century opera house and concert hall, and the blossoming, as we shall see shortly, of carefree, unedited experiment that was occasionally creative, often quite mad and always mind-bogglingly self-indulgent.

It would be a while before new classical music set the pace of change. Meanwhile, the war had brought about whirlwind developments in technology, some of which, such as the invention of magnetic tape for recording, would have a direct effect on music; others, like high-speed cars, planes and rockets found their giddy velocity reflected in music of revived, exhilarating energy. However threatened classical composers might have been by the inexorable rise of popular song in the jazz and swing era, it had been a light summer shower compared to the hurricane coming their way in the 1950s. And it was a hurricane with one unavoidable exhortation: *Roll over, Beethoven . . .*

8

The Popular Age II
1945–2012

The years 1939–45 will for ever be remembered as a turbulent turning point in world history. But at the same time, thanks in large part to the unprecedented movement and displacement of populations during this period, to American military presence in Europe and the Pacific, and to the United States emerging from the conflict as the economic and cultural dynamo of the world, American musical styles established themselves as the focus of change and growth in the decades following the war.

The war years signalled a watershed in music, as the swing variant of jazz gave birth to a new form, one that would sweep the planet like no other musical phenomenon before it: rock and roll.

The genesis of rock and roll can be traced back to a swing recording made in 1939 by the Benny Goodman Sextet, 'Seven Come Eleven'. On the surface of it, 'Seven Come Eleven' fits the mould of the classic swing number: energetic, well-organised, with symmetrical phrases, a predictable, reassuring, chugging-along rhythm generated by brushes on the snare drum, and distinct moments set aside for Benny Goodman's crystal-clear clarinet solos. Then, out of this run-of-the-mill swing exuberance, something emerges that is new in its sound, new in its execution and new in its improvisatory style. It is an electric guitar – an instrument invented in 1931 – played by a twenty-three-year-old African-American from Oklahoma, Charlie Christian, who co-wrote the song with Goodman. If you've never heard of him, now is the time to make up for the omission. His musical efflorescence was tragically brief, but this is the man who turned the chord-strumming, jobbing electric guitar into a high-wire, virtuoso lead instrument, from also-ran to star turn. If you were young in the 1940s, this Christian was your Messiah.

To our jaded twenty-first-century ears, Charlie Christian's solo on 'Seven Come Eleven' may not seem all that earth-shattering, but to musicians of the 1940s it was a green light. Jazz musicians took from it a fast, free-flowing, unpredictable stream of consciousness in sound, inspired by Christian giving emphasis (accent) to beats that would not normally have been strong and allowing the tune to stray like a river bursting its banks across open countryside, meandering across chords to which it was never intended to fit. Christian bends the strings as he solos, tweaking the notes above and below their standard tunings, not something one could notate very accurately – nor, indeed, would he have wanted to, as he attempted to give the guitar the cutting-edge energy of a tenor saxophone.

This frantic, somersaulting style turned within a few years into bebop, the elite modern jazz of the late 1940s and '50s. In bebop, whole tracks were devoted to helter-skeltering instruments, sometimes solo, sometimes in coordinated groups, tumbling across notes at high speed, wilfully oblivious of the harmonies to which they once belonged. If death-defying, off-piste skiing at high altitude down near vertical slopes had a musical equivalent, bebop would be it.

Bebop took a basic song shape, with its chord sequence and the ghostly outline of its tune lurking somewhere in the background, and used this as the oft-repeated foundation for an improvised solo from each member of the band in turn. Before bebop, the solos bore some resemblance – at least as they began – to the song's original melody and they also adhered to its key-family and chordal logic. Bebop defied these conventions on several layers: solos increasingly drifted away from the chord sequence and even the key-family of the original song, and they habitually veered off from the given song melody, too. Soon bebop musicians began dispensing with the blueprints of the standard songs and instead invented their own chord sequences and melodies – highly complex ones at that, sometimes derived from the note combinations of unusual chords.

Though the *ethos* of post-war jazz, with its celebration of freakishly talented individual skills, its infatuation with complicated chords and its ambitiously long, stamina-testing pieces, was always closer to that of classical music than of happy-go-lucky pop, the actual *sound* of bebop was about as far from what was going on in 1950s classical music as it was possible to be. Classical music in the mid-twentieth century was mostly about the brain and the intellect: the conceptual theory behind a composition had become more important than the sensory effect of the music. Bebop, though, was too fast, too instinctual, too trance-like to allow for much conceptualising or theorising. It was all about intuition, the moment, the feeling, the trip.

Post-war jazz relied for its forward-moving momentum on being daringly free with the regular, four-beats-in-a-bar pulse. Instead of emphasising the strong beats as the foot-tappingly predictable swing had done, bebop deliberately resisted, suspending the rigid reiteration of the regular pulse. Take as an example Cab Calloway's 1934 swing classic 'Jitter Bug' – the hit, incidentally, that caused the meaning of the expression *jitterbug* to change from someone suffering from alcohol-induced shakes to someone who dances to swing. Its steady, reliable beat acts as an anchor to the syncopated vocal line, while the rhythm guitar, bass and drums act as a unit to keep the clockwork of the pulse ticking along. Any stretches to the expected fall of the beat (that is, syncopation) are clearly audible against the main beat. In contrast, the steady 1-2-3-4 beat is virtually inaudible in the 1945 radio broadcast recording of 'Air Mail Special' by bebop pioneers Billy Eckstine and his Orchestra, giving way instead to syncopated, off-beat, high-speed brass phrases. Previously non-emphasised divisions of the pulse are now the principal motors of the rhythmic drive, with drummer Art Blakey playing furiously with ride cymbals and the kick-drum to serve up snapped, unpredictable accents in seemingly – though never actually – random beats. The overall effect sounds as if the drummer, formerly the guardian of the steady pulse, has been asked to improvise a solo from the first beat of the piece.

In the late 1940s, Billy Eckstine's big band boasted among its ranks some of the rising stars of the bebop era: Blakey, Charlie Parker, Dizzy Gillespie, Dexter Gordon and Fats Navarro. But while they were impressing each other on the road with their tightrope-without-a-safety-net virtuosity, there was another, quite opposite impulse emerging. It was a musical impulse that relied slavishly on hypnotic repetition and had an unbending loyalty to four steady beats, and it took the world by storm.

Although it grew out of swing and the pioneering electric guitar figures of Charlie Christian, early rock and roll announced its intention to go light on improvisation and heavy on rhythm guitar. Whereas bebop took from Christian's playing style the inspiration of his free-flowing solos, rock and roll took the sound of his accompanying – 'rhythm' – guitar grooves. If he had been a piano player instead of a guitarist, one might say bebop grew from the solos of his right hand while rock and roll grew from the accompaniment of his left. From the outset, of course, the functions of bebop and rock and roll were different and distinct, as were their respective audiences: jazz was for cool dudes to listen to, and rock and roll was for teenagers to dance and date to. And teenagers suddenly existed, apparently, after 1950.

Indeed, the affluence of post-war America – and eventually Europe – saw a generation of carefree teenagers with pocket money to spend, and they wanted to spend it on rock and roll. Transistor radios and Dansette record players opened a bustling new market for record companies and they began producing music specifically aimed at teenagers. Increasingly it became the case that albums were for adults and hit-parade singles were for the youth. The song generally identified as the first rock and roll record is 'Rocket 88', composed by Ike Turner's saxophonist Jackie Brenston and released in April 1951. (The song, which extols the virtues of the Oldsmobile 88 convertible as a metaphor for sexual prowess, was in fact based pretty unapologetically on two earlier tracks: 'Rocket 88 Boogie' (1949) by boogie pianist Pete Johnson, and 'Cadillac Boogie' (1947) by Jimmy Liggins.)

But before the new genre could become a universally addictive sensation it needed to undergo some fine-tuning, particularly in its choice of instruments. The major feature shared by rock and roll's prototypes is the swinging triplet of the piano. But this instrument's dominating role in churning out the oscillating left-hand chords or defining the 'walking' bass line in boogie-piano style – a more frantic contemporary of ragtime popular in the 1930s and '40s – was gradually taken over by the guitar on chords, with a double-bass (later bass guitar) dealing with the 'walking'. In addition the (at first unintentional) distortions of the electric guitar were later added deliberately, the sound blurring and fuzzing, and generally becoming 'dirtier' as its volume was cranked up in the amplifier.

All that was now needed to turn this cocktail into a mass youth movement with electric guitar at its throbbing centre was for some white guys to repackage this black music for an even wider audience. We have already witnessed black music being 'bleached' for greater commercial appeal a number of times, often to the dismay of its original performers. (The extent to which this had been true of jazz and swing led Art Blakey, who frequently hired white musicians, to observe somewhat resentfully that 'The black musician . . . his thing is to swing. Well, the only way the Caucasian musician can swing is at the end of a rope. Swinging is our field and we should stay in it.'[5]) But there was no stopping the inexorable takeover of rock and roll by big-name white musicians, and there were plenty of candidates willing to become the heart-throbs of a generation.

5 In conversation with drummer-writer Arthur Taylor (*Notes and Tones*, 1972).

First in line was a man who looks to us like an insurance salesman at his daughter's wedding karaoke, but who was to the upstanding middle class of the early 1950s the very incarnation of a rock and roll Satan: Bill Haley. He too jumped on the 'Rocket 88' bandwagon with a cover of the song, also in 1951. He and his Comets went on to have a series of enormous chart hits, including 'Shake, Rattle and Roll' in 1954 – originally composed, incidentally, by African-American Jesse Stone and previously recorded by African-American Big Joe Turner – and Max C. Freedman's 'Rock around the clock' in 1955, but they were eclipsed soon enough by the much more charismatic Elvis Presley.

The phenomenon of Elvis – good-looking, mildly rebellious, an expressive and versatile voice, a distinctive dancer, as good on film as on record, well promoted by a cunning team of managers and writers – is one that record executives have tried to emulate time and again over the course of the pop age. But Elvis did not bring just charisma and energy to the music scene; he also introduced two musical elements to the black Rhythm and Blues mix that was standard currency among American musicians of the early 1950s: the simplicity and liveliness of country music, known at the time as hillbilly or rockabilly, and the soul-searching yearning of gospel. This last ingredient, implausibly combined with uninhibited sexuality, was what gave his vocal renditions such quivering power, even when the subject matter was physical, rather than spiritual, love.

Unlike the giants of the 1960s, though – Bob Dylan and The Beatles for starters – Elvis did not carve out his larger-than-life identity through material he had actually composed himself, and by the time of his later Las Vegas residencies he was essentially a variety turn, reminding his inevitably older, richer audiences of their carefree youth. Dylan, on the other hand, though not gifted with Elvis's tremulous voice or elastic thighs, wrote the kind of lyrics that might change a whole society's way of seeing itself. Notwithstanding their chart success, his acute observations on modern society – 'Blowin' in the wind', 'The times they are a-changing', 'Only a pawn in their game' and 'The lonesome death of Hattie Carroll' – have rarely been matched in any field. That America's conscience, in the period of the Civil Rights movement and the Vietnam War, was pricked not by classical composers but rather by this awkward Jewish maverick with his guitar and harmonica – nothing more complicated than a folk singer, essentially – shows the extent to which musical tastes had changed by the 1960s. The signs had been there since the rise of radios and records in the 1920s and '30s, but now it was an inescapable reality: pop, be it folk, Blues, rock or gospel-based, was the music of the twentieth century.

The explosion in popular songwriting in the second half of the twentieth century is a joyous thing. But the sheer volume of songs being composed, albums being recorded and careers being launched at the dawn of the pop age should not blind us to the fact that, in purely musical terms, the vast majority of melodies, harmonies and rhythms were both relatively limited and relatively static in comparison to either jazz or classical music of the nineteenth and twentieth centuries. In a hundred years from now, with the dispassionate benefit of hindsight, it will be possible to describe large swathes of the pop, rock and soul repertoire as variants on the basic Blues template, with a straight four-in-a-bar drumbeat, a diet of between three and twelve chords, and a smallish smorgasbord of instruments to choose from: guitar, bass, keyboard, drums.

This is not to say that the ingenuity and character given to these meagre resources over the past few decades has not been staggering, nor that the journey from (apparently) innocent teen fun in the late 1950s to the sophistication and diversity of the modern pop industry is not remarkable in itself. But pop has certainly remained true to a number of tried and tested templates since its early days; one might even say the ground rules for the way commercial pop would work were laid down from the very beginning. Talent contests and megalomaniac record producers have always paired ingénue wannabes with experienced songwriters, for instance, cashing in quickly on success before the public's appetite for novelty fades. Rags-to-riches ascents are inevitably followed by equally rapid riches-to-rags descents, while established set-ups such as the high-school girl group – early pioneers were The Marvelettes, The Ronettes and The Shirelles in the early 1960s – are still very much with us today.

But against this tradition of pop history repeating itself, certain artists have stood out for their engagement in a deeper exploration of the popular song form – even finding success with these unconventional endeavours in an industry increasingly motivated by money. As had been the case in earlier centuries – with classical composers such as Bach, Handel, Mozart and Mahler – the pop era composers who made the most profound impact over time were those able to synthesise and absorb the many styles and influences around them, wrapping them up in something of their own. Stevie Wonder, surely one of the greatest of all twentieth-century musicians in any field, was one such gatherer of styles. The fusion of influences that characterised his music proved both irresistible and irreversible: we can hear his masterly hand behind almost all modern black music, even if his deeply felt spirituality has largely been stripped out along the way. In his landmark albums of the 1970s, Wonder combined the prevailing Blues and gospel-influenced pop he had grown up singing in his childhood Motown days (such as 'Signed, Sealed, Delivered, I'm Yours' and 'For Once in My Life') with the exhilarating dance rhythms and sultry jazz chords of central and southern America, which he had discovered as a young adult. The most influential of these exotic beats came from the dynamic rhythmic hub of Cuba.

The distinctive Cuban dimension in Latin American music that so inspired Stevie Wonder and others had only really escaped from its island home at the beginning of the twentieth century. Around the time that ragtime and the Blues were giving way to jazz in mainland America, a form of music called *son* was becoming popular in Cuba. *Son* was a hybrid African–European song type that could be danced to, and it comprised three main rhythmic layers: a bass line that determined the (mostly) minor-key chord sequences of 'primary colour' chords I, IV and V, and which moved at a slightly slower pace; an eight-beat repeated syncopated pattern that worked as an embellishment against a simple reiterated 'clave' (both a term for a repeating pattern and the percussion instrument that might play it); and a piano or guitar figure, also shaped into eight-beat patterns, which glued together the bass and percussion components. From *son* an abundant range of dance and song types blossomed: *danzón*, rumba, guaguanco, yambu, bossa nova, mambo, chachacha, conga, and eventually salsa. These forms came to have enormous influence on twentieth-century music, first in the Americas and then in time around the world, through popular music of countless genres. But what was it about the three-layered Cuban *son* rhythm pattern that was so seductive?

For one thing, Cuban folk songs fused a European-style chordal guitar accompaniment with an African approach to rhythm, whereby patterns would be layered one on top of another – rather like the polyrhythm we encountered in Stravinsky's *Rite of Spring*. In a sense, layered rhythm patterns were a percussive version of harmony: each player's individual pattern fitted to the ones already up and running until there might be four, five or six different repeating rhythmic phrases operating at the same time. To African drums, the Cubans gradually added an array of percussion instruments that were native to the region, such as the claves and the maracas. (The urge to complicate a rhythmic pattern was so great in Cubans, in fact, that Havana dock workers were famous for making up highly sophisticated percussion improvisations from the packing cases and trunks they had stacked all around them, each docker adding his own variation to the whole. These impromptu packing-case sessions were still being performed in the 1960s.)

Secondly, there was a particular type of syncopation that originated in *son* that proved irresistible to late-twentieth-century ears.

This syncopation is now so common in all popular music that it has quite forgotten its Cuban roots. It is a kind of mirror image of swing, and although it hasn't got a name one might call it 'lurch'. We have already heard swing performers of the jazz scene holding back the melody a little to give it a degree of elasticity against the main beat, a syncopation brought about by delaying the expected fall of the pulse. In Cuban *son*, however, the melody is elastic in the other direction: it *anticipates* the main beat. Nowadays, this kind of 'pushed' melody – where the melodic line nudges ahead of the beat – has become so commonplace that singing without it would sound odd, stiff and stilted; it is virtually unheard-of in the classical world but I doubt there is a single pop song since the Second World War that does not make use of it. In Beyoncé's 'If I Were a Boy' (2008), for example, the anticipation can be heard as she arrives (too early) on the word 'boy' – the main underlying beat she technically should arrive on follows shortly afterwards. Likewise, Adele's 2008 cover of Bob Dylan's 'Make You Feel My Love' ends each line of the first verse on two anticipated beats: 'blowing in **your face** . . . on **your case** . . . warm **embrace**'.

In Cuban *son* it is not just the melody, whether played on a trumpet or sung, that pushes ahead, but also the bass line. Indeed, the fact that the bass jumps ahead of the beat is what gives *son* such a powerful dance feel: it almost pushes your feet to move. The definitive introduction to this style is the work of the prolific composer and bandleader Ignacio Piñeiro, who made a number of *son* recordings with his Sexteto – later Septeto – Nacional between 1927 and 1935. One of them, 'Échale Salsita' (1930), even gave birth to the term, and later genre, *salsa*. Easily the most famous *son*, 'Guajira Guantanamera', attributed to Joseíto Fernández, is practically the national song of Cuba (as well as the tune of choice for a variety of football chants around the world). In this classic, as well as in the other early *sons*, the gently strumming guitars play the regular, pacesetting beats, and the voice and bass then nudge ahead of every 'downbeat' – that is, the strong first beat of any group or bar. Meanwhile the percussion instruments layer on another set of patterns, African style.

There was a seductive sway to this type of syncopation that complemented the sexy, body-to-body, hip-orientated nature of Cuban dance; being 'forward' fits neatly with both the physical and musical nature of Cuban rhythm. Nothing could be further from the non-contact European court dances with which the colonial sugar-cane and coffee-plantation owners had wiled away their evenings before Cuban independence. But the interesting thing about this irresistible new form of syncopation is that the early Cuban prototypes that started spreading across the Americas in the 1930s and '40s did not ride roughshod over the pulling, delaying swing of jazz; rather the two styles merged and combined, offering a whole new palette of musical possibility.

Nobody mined the ambiguities available in these seemingly contra-dictory syncopations with more dazzling panache than Stevie Wonder, combining – often within the same song – the relaxed Latin feel of them with the steady, pressing groove of urban black soul music; a prime example is the infectiously jerky 'Don't you worry 'bout a thing'. But while Wonder was a pioneer of twentieth-century musical fusion – from jazz chords ('You are the sunshine of my life', 'Isn't she lovely?'), Latin rhythms ('Ngicuela – Es Una Historia – I am Singing'), classical pastiche ('Pastime paradise', 'Village ghetto land'), swing-era pastiche ('Sir Duke'), gospel anthems ('Heaven help us all', 'Love's in need of love today') and Motown grooves ('Superstition', 'Higher Ground') – even he, inspired as he was by the sacred music of his childhood, never thought to incorporate a German Lutheran hymn tune that had been harmonised by Bach into a pop song. This was the idea of one of his most brilliant contemporaries, Paul Simon, with his knowingly entitled 1973 hit 'American Tune'.

Simon's choice of hymn was in fact rather apt. The origin of the hymn, 'Ich will hier bei dir stehen' (I will stand by you), gener-ally known in English as 'O Sacred Head Sore Wounded', is medieval, but its tune started life as a secular love song from around 1600 called 'Mein G'müt ist mir verwirret', which loosely translates as 'All shook up'. We saw in an earlier chapter that Martin Luther's enthusiasm for congregational singing prompted the early Lutheran Church to borrow favourite tunes, often popular folk songs, and give them holy words, so in a sense Paul Simon's expropriation of the tune was simply returning it to its populist, unholy roots.

And indeed the overriding emotion of 'American Tune' is an understated patriotism that is characterised not by cynicism but rather by gratitude. It is a song about – and for – the ordinary people of a nation struggling to reconcile the growing pains of diversity with a boom in affluence and technology, to understand what its stars and stripes actually represented at the same time as planting them on the moon. There was a quarrelsome, ill-at-ease atmosphere at play in the post-war United States – 'you can't be for ever blessed' – but Simon's song is representative of a sort of social contract between the vast melting pot of cultures and backgrounds who 'come in the age's most uncertain hours and sing an American tune'. It is an attitude he shared with, among many others, George Gershwin, Irving Berlin, Elmer Bernstein, Aaron Copland, Bernard Herrmann, Benny Goodman, Leonard Bernstein, Stephen Sondheim, Burt Bacharach, Philip Glass, André Previn, Neil Sedaka, Neil Diamond and Bob Dylan – all the children or grandchildren of Jewish immigrants.

While the United States was by no means unique in embracing a diverse human melting pot, its size and prominence on the world stage pushed its racial and cultural tensions into the spotlight in the 1960s and '70s. In many ways this was a good thing for the nation's artistic output: it is certainly fair to claim that popular music played a significant role in allowing communities to embrace their differences, to find common cause with one another and to celebrate the heterogeneity of their origins. It should not surprise us at all that some of the richest fusions of genres took place in the arena of American music.

'American Tune' was not Paul Simon's first attempt at integrating disparate styles of music – Simon and Garfunkel's monster hit of 1970, 'Bridge over troubled water', had brought together folk and gospel elements, a ravishingly full grand piano and a large classical orchestra – nor was it his last. In 1986 he released arguably his most radical melding of previously unconnected genres in *Graceland*, a collaboration with South African singing group Ladysmith Black Mambazo and others. The project was not without its controversies: the recording process technically flouted a UN embargo on Apartheid South Africa, while the question of whether due credit had been given to all participants was reminiscent of the debate that had surrounded Dvořák's *New World* symphony. But from a musical point of view, *Graceland* was quite extraordinary, mixing the irrepressibly energetic township sound with folk styles popular in the Southern United States, such as Cajun, zydeco and Tex-Mex; the album's title, of course, is a reference to Elvis Presley's home in Memphis, Tennessee. It achieved incredible international success, any qualms about its genesis assuaged by the reassurances of Joseph Shabalala, founder of Ladysmith Black Mambazo, that *Graceland* was a sincere, non-exploitative collaboration that had given a worldwide platform to the voices of black Africans whose only freedom at that time was the exuberance of their hitherto largely unnoticed music.

Time and again in the rich tradition of fusing musical genres we have seen composers draw on little-known folk styles – as Paul Simon did on *Graceland* – or trawl through music's attic in search of inspiration. While Simon and Garfunkel and Bob Dylan were prominent members of the 1960s movement that sought to explore the possibilities of regional American and Anglo-Celtic folk music, they were outdone in terms of sheer volume of experimentation by the leading pop group of the period – and indeed of all time – The Beatles.

Between their first love, rock and roll, and their late-1960s infatuation with drug-induced psychedelia, The Beatles embraced

Anglo-Celtic folk music and ancient folk modes, notably bringing them together in 'Eleanor Rigby'. They plundered the tongue-in-cheek novelty song style of music hall and vaudeville in 'When I'm sixty-four' and they played with tape-looping and other electronic experiments of the 1960s avant-garde in 'Tomorrow never knows', a song that also featured both a drone – recruited back into service for the first time since the thirteenth century – and voices run through a 'Leslie speaker', a Doppler-effect sound processor originally developed in the 1940s for Hammond organs. They ventured eastwards into Indian music and instruments – as in 'Within you, without you' and 'Norwegian Wood' – prefiguring the later boom in world music, and westwards for close-harmony vocal arrangements, used for example in 'Nowhere Man'. They invited back into popular music the sounds of the classical orchestra ('A Day in the Life'), brass band ('Sergeant Pepper's Lonely Hearts Club Band'), string quartet ('Yesterday') and harp ('She's Leaving Home'), as well as instruments long since consigned to the curiosity cabinet: harpsichord ('Fixing a hole'), melodeon and fairground organ ('Being for the Benefit of Mr Kite'), harmonium ('We can work it out'), the eighteenth-century 'piccolo' trumpet ('Penny Lane'), recorder ('Fool on the Hill'), ukelele and banjo ('Honey Pie'). Of course they did not overlook an array of instruments recently invented, and in many cases since abandoned, such as the Mellotron ('Strawberry Fields Forever'), the Selmer Clavioline ('Baby You're a Rich Man'), the twelve-string guitar and the synthesiser, these last two becoming rock staples ever after.

The Beatles became the most famous and successful musicians of the twentieth century mainly because their songs were youthful, catchy and imaginative, and because everyone who heard them – millions of people across the planet – felt the world was a better place. And by becoming such an international phenomenon, everything they chose to do by way of musical adventure flowed generously into the mainstream, so they acted – thanks to modern communications – as conduits of experiment and diversity on an unprecedentedly rapid scale. To be sure, the studio albums The

Beatles created with producer George Martin between 1965 and 1970 – *Rubber Soul, Revolver, Sergeant Pepper's Lonely Hearts Club Band, Magical Mystery Tour, Yellow Submarine, The White Album, Abbey Road* and *Let It Be* – are like a vast, joyful, kaleidoscopic journey through musical history. The message their irrepressible creativity sent out to the young at heart, swimming in teenage pop culture, was that the old stuff still had a role to play, that music's past was relevant, enthralling and engrossing.

What John Lennon, Paul McCartney and George Harrison achieved as composers had an impact way beyond the internal fashions and rejuvenations of pop itself. At a time when classical music was grappling with what it was supposed to sound like and what its fundamental building blocks should be, The Beatles (intuitively, not intentionally) reaffirmed the supremacy of the Western system of key-families, the interlocking jigsaw of harmony and melody that had worked for the likes of Bach, Schubert and Mendelssohn. They were the most unlikely saviours of old-fashioned music, but that's undoubtedly what they were.

This may seem a bold statement, but a look at the concerns of the classical community of the 1950s and '60s reminds us just how radical The Beatles' revolution was to the plight of Western music. The composer-conductor Pierre Boulez, the leading European spokesman for the vanguard of modern classical music during The Beatles' heyday, is a useful weathervane of prevailing attitudes to what composers believed was the moribund condition of the musical tradition they had inherited. In an angry 1963 publication called *Penser la musique aujourd'hui* (Thinking of today's music), Boulez articulated his disenchantment with more or less all the organising features of Western music – melody, harmonic progression, dance rhythm, repetition – and with virtually all music written before 1900, which was 'nostalgic' and 'bourgeois'. (A fair amount of post-1900 music was likewise victim to his venom, Erik Satie being singled out as a 'spineless dog'.) Boulez promulgated a form of 'total' serialism, in which Schoenberg's twelve-tone idea – the removal of all repetition and therefore of hierarchy in the scale of notes – would be extended to rhythm, note duration, dynamics (degrees of volume) and even ornamentation. Any living musicians who did not fully immerse themselves in this system were 'USELESS'. But while Boulez's iconoclasm was attractive to some students of twentieth-century classical music, who venerated his 1957 composition *Le Marteau sans maître* (The Hammer without a Master), most neutral listeners then as now found both his polemic and his music thoroughly impenetrable.

Lennon and McCartney were, no doubt about it, intrigued by certain experimental aspects of avant-garde classical music, but in the main their creativity was directed – perhaps surprisingly, given their status as the supreme representatives of the younger generation – backwards in time. The kiss of life they gave to long-lost and hitherto unfashionable musical styles reintegrated them with the popular mainstream at a time when one might have expected modern sounds like Boulez's to rise to the fore.

Classical music was in trouble, and by the whirlwind conclusion of The Beatles' adventure, it looked as if the words of one of their early Chuck Berry covers, 'Roll over Beethoven', were actually coming true. This was a time in which the most extraordinary and bizarre sonic experiments were being conducted at the cutting edge of classical music, but what need did an ordinary music lover have for the complicated, uncomfortable results of these ideas in their raw, unfiltered state – complete with incomprehensible theories and analyses – if they could enjoy sonic experiments that had been integrated into a Beatles track? Mischievous though it undoubtedly was to include classical composer Karlheinz Stockhausen on the cover of *Sergeant Pepper*, how many of its millions of buyers would have sought out and relished the latter's *Zyklus* (1959), in which a lone percussionist appears to strike instruments at random for anything between eight and fifteen minutes? Its spiral score is laid out graphically, has no set starting point and can be read left to right, right to left, upside down or back to front. The player is expected to respond to the sketched-out instructions 'spontaneously'. There is no doubt that Stockhausen left an impressive pioneering legacy, but it did little for classical music's reputation – or popularity – that one of its most distinguished composers was creating music out of what sounded to most people like a small child thrashing about unpredictably in a room filled with objects to be struck.

While modern classical music had its challenges, older music was encountering its own difficulties in the twentieth century, despite – or indeed because of – an explosion in recordings in the 1960s. The success of the classical recording industry, improved long-player technology and an understandable desire to expand the market and broaden listeners' horizons had led to the rediscovery and release of music that pre-dated the 'core' classics (broadly defined as Haydn to Sibelius). This development was a huge bonus, with music of the eighteenth, seventeenth and sixteenth centuries first in line for resuscitation, followed by music from even earlier periods. Alongside this fresh boost of material came a desire to try to reproduce as accurately as possible the sounds that the original composers might have heard – a movement searching for 'authenticity'.

Much of what was discovered in this search, from the late 1960s onwards, was to feed directly and irreversibly into performance practice of earlier music, for example the use of older-style – often replica – instruments, or of bowing techniques on violins, violas and cellos. Modern metal and synthetic materials for strings were replaced with the older animal gut that had been in use prior to the nineteenth century, and more recent changes to the design of instruments – to make them sturdier, louder or more consistently in tune – were reversed. It was determined, amid much debate, that the pitch of modern notes was appreciably higher than that in the time of Bach, so his works and the works of other composers of his period were transposed downwards accordingly, to make them sound more authentically 'eighteenth-century': an A became an A♭, and so on.

The yearning for authenticity did not stop there. In the 1950s

and '6os it was commonplace to record or perform a cantata by
Bach or an oratorio by Handel with a large chorus and a Mahler-
sized symphony orchestra using contemporary instruments –
perhaps three times as large as the group Bach would have
employed – but by the 1980s this had become a rarity. Small
ensembles playing 'Baroque' instruments at lower pitch had
become the norm. The urge to make performances 'authentic'
gradually spread to music of Mozart's and Haydn's period, and
recently, for example in the recordings made in the late 1990s and
early 2000s by the Orchestra of the Age of Enlightenment, to the
orchestral music of Felix Mendelssohn, composed in the 1840s.

This mostly invigorating, positive trend was not without its
drawbacks. For one thing, where does one draw the 'authentic'
line? Handel's operas, for (an albeit extreme) example, all feature
leading roles for castrati: in order to hear as faithfully as possible
what Handel heard, should this barbaric custom not be reintroduced? Likewise the concept of an 'authentic' (replica) Baroque
violin: the very notion assumes that the violin of the period 1600–
1750 was a standardised, unchanging instrument across Europe,
which of course it was not. Different composers would have had
different sounds in mind when they composed for the violin.

But perhaps the weightier question surrounding the new enthusiasm for reviving the classics is the effect of flooding the record
market with such a glut of 'new' material, the enormous back
catalogue of music from the eighteenth to twentieth centuries
now joined by music stretching back as far as the thirteenth. Even
by 1970, *hundreds* of recordings of the same clutch of works by
Beethoven were available, to name but one nineteenth-century
composer, bulging the shelves of the (then) relatively numerous
High Street record shops. Radio programmes analysed the merits
of different interpretations of the same pieces, while there were
always new reasons to hear, say, Mozart afresh, thanks to the
selling point of newly researched performance techniques. People
were enjoying classical music, certainly, but what this mountain
of material demonstrated was a near fatal shift in classical music

away from the new to the old. Live concerts in the nineteenth century had typically presented mostly premières, with some familiar favourites sandwiched in alongside them. At a concert in February 1814, for example, Beethoven presented the première of his eighth symphony alongside a performance of his seventh, which itself was only two months old. No one at the time thought this unusual. By the mid-twentieth century, however, the tables had been turned: old favourites became the bread and butter of live concerts, with new works squeezed in between them apologetically.

The weight of the past and its majestic legacy weighed very heavily on the shoulders of young and untested twentieth-century composers in the classical tradition, since they were competing for audiences and promoter attention with an ever greater body of 'masterworks' from the past, rather than – as their predecessors in previous centuries had – simply the works of their parents' generation. It would not have occurred to The Kinks, The Beatles or The Beach Boys in 1967 to be inhibited by the prior successes of Elvis Presley, Buddy Holly or Lonnie Donegan, still less by the popular songs of Cole Porter in the 1920s or the minstrel songs of Stephen Foster of the 1850s – nor would concert and record promoters have been reluctant to take a risk on them because they were not Presley, Porter or Foster. But this was the great divide between the two genres: in pop, being new was a bonus; in classical, it had become a hurdle.

Classical music's infatuation with mining the riches of the distant past only reinforced the popular impression that it was backward- rather than forward-looking. All around its besieged citadel, live music was booming as never before, but only in genres in which it was acceptable – desirable, even – to move with the times. That is not to say that some classical musicians did not attain fame and success, but these were mostly singers, conductors and virtuoso players, making their names with Verdi, Mahler, Mozart or Wagner. Meanwhile the 'big' international names among classical composers of the 1960s – Olivier Messiaen, Pierre Boulez, Milton Babbitt,

Morton Feldman, Luigi Nono, Karlheinz Stockhausen, Hans
Werner Henze, Witold Lutosławski, Krzysztof Penderecki, Dmitri
Shostakovich, Benjamin Britten, John Cage, György Ligeti, Igor
Stravinsky – had what one might call a Sunday-supplement visi-
bility: their new works were reviewed and discussed in the broad-
sheets, large cultural institutions commissioned them, publicly
funded radio stations played them, universities studied them, but
the general public was largely unaware of, and uninterested in,
their music. None of these composers was as well known as their
counterparts in film music: John Barry, Jerry Goldsmith, Maurice
Jarre, Alfred Newman, Ennio Morricone, Nino Rota, Bernard
Herrmann, Miklós Rózsa and Michel Legrand. But nowhere was
the rout of classical music's previous position of dominance more
clearly seen than in musical theatre.

The musical had, as the twentieth century matured, gratefully
filled the vacuum created by opera's self-imposed exile from acces-
sibility, an attribute it had successfully maintained from the 1630s
to Puccini's last operas in the 1920s. The musicals of Rodgers and
Hammerstein, Cole Porter, Ira and George Gershwin, Rodgers
and Hart, Lerner and Loewe, Frank Loesser, Leonard Bernstein,
Kander and Ebb, Stephen Sondheim, Stephen Schwartz, Andrew
Lloyd Webber and others retained the affections of a large portion
of the ticket-buying public, while at the same time broadening
the scope, ambition and stylistic edge of the musical form.

   This is particularly true of Stephen Sondheim, whose disdain
for both high opera and tacky pop drove him to create a sound
that lay comfortably and distinctively equidistant between the two:
an instinct that was typically twentieth-century. Sondheim had
learnt his trade by writing lyrics for *West Side Story*, which opened
in 1957. That *West Side Story*'s composer was Leonard Bernstein
– easily America's most famous twentieth-century classical musician, a conductor-composer-broadcaster of giant status and prestige – should have sent out a loud and clear message that, for all
the popularity of the older classical repertoire, newer forms of

entertainment driven by Broadway and Hollywood were now monopolising key musical talent. Bernstein's score for *West Side Story* derived its energy from a sassy fusion of jazz, vaudeville, Broadway pizzazz, Latin American popular dance – and his own spectacularly accomplished classical training, which is evident in, among other elements, its sophisticated structure and recurrent musical themes. Though Bernstein himself composed other musicals, *Wonderful Town* and *Candide* among them, it was his young lyricist Sondheim, also a composer, who most enthusiastically took on the challenge laid down by the genre-hopping adventurousness of *West Side Story*. Over the ensuing half-century he wrote a series of brilliant, unusual and thought-provoking Broadway musicals, from the kabuki-theatre-influenced *Pacific Overtures* (1976) to the Victorian music hall thriller *Sweeney Todd, the Demon Barber of Fleet Street* (1979), and from *Sunday in the Park with George* (1984), inspired by a Georges Seurat pointillist painting, to an exploration of the darker side of children's fairy tales in *Into the Woods* (1986).

The opening of a Sondheim musical would typically attract the kind of attention among the educated classes and in the media that a new novel, a new play, a new art exhibition or a daring new piece of architecture might expect. By the second half of the twentieth century this was certainly not the case for premières of new operas or symphonies. Classical music seemed definitively – resentfully – sidelined.

But then, in 1970s America, a strange thing happened. Two parents, contemporary pop and contemporary classical, gave birth to a child that was a perfect mix of them both. The child's name was minimalism, and its arrival heralded a sea change in the relationship between musical genres. It ushered in an age of musical convergence: our age.

Minimalism had in fact begun to emerge, rather quietly, in the 1960s, but it made a louder entrance in the 1970s, spearheaded by American composers Terry Riley, Steve Reich and Philip Glass. Steve Reich has been described as the single most influential composer of the late-twentieth century, bringing fresh ideas and impetus to both popular and classical music. It is a big claim, but one that is wholly justified.

Where The Beatles had plundered music hall, centuries-old Anglo-Celtic folk and the sounds of the 1960s electronic avant-garde, Steve Reich derived his inspirations from African drumming and Balinese gamelan music. He found that the hypnotic, seemingly repetitive and endless patterns of these drum- and mallet-based styles did not in fact stay the same: instead they changed subtly with each reiteration of the phrase. He sought to apply this developmental approach to Western music, creating pieces – initially mostly instrumental – that superficially sounded as if they were made up of a phrase being repeated hundreds of times, but which in reality altered slightly with each new cycle until the original phrase had become something quite different.

In its crudest form, this exploitation of 'phasing' could be demonstrated by setting off two pendulum metronomes at exactly the same time and precisely the same speed. Because these pre-digital age instruments were subject to tiny variations in their mechanisms, minute differences in the metals used or fractional discrepancies in pendulum weights would result in the two metronomes staying exactly 'in time' with one another for only a short while: after thirty seconds or so, one would be ticking marginally faster than the other. Over further minutes the discrepancy would widen until the two machines were tapping out a rhythmic pattern in the difference between their two beats. This was essentially the idea that Reich pursued, albeit with more complex initial patterns. At first he used electronic techniques to make incremental transformations to a pattern, later having live players and acoustic instruments *imitate* this effect under his very specific and detailed configuration.

The result of these experimental techniques was that the forward-moving logic of chords – what we called 'harmonic progression' or 'musical gravity' when we first encountered it in earnest in the seventeenth century – was stopped in its tracks. A new logic of repetition and incremental variation took its place. Stravinsky's style – the jerky jigsaw of adjacent, unrelated musical segments – was also abandoned. Instead, Reich employed a method of driving music along through constantly evolving reiteration, which was quite alternative to the tried and tested Western formulas perfected over several hundred years. It was utterly radical and, for many musicians and listeners at the time, baffling.

Reich was fascinated by the creative possibilities of splicing up tape recordings and putting them back together again in collage or repetitive sequence, inspiring, among others, The Beatles to do likewise. He is the godfather of the technique known as 'sampling', whereby a fragment of recorded sound is chopped up and recycled back into a musical pattern of some kind: it is the bedrock of practically every hip-hop track you have ever heard, and it is even more ubiquitous in dance music than the electric guitar was in the 1960s. Its genesis can be traced to Reich's 1965 work, *It's gonna rain*, in which he takes the taped sermon of a Pentecostal street preacher and chops up segments of it to make rhythmic cells that are repeated again and again.

Bearing in mind the all-conquering nature of popular music in the twentieth century, it is important to note that Steve Reich, a classically trained composer who grew up with and was influenced by progressive rock music, handed down techniques in sound that were to feed back into popular music. A two-way relationship between musical zones was once again functional.

And this interchange wasn't confined to Reich: David Bowie integrated minimalist styles from Reich and his fellow New Yorker Philip Glass into his 1977 album *Low*, recorded at the Château d'Hérouville in France and completed in the shadow of the Berlin Wall. Fifteen years later, Glass composed a *Low* symphony based on material from the Bowie album. Neither Bowie nor Glass could be described as marginal figures in their respective popular and classical worlds: this was a major breakthrough for music in a century otherwise characterised by division.

★

Recent decades have seen this melding of the two traditions become more permanent and profound, a process enhanced and accelerated by film music, which has become a playground for the intermingling of the DNA of minimalism and contemporary popular music. Convergence has increasingly characterised contemporary music-making of all kinds in the years since The Beatles announced an ambitious new era for mainstream pop music with *Revolver*. The cross-genre ventures of Frank Zappa, for example, such as *Freak Out!* (1966) and *200 Motels* (1971), which mixed hard rock with orchestral sound and avant-garde techniques, made their impact on the fringe of the mainstream and caused considerable logistical (and legal) difficulties for Zappa and his classical collaborators. Thirty years later, cross-genre recording and performing had become so routine as barely to raise comment. Deep Purple's founder and keyboardist, Jon Lord, turned to writing classical music in the 1990s after a long and successful career in rock. Damon Albarn, co-founder of Blur and Gorillaz, premièred his opera *Dr Dee* in Manchester in the summer of 2011; it was also performed at English National Opera's London Coliseum as part of the London 2012 Festival. Coldplay's 2008 'Viva la Vida', a huge worldwide hit, prominently features a string quartet arrangement, as 'Eleanor Rigby' had back in 1966. In 2006 Sting released *Songs from the Labyrinth*, his reworking of the songs of John Dowland, whom we encountered back in the sixteenth century, in collaboration with Bosnian lutenist Edin Karamazov, and in 2010 and 2011 he undertook his *Symphonicity* world tour, performing his songs with a symphony orchestra.

Lord, Albarn and Sting are not isolated cases: this is a trend being replicated all over the world. Whether it wants it or not, classical music's isolation from the commercial mainstream is history. And what all these developments indicate is that the future of music is likely to produce compositions that are harder and harder to categorise: a hybrid third genre of 'contemporary' music will prevail that has no tribal allegiance to conservatoire or club. The specific and particular musical journey that has been labelled

'Western' despite its many Eastern, Northern and Southern elements and influences – from, say, Kassia of Constantinople's ninth-century chants to John Adams's opera *Doctor Atomic* of 2004 – is giving way to a World musical culture of infinite colour and possibility.

Most of the modern music in which convergence is most active has thrived in a relatively prosperous, educated milieu, dominated by the United States and Europe, where something approaching a cultural consensus exists. But just as the Blues, ragtime and jazz emerged among the poor, disconnected communities of the American South, there is a modern-day equivalent that was likewise born in areas of deprivation: hip-hop.

Like its predecessor forms, hip-hop grew from obscurity to ubiquity within a few decades, starting out among frustrated and alienated African-American and Latin American youngsters in the Bronx in the 1970s, but since becoming the chosen genre and musical badge of identity of marginalised youth everywhere. Though its pioneers, notably Jamaican-born DJ Kool Herc (Clive Campbell), had hoped to draw young people away from gang culture by immersion in the dance and rap craze of hip-hop – and initially succeeded – hip-hop has never entirely rid itself of an association with gun culture, sexism, racism and a contempt for education, even if many of its iconic performers have contradicted this unfortunate aspect of its scene. Its terminology and rapped lyrics were at first intentionally impenetrable (or offensive) to uninitiated listeners – just as the Blues and jazz had once been – but with its enormous popularity among young people of all backgrounds, its language, break-beat dancing and graffiti became familiar by the 1990s. Its DJ-led techniques of song mixing, splicing and sampling gave it, from the start, an inbuilt propensity to absorb other styles, and its influence – particularly its favoured rhythmic grooves – invigorated the creativity of thousands of musicians in other branches of contemporary music, from Blondie's 1981 hit 'Rapture' to the Jay-Z/Alicia Keys modern standard of 2009, 'Empire State of Mind'.

More intriguing still is the recent fusion of hip-hop with Bhangra – a British pop-Punjabi folk cross-genre that emerged in the 1980s – which has formed a bridge between two vast musical empires, Western and Asian, that may yet prove to have an even deeper impact on the world's busily colliding youth cultures than its parent form. It is probably only a matter of time before one of the world's leading classical composers premières an opera based on Dizzee Rascal's 'Boy in da Corner' or writes a symphony on themes from Kanye West's 'My Beautiful Dark Twisted Fantasy'.

Of course, not everyone has welcomed the meltdown between classical music and the diverse forms of popular music. The spearhead of both fields has become unapologetically mechanised and electronic in character, a trend that alarms all those who cherish the spontaneity and humanity of unplugged music, whether classical, folk or genres from other cultures. It is not a new fear.

Around the time of the 1930s Depression, much of the blame for the world's problems was heaped at the door of job-threatening modern technology, a fear exploited in such films as Fritz Lang's *Metropolis* (1927), Charlie Chaplin's *Modern Times* (1936), and René Clair's *À nous la liberté* (Freedom for us, 1931). The latter features a score, choruses and songs by Georges Auric, and tells the story of a mischievous protagonist, an escaped ex-convict, who steals some money, becomes rich, and sets up a record and record-player factory. Thus the technology of *music*, of all things, was satirically portrayed as the ultimate triumph of hard-hearted commerce over humanity.

The danger of humankind being swallowed up by its own inventions – machines usurping the natural sound of our voices and the instruments we have crafted over the centuries – is an idea that has been explored often, even by those most intrigued by the possibilities of electronic processing. Radiohead's haunting 2000 song 'Kid A', for instance, the product of a thoroughly convergent set of electronic and minimalist musical ingredients, uses an electronic instrument invented in 1928, the *ondes Martenot*, to articulate what might be the distressed cry of a human clone. The ondes Martenot had previously been a favourite instrument of classical composer Olivier Messiaen, featuring as a prominent solo part in his magnificent, dissonant and joyous *Turangalîla-Symphonie*, which was first performed in December 1949 (and conducted by a young Leonard Bernstein). Manipulating the human voice through electronic processes had been around in recording since at least 1947, when *Sparky's Magic Piano*, a children's story on shellac disc, used a device patented as the 'Sonovox' to create the impression of a talking or singing piano. Subsequent developments included the vocoder, a keyboard-based voice processor used prolifically in pop after Wendy (then Walter) Carlos and Robert Moog's vocoder had been heard to disturbing effect in Stanley Kubrick's 1971 film *A Clockwork Orange* – particularly in the soundtrack's rendition of the 'Ode to Joy' from Beethoven's ninth symphony. 'Kid A's atmosphere, rather like that of *A Clockwork Orange*, is of a futuristic dystopia where humanity has become lost and fearful.

But music never ceases to surprise us with its trends and about-turns. Since the 1990s, just as – or perhaps because – we seemed to have lost ourselves in worrying about becoming slaves to machines, there has been a dramatic increase in the popularity of reflective, acoustically spacious spiritual and sacred music. This wave of contemplative, unhurried music surged into the public's consciousness with the rediscovery of the previously little-known plainchant-inspired works of the Estonian Arvo Pärt, such as his *Cantus in Memoriam Benjamin Britten* (1977). Likewise the *Symphony of Sorrowful Songs* by Pärt's Polish contemporary Henryk Górecki, composed in 1976 but not a worldwide bestseller until 1992, thanks to the championing of British radio station Classic FM. More recently, in 2009, the CD that spent half a year at no. 1 in the Specialist Classical Charts was *Enchanted Voices*, my own setting of the New Testament's Beatitudes, in Latin, for eight sopranos, solo cello, chamber organ and handbells: a re-imagining of ancient chant for the twenty-first century. That outcome, never mind that musical proposition, would have been inconceivable to classical composers of the 1960s, when I was a boy chorister at an Oxford college.

What the musical past tells us is that it doesn't do to worry too much about what happens next. For every movement there is a counter-movement, for every fear a reassuring hand on the shoulder. Even as we struggle with the existence or abolition of God, we seem to have more music than ever to answer our need for a spiritual dimension.

In the closing years of the Victorian Age, composers and musicologists went backpacking around Europe and America recording and notating the folk music being sung, played and danced to in remote rural communities, most, if not all of whom have since disappeared, taking the rest of their music and culture to the grave with them. In the 1970s and '80s the English explorer-composer David Fanshawe did the same for more distant peoples in developing countries, saving for ever the sounds of their voices and rituals, now silent. The endeavour of these pioneers was a noble and timely one, and much of what they heard found itself reintegrated into new musical works and styles.

How long, then, will it be before our musical culture will be shuddering towards extinction, needing some earnest lover of the old and the 'authentic' to rescue our songs and symphonies from oblivion? Is the internet free-for-all going to kill off the very musical endeavour most beloved of its young pirates? After all, if someone is caught stealing from a shop in broad daylight, society unhesitatingly deems this a crime worthy of retribution, yet when music is downloaded illegally from the internet without remuneration it is seen as a harmless, victim-free 'right'. Not paying someone for their music is what happened in the seven or so centuries before 1900, when composing was the job of a tiny handful of white men who had other ways of supporting themselves. Only a fool would want to see the return of that closed, fusty world.

Yet the age of technology and communication has also made

music a much more open exchange between maker and listener. It is gradually reassuming a role it had for thousands of years: a free-flowing, unwritten, spontaneous, aural tradition based entirely on the lives, loves, hopes and fears of ordinary people. The more complicated adventures undertaken by composers with notation, orchestras, opera singers, conductors, musicological analysis and the rest are still vital parts of music's main body, but they are not in truth its central purpose. What used to be called 'classical' music has become a nursery for experiment: a fascinating, unpredictable, whimsically creative laboratory for the super-interested, funded by taxpayers the world over, feeding profusely into the general flow of musical activity.

Throughout the last thousand years of innovation and techno-logical development in music, at regular intervals composers at the cutting edge have found inspiration, new energy and source material from the limitless underground reservoirs of folk and popular music that were always around them, like the vast aquifers which hold so much of humanity's water supply beneath the earth's thin surface. Just as Bach borrowed favourite Lutheran hymn tunes – themselves derived from unholy folk songs – or as Chopin mined his native Polish dances, Scott Joplin and George Gershwin took the bar-room piano styles of their day and converted them into polished gems for the concert hall, the musical language we have inherited from the past is once again being renewed by mingling in the crowded bazaar of popular music's marketplace.

The young musicians in modern conservatoires, music colleges and universities study in an environment that fosters respect for and engagement with a multitude of genres and traditions. They also know they need not shudder in fear at the thought of music-making that is not slavishly dependent on the printed page. J. S. Bach was probably the cleverest composer who ever lived, but he gave his performers almost no detailed instructions as to how they might play his sublime music. He hastily scribbled down the notes and left them to it. It is as if he is saying, 'trust me, and play'.

We, more than any previous generation, can readily identify with Bach's request. We press 'play' and a million styles, sounds, aural colours, echoes and voices breeze in towards us as if through an opened window. We are like children with a thousand games at our fingertips. We have, at last, reached a point where there are no wrong or right decisions about what music we may or may not enjoy – just one gratifyingly simple instruction: 'play'.

Playlist

Extended Spotify playlists for each chapter can be found on my website: www.howardgoodall.co.uk

1. The Age of Discovery

Kassia of Constantinople/Byzantium: 'Ek rizis agathis' (ninth century)
Early Byzantine chant with modifications, ornamentation and parallel voices

Hildegard of Bingen: 'Columba aspexit' (twelfth century)
Early 'composed' (original) sacred music with drone in organum style

Pérotin the Great: 'Viderunt omnes' (1198)
Experiments in chordal harmony for four voices

John Dunstaple: 'Quam pulchra es' (c.1400)
The introduction of major and minor thirds and triads

2. The Age of Penitence

Traditional: 'In dulci jubilo' (fifteenth century)
An early example of the lauda or carol: holy words set to jaunty folk-dance tunes, mixing Latin and 'modern' languages

Josquin des Prez: *Miserere mei, Deus* (*c.*1503)
A significant early piece in Western music in which the lyrics were important and thus made audible, rather than overly melismatic

William Cornysh: 'Ah, Robin' (**early sixteenth century**)
Courtly song evoking the difficulties of love through nature

Jacques Arcadelt: 'Margot, labourez les vignes' (*c.*1560)
Typical of the catchy chansons that enjoyed great popularity in Europe and expedited the rise of secular music

Giovanni Palestrina: *Missa Papae Marcelli* (1562)
An example of the use of closely related chords to create a sense of stability within a piece: one of the musical outcomes of the Counter-Reformation

William Byrd: 'Infelix Ego' (1591)
A cry of lamentation in the midst of religious turmoil by a Catholic in Protestant England

John Dowland: 'Flow, my tears' (*c.*1597)
One of the first 'modern'-sounding three-minute songs

Claudio Monteverdi: 'O Mirtillo, Mirtillo anima mia' (1605)
The deliberate use of clashing chords to create dissonance and suggest pain: word-painting in sound

Claudio Monteverdi: *Orfeo* (1607)
The 'musical fable' that successfully introduced the new musical form of opera

Giovanni Gabrieli: 'In ecclesiis' (1615)
Polychoral music for St Mark's, Venice

Claudio Monteverdi (or assistant): 'Pur ti miro, pur ti godo'
from *The Coronation of Poppea* (1643)
A sensual, voyeuristic duet from an opera whose radical political and emotional content marked new territory for the form

3. The Age of Invention

Jean-Baptiste Lully: 'Le Bourgeois gentilhomme' (1670)
The rise of the overture, derived from ballet, which marked the beginnings of the symphony

Henry Purcell: 'Evening Hymn' (1688)
The use of a repeated chord sequence to give the music an inner forward momentum, with a ravishing meandering tune above

Arcangelo Corelli: *Christmas* concerto (*Concerto grosso Op. 6 No. 8: Allegro*) (c.1690)
An example of musical contrast or chiaroscuro: in this case a *concertino* of two violins and a cello alternating with a larger ensemble or *ripieno*

George Frideric Handel: 'Lascia ch'io pianga' from *Rinaldo* (1711)
An early example of the Italian operas Handel composed for the London stage

Johann Sebastian Bach: *The Well-Tempered Clavier Book 1 & 2* (c.1722)
Bach's demonstration of Equal Temperament

Johann Sebastian Bach: 'Air on a G String' (c.1722)
Uses a perennially popular chord sequence that has been reprised in, among many others, Procul Harum's 'Whiter Shade of Pale', The Moody Blues' 'Go Now', Bob Marley's 'No Woman No Cry' and Billy Joel's 'Piano Man'

Antonio Vivaldi: *The Four Seasons* (1723)
The refining of the concerto to a single violin being played against the *ripieno*

George Frideric Handel: 'Zadok the Priest' (1727)
English ceremonial choral style in celebration of national identity

Johann Sebastian Bach: *St Matthew Passion* (1729)
A masterful combination of dance rhythms, the Italian concerto

style, a French-style proto-orchestra, the Circle of Fifths and fugal counterpoint with an architecture based on Lutheran congregational hymns

George Frideric Handel: 'Hallelujah' chorus from *Messiah* (1741)
A well-known example of the kind of crowd-pleasing choruses written around this time for an increasingly commercial music market

George Frideric Handel: 'Will the sun forget to streak' from *Solomon* (1748)
A prime example of the wisdom and compassion inherent in Handel's music, a trait he shared with Bach

4. The Age of Elegance and Sentiment

Carl Philip Emmanuel Bach: 'Flute Concerto in B flat' (1751)
A new, clearer, simpler style in a concerto for his employer, flautist and patron of the new wave of music, Frederick the Great of Prussia

Wolfgang Amadeus Mozart: 'Serenade No. 10: Gran Partita' (*c*.1781)
An example of Mozart's desire to ennoble humanity through his music, in a period of widespread turmoil and misery

Wolfgang Amadeus Mozart: 'Dove sono' from *The Marriage of Figaro* (1786)
A masterclass in melody: an aria based around the notes of the tonic, in this case C, E, and G

Josef Haydn: 'Symphony No. 88, II: Largo' (1787)
Subtle use of quasi-symmetrical balancing melodic phrases

Josef Haydn: 'Symphony No. 99, IV. Finale: Vivace' (1793)
The playfully vivacious music Handel was composing while the Terror raged in Paris and the King and Queen of France were being executed

Ludwig van Beethoven: 'Funeral March' from *Eroica* (1804)
A new seriousness in Beethoven's approach that marked a transition into music that confronted its audience; mere entertainment would no longer suffice

Ludwig van Beethoven: 'Symphony No. 7, II: Allegretto' (1811)
The dawn of a new age: super-sized musical arrangements that were larger and louder than anything previously heard

John Field: *First Book of Nocturnes* (1812)
The piano as a vehicle for music that did not obey the strict formal rules of 'Sonata Form', and the template for the nineteenth century's love affair with the instrument

Ludwig van Beethoven: 'Symphony No. 9' (1824)
The clarion call for all nineteenth-century musicians: music might change the world

Ludwig van Beethoven: 'String Quartet No. 14, Opus 131, I: Adagio ma non troppo e molto espressivo' (1826)
Profoundly deaf and ill, Beethoven retreated into an inner world and wrote what sounded like music from a bleak and unsettling future

Franz Schubert: 'Auf dem Flusse' from *Winterreisse* (1827)
A perfect example of the use of nature in song as a metaphor for a composer's feelings

Felix Mendelssohn: *Fingal's Cave* (*The Hebrides*) (1830)
An effervescent example of music being about something extra-musical, in this instance a place

Frédéric Chopin: 'Nocturne in E flat, Op. 9 No. 2' (1830–2)
The nocturne the teenage Clara Wieck played to Chopin in Paris in 1832. She was to be his, and Schumann's and Brahms', greatest champion on the concert platform

Robert Schumann: 'Im wunderschönen Monat Mai' from *Dichterliebe* (1840)
One of the many touching love songs Schumann wrote with a

real, non-idealised woman in mind: his wife, Clara Wieck Schumann, herself an accomplished pianist

5. The Age of Tragedy

Hector Berlioz: *Symphonie fantastique* (1830)
The start of the nineteenth century's craze for music about death, destiny and supernatural love

Franz Liszt: *Hungarian Rhapsody No. 2* (1847)
An early example of the rise of 'Nationalism', generally written by middle-class composers who had little understanding of true folk music

Franz Liszt: *Totentanz* (1849)
Liszt's Hallowe'en-style music influenced contemporaries including Saint-Saëns and Grieg as well as, in our own time, film composers such as Danny Elfman

Giuseppe Verdi: 'Addio, des passato' from *La Traviata* (1853)
Verdi focuses the melodic style of popular Italian opera onto 'realistic' contemporary moral issues

Richard Wagner: 'Liebestod' from *Tristan und Isolde* (1859)
While most of Wagner's supposed innovations came from Liszt, he composed better tunes – this one also about death, doomed love and destiny – and has retained a stronger appeal

Pyotr Tchaikovsky: *Swan Lake No. 20, Hungarian Dance: Czardas* (1877)
Another well-known example of the integration of pseudo-peasant styles into classical music, and of Russian fascination with dance – in this case the popular csárdás of Eastern Europe

Franz Liszt: *The Fountains of the Villa d'Este* (1877)
Written just three years after the First Impressionist Exhibition, this piece is akin to a sort of 'impressionism' in music, pre-dating Debussy's 'impressionist' piano works by over twenty years

Richard Wagner: *Parsifal* (1882)
A masterwork, and an early use of extreme chromaticism, although its proto-Nazi philosophy and uncomfortable racial overtones have done much to make Wagner a troubling character

Antonín Dvořák: *New World* **symphony** (1893)
A much-loved classical favourite but one of the most controversial uses of ethnic imitation – although Dvořák denied having 'borrowed' Native American melodies

Claude Debussy: 'Gardens in the Rain' (1903)
It is generally Debussy rather than Liszt who is credited with musical 'impressionism', even though he composed this piece three decades after the Impressionist painters appeared

6. The Age of Rebellion

Modest Mussorgsky: *Pictures at an Exhibition, I. Promenade* (1874)
Mussorgsky was unusual in his lack of formal musical training, as a result of which he was perhaps the most original composer of the late nineteenth century

Erik Satie: First *Gymnopédie* (1888)
Inspired by a desire to reduce pomposity and excess in music, this was a first indication of a backlash against Wagner

Nikolai Rimsky-Korsakov: *Scheherazade* (1888)
One of a series of Russian operas that cashed in on an obsession with the Empire's Asiatic and Slavic folklore

Edward Elgar: 'Nimrod' from *Enigma Variations* (1899)
Self-consciously backward-looking in its thematic intentions, this typifies a late-nineteenth-century trend for music that yearned for the past

Scott Joplin: 'Maple Leaf Rag' (1899)
An early example of ragtime syncopation

Gustav Mahler: 'Nun will die Sonn' so hell aufgeh'n' from *Kindertotenlieder* **(1901–4)**
Unlike many contemporaries, Mahler abandoned the smokescreen of euphemism and addressed difficult issues – here the deaths of children – head-on

Claude Debussy: *Estampes, I. Pagodes* **(1903)**
Debussy allowed his chords to reverberate and overlap in order to evoke the sound of the Javanese gamelan

Richard Strauss: *Salome, Scene 4. Dance of the Seven Veils* **(1905)**
Strauss's starkly modern opera set a new standard for ear-splitting dissonance

Gustav Mahler: *Das Lied von der Erde, VI. Der Abschied* **(1908–9)**
Mahler's instruction is for the final, long chord to fade away imperceptibly; Benjamin Britten described it as 'imprinted on the atmosphere'

Igor Stravinsky: *The Rite of Spring, VII. Dance of the Earth* **(1913)**
The zenith of musical modernism in the early twentieth century, this shows Stravinsky having 'everything at once' – including African-style cross-rhythms – rather than developing a tune gradually

7. The Popular Age I

George Gershwin: *Rhapsody in Blue* **(1924)**
Jazz meets classical music in this revolutionary piece that was sneered at by highbrow critics but loved by audiences

Bertolt Brecht and Kurt Weill: *The Threepenny Opera, II. Die Moritat von Mackie Messer* **(1928)**
A savage critique of capitalist society in accessible musical form

George Gershwin: *Porgy and Bess* **(1935)**
A musical with social conscience, this was notable for its sympathetic but clear-eyed portrayal of underclass life

Carl Orff: *Carmina Burana* (1937)
The cultural calling-card of a composer who cooperated with the
Nazi regime

Abel Meeropol: 'Strange Fruit', recorded by Billie Holiday (1939)
Emotionally charged and socially progressive coming-of-age for
the popular song

Michael Tippett: *A Child of Our Time, VIII. Steal Away* (1939–41)
Interspersing quasi-operatic narrative passages with African-
American spirituals, this response to the horrors of war was
inspired by the real-life assassination of a German diplomat by a
Jewish refugee

Dmitri Shostakovich: *Leningrad* symphony (1942)
Dedicated to the people of his besieged home city, this was musical
patriotism and morale-raising for a mainstream audience

Aaron Copland: *Appalachian Spring* (1944)
American musical patriotism and morale-raising in a ballet score
with enduring appeal

8. The Popular Age II

Leonard Bernstein and Stephen Sondheim: *West Side Story* (1957)
Groundbreaking musical fusing Latin-American, jazz, Broadway
and classical styles

Bernard Herrmann: *Psycho* original soundtrack (1960)
Herrmann's reinvention of film scoring techniques, with hard-
edged string orchestra accompanying Hitchcock's black-and-white
horror masterpiece

Bob Dylan: 'The times they are a-changing' (1964)
Musical challenge to the prevailing United States political establishment

The Beatles: *Revolver* (1966)
A radical overhaul of the possibilities of pop, with daring integration

of classical, avant-garde, folk and world idioms, studio technology
and mainstream rock and roll

Stevie Wonder: *Innervisions* (1973)
Motown soul inventively merged with Cuban rhythmic patterns

Steve Reich: *Music for 18 Musicians* (1974–6)
Minimalism joined the gap between pop and classical and made
classical-inspired music more relevant for the modern age

Stephen Sondheim: *Sunday in the Park with George* (1984)
Expanding the expectations of the stage musical: a musical narra-
tive based on Georges Seurat's 1884 pointillist painting *A Sunday
Afternoon on the Island of La Grande Jatte*

Paul Simon and others: *Graceland* (1986)
South African *iscathamiya* (unaccompanied Zulu group-singing
genre) brought into colourful collision with folk and country styles
of the southern United States

John Adams: *Nixon in China* (1987)
Opera reconnected to contemporary current affairs

Steve Reich: *Different Trains* (1988)
Classical concert work for a string quartet, shaped around sound-
sampling of taped conversations

Danny Elfman: *Batman* **original soundtrack** (1989)
Lisztian neo-Gothic power demonstrated the continued vibrancy
in the cultural mainstream of the 'classical' heritage of the
symphonic sound

Dario Marianelli: *Atonement* **original soundtrack** (2007)
Genre-defying layering of styles, one on the other: the orchestral
past and present co-existing in a modern film score

Howard Goodall: *Enchanted Voices* (2009)
Newly composed twenty-first-century reappraisal of ancient plainchant

(Highly Selective) Further Reading

Oxford History of Western Music, Richard Taruskin (Oxford University Press, 2005)

The Triumph of Music: Composers, Musicians and their Audiences, Tim Blanning (Allen Lane, 2008)

A History of Western Music, J. Peter Burkholder, Donald Grout, Claude Palisca (W. W. Norton, 2009)

The Rise and Fall of Popular Music, Donald Clarke (St Martin's Griffin, 1995)

Music: A Very Short Introduction, Nicholas Cook (Oxford University Press, 1998)

Roots of the Classical, Peter Van der Merwe (Oxford University Press, 2004)

Origins of the Popular Style, Peter Van der Merwe (Oxford University Press, 1989)

This is your Brain on Music, Daniel Levitin (Atlantic Books, 2007)

The Unanswered Question, Leonard Bernstein (Harvard University Press, 1990)

Vindications, Deryck Cooke (Cambridge University Press, 1982)

Unheard Melodies, or Trampolining in the Vatican, Paul Drayton (Athena Press, 2008)

Johann Sebastian Bach, Christoph Wolff (Oxford University Press, 2001)

Evening in the Palace of Reason, James Gaines (4th Estate, 2005)

Wagner and Philosophy, Bryan Magee (Penguin, 2001)

The Twisted Muse: Musicians and their Music in the Third Reich, Michael H. Kater (Oxford University Press, 1997)

Composers of the Nazi Era: Eight Portraits, Michael H. Kater (Oxford University Press, 2000)

The Reich's Orchestra: The Berlin Philharmonic 1933–45, Misha Aster (Souvenir, 2010)

On Russian Music, Richard Taruskin (University of California Press, 2009)

Revolution in the Head: The Beatles' Records and the Sixties, Ian MacDonald (Pimlico, 1995)

Between Old Worlds and New, Wilfrid Mellers (Cygnus Arts, 1997)

The Rest is Noise, Alex Ross (4th Estate, 2007)

Listen to This, Alex Ross (4th Estate, 2010)

Picture Credits

Painting from the Chauvet cave, southern France (© culture-images/Lebrecht)

Bone flute from Hohle Fels (AFP/Getty Images)

Lur (after Danish example, about 1000 BC), made by Victor-Charles Mahillon (© Museum of Fine Arts, Boston (Leslie Lindsey Mason Collection)/Lebrecht)

The Schøyen Collection MS 2340: Lexical list of harp strings, Sumer, twenty-sixth century BC (The Schøyen Collection, Oslo and London)

Egyptian wall-painting featuring musicians (© Lebrecht Music & Arts)

Ancient Greek krater from the fifth century BC (Getty Images)

An organist and a horn player entertain at a Gladiator match (Museum für Vor und Frühgeschichte, Saarbrucken, Germany/The Bridgeman Art Library)

The Schøyen Collection MS 1574: St Gallen diastematic staffless neumes, Austria or Southern Germany, twelfth century (The Schøyen Collection, Oslo and London)

'Musica enchiriadis', Msc.Var.1, fol.57r (Staatsbibliothek Bamberg/photo: Gerald Raab)

View of the south transept of the Cathedral of Notre Dame, Reims (© Paul Maeyaert/The Bridgeman Art Library)

Portrait of a Musician, possibly Josquin des Prez, c.1485 by Leonardo da Vinci (Ambrosiana, Milan, Italy/The Bridgeman Art Library)

Girolamo Savonarola (1452–98), Dominican priest and, briefly, ruler of Florence (Lebrecht Authors)

Al'Ud (lute) (© Museum of Fine Arts, Boston (Leslie Lindsey Mason Collection)/Lebrecht)

The Lute Player, c.1595, by Caravaggio (Hermitage, St. Petersburg, Russia/The Bridgeman Art Library)

The Cittern Player by Gabriel Metsu (Gemaeldegalerie Alte Meister, Kassel, Germany/© Museumslandschaft Hessen Kassel/The Bridgeman Art Library)

Violin made by Nicolo Amati (© Museum of Fine Arts, Boston (Gift of Arthur E. Spiller, M.D)/Lebrecht)

Organ from Notre-Dame de Valere (Bridgeman Art Library)

Clavemusicum Omnitonum (De Agostini Picture Library/The Bridgeman Art Library)

Ballet costume worn by Louis XIV as Apollo (© Lebrecht Music & Arts Photo Library)

Title page of 'The English Dancing Master' by John Playford (© Lebrecht Music & Arts)

The first page of musical manuscript from Johann Sebastian Bach's 'Well-Tempered Clavichord' (Getty Images)

'The Military Prophet; or a Flight from Providence', 1750 (© Museum of London)

Ranelagh Gardens, Interior of the Rotunda by Canaletto (Private Collection/The Bridgeman Art Library)

Scene from Haydn's opera 'L'incontro improviso' (© Lebrecht Music & Arts)

Paganini playing the violin (© Lebrecht Music & Arts)

Clara Wieck Schumann (The Art Archive/Schumann birthplace/Collection Dagli Orti)

IR 65 Johannes Kreisler (Staatsbibliothek Bamberg/photo: Gerald Raab)

Caricature of Franz Liszt playing the piano (Archives Charmet/The Bridgeman Art Library)

Engraving after Wilhelm von Kaulbach's *Battle of the Huns* by Eugène Delacroix (© culture-images/Lebrecht)

The Standard Bearer by Hubert Lanzinger (Peter Newark Military Pictures/The Bridgeman Art Library)

Third Reich stamps featuring Wagner operas, 1933

Advert for an appearance of The Fisk University Jubilee Singers (© Look and Learn/Peter Jackson Collection/The Bridgeman Art Library)

Four women dancers in Javanese Village, Paris Exposition, 1889 (© Niday Picture Library/Alamy)

Narcisse, costume design by Leon Bakst for Sergei Diaghilev's *Ballets Russes*, 1911 (© Leemage/Lebrecht Music & Arts)

Vaslav Nijinsky in Claude Debussy's L'Après Midi d'un Faune, Ballets Russes, seventh season (© De Agostini/Lebrecht Music & Arts)

Paul McCartney in a studio to record 'The Family Way', November 1966 (Getty Images)

Steve Reich (Boosey and Hawkes/ArenaPAL)

Paul Simon sings with Ladysmith Black Mambazo at Library of Congress Concert, Washington, DC (© Chris Kleponis/epa/Corbis)

Acknowledgements

Grateful thanks to David Jeffcock, Francis Hanly, Jan Younghusband, Paul Sommers, Caroline Page, Martin Cass, Will Bowen, Justine Field, Adam Barker, Tony Bannister, Colin Case, John Pritchard, Iain McCallum, all of whom helped create – with many other skilled colleagues – the BBC TV series, and for the book, Silvia Crompton, Becky Hardie, Cat Ledger, Caroline Chignell, Peter Bennett-Jones, John Evans, and for unerring support and musical encouragement during the period of this mammoth undertaking, Val, Daisy and Millie Fancourt, Kathryn Knight, Tim Brooke, Richard Paine, Richard King, Stephen Darlington, Darren Henley, Melvyn Bragg, Simon Halsey, Claire Jarvis, Pru Bouverie and my parents, Geoffrey and Marion Goodall.

Index